Sarajevo's Elusive Spring

By

Sami Tischler

Sami Tischler

Copyright © 2025 Sami Tischler.

All rights reserved.

No part of this publication may be reproduced, stored in a retrieval system, or transmitted in any form or by any means, electronic, mechanical, photocopying, recording, or otherwise, without prior written permission of the copyright owner, except in the case of brief quotations used in reviews or articles.

Dedication

To friends no longer alive and those scattered around the world.
Desperately missing Chuck, Gev, Hardi, Karlo, Zizi, Chief, Slav.

Sami Tischler

Acknowledgment

To Mia, lifelong companion, for her warmth, big heart, and tolerance spilling out of it.

To Australian book publishers for their great editing and collaborative production work on this book.

Sarajevo's Elusive Spring

Table of Content

Dedication iii

Acknowledgment iv

Jatza (Angie) 9

Township Violence 13

The Last Dance 17

Slav 20

Sam 24

Chuck 28

Hardi 31

Professor Philip 33

Dumped by Imam's Daughter and the Moonlight Beauty 36

With Chief in Dubrovnik 41

Travel, Travel, Travel, Everybody Travels to the Coast! 45

In the Scrap Yard 47

Adriatic Coast 53

Dumped in Drvenik 55

I Met my Ex at the Beach. 57

Wandering, Foraging, Partying 59

Mitzy 62

Passport 66

Third Time Lucky 74

School is Over 88

Where to Go, the Question is Now 99

Boom Boom 106

Accidentally in Istanbul 108

Back on the Road Heading West.....................................114

Through the Dust & Across Borders in the Company of Brothers.118

Go, Go, West! 124

Venice 129

Driven Up the Alpine Wall..133

The Empire..140

Threesome in the Forest 147

Day and Night on the Loony's Farm...............................154

Reality of a Breakup 162

Back in Helga's Hands & Between Her Legs 165

Munich 170

Some Welcome and Lack of It 173

Hans' Sweetheart 178

France, here we Come! 183

Mao's Death in Paris...187

Paris →Nancy → Antwerp → Brussels → Rotterdam ...189

Hustling in Chambery 195

Back in Italy on an Iron Horse 200

Karlo 203

Sarajevo's Elusive Spring

Time Travel to Ledići on Foot 205

House Arrest 212

Freed But Handcuffed 214

Višegrad, Narrow Gauge Narrow Minds 217

Exiled from the White City 221

Bold in Sarajevo 227

Senta 230

Getting Out of There 237

Time to Go Back 242

Field Manoeuvres 247

Far Away from Home in Raška 252

Forbidden City Novi Pazar 256

Smak Concert 258

Aliens in Raška 262

Yet Another Transfer, Army Lock Up 267

Army, the Slow River 272

Three Amigos on the Road 275

Rašo 276

Germany Revisited 278

Still in Germany 283

Back at Home + Baba's Harem 285

Employed and Settled? 287

The Princess 289

R. 297

Princess and R. 303

Free in Sarajevo, Heading East Again 308

Untimely Troubles with Baba's Harem on the Road 321

Mia 326

My Mia 330

From Bad to Worst 334

Out of the Trouble Zone 341

Sort of an Epilogue 348

Back in Ledići 353

Jatza (Angie)

I had just finished primary school and, apart from secretly falling in love with girls at school, I hadn't had one I could truly call mine yet. I often hung around a neighbour's house for the company of their daughters, and even more so for their young, blonde visitor. The blonde cousin lived in a block of flats in town.

In the 1960s, all of us living in our own houses on the edge of town were considered lower class compared to those living in government owned flats in the township of Joša, only 0.5 km away.

I had spent the last two years at school sharing a bench with Alexandra. She was the daughter of the local pharmacist. They had previously lived in the Capital. "Jaca" spoke with a posh Belgrade dialect and had the manners of a metropolitan girl. She was super cool with her almost translucent white skin, short straight black hair, and indigo dark eyes. For some reason, she chose to share the bench with me. I learnt not to be shy around her, and we had some frivolous moments in class and during the breaks.

My male friends were mostly good students, but unruly and rebellious. Boya was an exception. He struggled with schoolwork but grew faster and stronger than the rest of us. From time to time, I ganged up with my mates. We'd spend wild hours together in our various neighbourhoods. They never came to my street to play, I was always the one taking the risk of crossing their turf. These were actual ganglands, with defined territories and rules.

Jatza, the pretty young blonde, frequently wandered into my street to hang out with her cousins. She caught my eye, and I started chatting her up. I didn't know if I was making any progress. She seemed a bit snobbish, reserved, and half-interested. I was beginning to think my efforts were wasted.

Surprisingly, one day as the school year was drawing to an end, she invited me to their school disco to mark the close of the year. I slipped on my brand-new Italian *Super Rifle* jeans, my first ever pair. I wore dark blue Chinese sneakers and a sailor-striped blue and white T-shirt. The famous hit "Angie" by The Rolling Stones had just been released. They played it over and over as we danced in a close embrace.

We had a great time. Her small blond headed fragile figure, so close to mine made me lightheaded. I was a year older and must have impressed her girlfriends with my height and the outfit. I was almost walking on air when I strolled home after the party. I felt so grown up. Finally, I had a girlfriend of my own. She was blonde, cute, petite, laughed a lot, and at first, seemed very happy to have me around.

We met a couple of times in my street and with her nieces. But it became exhaustingly tedious. I had to compete with her two young relatives for attention, and her attitude towards me shifted from cocky to spiteful. The challenge was outwitting three unpredictable, cheeky teenagers.

Then, without warning, she stopped coming into my street. The summer holidays had just begun, and I had already lost my girlfriend.

I decided to look for her in town. I roughly knew where she lived. I wandered around a block of flats, hoping to catch a glimpse of my elusive girlfriend. A group of young kids materialized out of nowhere and surrounded me.

"Who are you looking for?" It was clear they weren't offering help, and their questions could lead to trouble. One of them stepped forward.

"You're looking for Jatza, aren't you?" he hissed, his question sounding more like a threat. I noticed his left arm hung uselessly in its sleeve. I couldn't take his move too seriously, his disability wouldn't give him much of a chance in a street fight, if that's what he was after. But I wasn't looking for trouble. I was on a mission. I was in love with the young blonde, desperate to get just a minute alone with her.

Sarajevo's Elusive Spring

"Yes, I'd like to see her. That's why I'm here," I said, trying to be as non-threatening as possible. I realized I was facing a gang on their own turf, no need to provoke them.

"Listen, you little peasant," the boy with the disabled hand snapped. "Jatza is my girlfriend, and you'd better get the fuck out of here before you get beaten!"

The rest of the gang circled around me like a pack of hyenas, shoving and poking me in the side and back. This kind of aggression wasn't unfamiliar to me. I'd dealt with young thugs before. I'd fought my way out of an ambush or two at the end of a movie night with my street mates.

My strategy was always the same: pretend to be naive, show no interest in fighting back, but build up the anger inside and then explode violently and unexpectedly. I'd jump on the most dangerous one and hurt them, punching, kicking, biting. Then I'd break through, disappear into the darkness, and make a run for it. Risky, but it usually worked at night. The notoriously poor street lighting gave me the advantage of vanishing into the night.

But this time, in broad daylight, that wouldn't work. I was far from home, and I couldn't run to the safety of my street. They weren't giving me any options. Surrounded on the pavement, I waited for an opening, my mind racing, trying to decide who I'd hit first.

"Hey, you young monkeys, what the fuck do you think you're doing?" came a familiar voice from behind.

My schoolmate Boya had appeared, already tall and strong, wearing the ugliest version of his face for the occasion. The young thugs backed off. Boya commanded respect. It gave me the chance I needed. They took theirs and slipped away.

Boya threw his rugged arms and massive hands around my tall frame, and we walked off together like the best mates we were. Jaca must have watched the whole scene from her second-floor window, behind the lace curtain like a medieval princess.

Sami Tischler

I never worked out whether she left me of her own will or her boyfriend banned her from seeing me. The next time I saw her, she was holding hands with the boy who led the confrontation that day.

She could have passed the verdict to my face if she'd had any decency. I'll never know if she flirted with me just to make him jealous.

I was lucky to walk away from that whole affair unharmed. It was one of those rare times a school friend had my back, and that was what really mattered.

My mate Boya grew up to become a serious criminal and plied his trade in northern Italy. By the age of 21, he was shot dead in an armed robbery gone pear-shaped.

Township Violence

Going out to the movies was a risky business. Any confrontation or reaction to harassment from town gangs usually led to getting attacked afterwards in the dark car park behind the cinema. My friends, neighbourhood boys my age, were cowards when it came to making a stand. They had big mouths and happily hurled abuse during the screening when harassed. I was usually left alone during the show. Tension would grow over the length of the session. If you were picked out as a suitable victim, you'd get confronted afterwards in the darkness around the exit.

Authorities never understood that proper lighting and a police officer on duty at the back of the cinema could've saved many of us teenagers from injury and the hurt of being beaten and humiliated. My friends had a habit of deserting the battlefield after a slap, a kick up the arse, or an aggressive verbal insult. They'd provoke the enemy and leave me to fight the war on my own. Most of the time, I had no idea who or what I was fighting for. After all, I went to the cinema to watch a movie. But I was often left there in the dark to fight on their behalf.

I grew tall and strong, and many were keen to test themselves against me. I have the spiteful nature and pride of my mountain ancestors. I couldn't resist responding to provocation and had to have the last word in a verbal exchange. This inability to keep my mouth shut and tendency to be the last one on the barricade followed me through life. To be honest, I'm lucky to be alive, and have managed to live with a broken cartilage in my nose. At 64, a specialist finally diagnosed the problem.

I've walked out of street fights with bruises, a bloody nose, and pain all over my body, just because I had to fight gangs. I can hardly remember losing a one-on-one fight. I don't recall losing a fight when I had someone covering my back either. Unfortunately, I fought many on my own against gangs, abandoned by those who had started the trouble in the first place.

Sami Tischler

Those early fights in the Township were the worst. Even if you won one or managed to escape the beating, as I did several times, it wasn't the end of your troubles. All essential facilities sat in the territory of the gangs operating in the Town's centre. They hung around the shops, markets, school, cinema, soccer fields, parks, playgrounds, and the main bus stop. It was virtually impossible to avoid revenge.

After one visit, my cousin Gev figured out that the disco club in town played great music and that the girls were gorgeous. He got me excited about it. We went out together a couple of times. The girls seemed interested, but the older thugs who managed the club on behalf of the Youth Association weren't impressed with his looks, dance style, or cockiness. One night, he came alone, danced a lot with a great-looking girl, and, as he walked her home, a gang of thugs confronted him and started a fight.

Considering he was there by himself, he did okay. He had swelling all over his face, black and blue, and pain in different parts of his body for a long time. He was lucky he knew the area and managed to outrun the gang by heading towards our house. He didn't make it to my parents' place but managed to escape through the fields towards the river. He followed the willow thickets along the banks and made it to the bus stop just outside town. Gev caught a bus back home.

Apart from the bruises, he destroyed his best pair of Italian moccasins, his good shirt was ripped and bloodied, and chunks of his long hair were torn out.

The town "Joša" wasn't the only place where this kind of violence happened. Gev lived above the Old Town in Sarajevo and had to deal with the same rubbish every time he headed into the city to shop, go to the cinema, or get to work. Gev was an apprentice motor mechanic and lived in a part of the Old Town where the government sold land that was difficult to build on. My Aunt Golda, Gev's mother, and his father built a house against a limestone cliff in the late 1950s. In the basement, they discovered a spring, which they concreted and drained.

Sarajevo's Elusive Spring

It proved a real treasure.

On days when the local government rationed water due to the city's rapid development and overpopulation, the spring gave them an unlimited and free water supply. During the Ethnic War in Bosnia in the early '90s, it saved them, my parents and my sister's family, from having to risk sniper bullets while fetching water in the Old Town. The Serbian army encircled the city, blocked all roads, cut off gas, water, and electricity, shot at anyone they could see, and bombarded the city relentlessly for nearly four years. The only water available came from the polluted river Miljacka or from several natural springs, well known to the trigger-happy enemy forces, who fired mortars at those locations. Perfect opportunities to cull the civilian population already sentenced to a slow death.

Back when we were teenagers, a volatile mix of Bosnia's population lived happily together, enjoying the fruits of the Socialist Revolution, Unity and Brotherhood. Gev's neighbourhood wasn't much different to mine. When I stayed at his place, usually during school holidays, we'd spend heaps of time in Nine's bedroom. He lived with his grandmother and had a great collection of progressive Western music. Gev bought a record player and started collecting vinyl LPs. We'd listen to Pink Floyd, Deep Purple, and Black Sabbath for hours. Sarajevo's "Indexi," Josipa Lisac, and "Time" from Zagreb were our Yugoslav favourites.

When we were together, we never feared anyone. Gev wasn't keen on the disco in my Township after his "lucky" escape, so we went to the legendary "Club Cactus." I still remember my first time there. I was lucky enough to see a DJ called Šukrija spinning records. He only played progressive rock. That night, he played Roxy Music. I'd heard of the band but barely knew any of their songs. It was 1972. The whole club was jumping. I didn't recognise a single person in the massive crowd. The way they looked, danced, and acted seemed unreal, completely liberated.

Sami Tischler

Apart from "Paranoid" by Black Sabbath and a few well-known dance tunes, most of the music was totally new to me. I loved the vibe of the place and the fact that you could cut loose in the semi-darkness of the club and dance the night away however you liked. No one hassled you about your appearance or how you reacted to the sound being masterfully driven by DJ Šukrija.

Gev already seemed to have made a few friends. He was always hunting down new records for his small collection. Gev was "cashed up," earning his apprentice's wage, and could afford the absurd prices they went for. His mother, Golda, would've thrown him out of the house if she knew what he was paying for those "Satanic songs."

The Last Dance

My parents weren't happy or supportive about my new interest in music and disco clubs. They were even less excited about my soirées into the city at night. I couldn't really afford it too often on my small pocket money anyway. I started going out to the local disco, met a few local freaks, and one of them acted as the "Chief". Chief developed a kind of liking for me.

There was a group of us who would get up and dance to a small selection of music we liked. The rest of the time, we smoked cigarettes, talked over extremely loud music and drank very little. When the DJ played our tunes – which was generally reduced to a few sets of 15 minutes – we'd get up and do the craziest stuff possible. We shook our heads to the beat, played air guitars, air saxophones, jumped to the rhythm, while the fashionably dressed socialist youth gaped and wondered if we were under the influence of some unknown drug.

We took no drugs. We would have if they were around.

This scene lasted for some time, because the club was meant to be offering a dance venue for the youth indiscriminately. It was subsidized by the government and all those working there were paid by the Youth Association. However, there was a section of staff – small-time local thugs – who didn't like this new trend, our long hair, our dance moves, our dressing style, and the fact that we weren't drinking enough. We got frequently harassed.

"Security Guards" would come to the dance floor and warn us for "shaking our heads" to the beat. After two warnings, they would kick you out of the club. The most humiliating part was a written ban on an empty packet of cigarettes. The whole thing was becoming ridiculous and the way we were bullied grew increasingly aggressive. You'd get pushed, sworn at with obvious hatred and intent. It was clear they didn't want us there.

Chief had a disability which provided a certain level of protection from heavy physical handling. Verbal abuse, name-calling, threats and every other form of humiliation were on the menu. He wrote poetry, owned a great collection of psychedelic music, enrolled to study Philosophy at uni but left the course claiming it to be a waste of time.

He was very well connected into Sarajevo's underground freak culture, played guitar, but never played any covers. He only played his own material, and we often jammed in neglected areas of parkland around our Town. He screamed his own rebellious blues and drove wild boogie grooves on a cheap, beaten-up guitar. I played rhythm on cardboard boxes, tin cans, and wine bottles.

He managed to push for an evening of poetry in the Disco Club. Most of his poetry was hard to comprehend, but the anger, rebellion, and criticism of the social aberration we were surrounded by were more than obvious. He got into the DJ booth and spoke his poetry over segments of Pink Floyd soundtracks.

We, the freaks, loved it – but the rest of the crowd didn't. He forced his performance to the end by out-yelling the angry clientele and screaming his poetry into the microphone. He had an obvious advantage having control of the sound.

At the end, it felt as if we had disturbed a hornet's nest and there was no return.

Collectively escorted out of the Club, we were followed through a dark alley to the main street by a large band of thugs who kept pushing, shoving, kicking, punching, and encircling our group. We decided not to return any punches, mainly for our own safety. We felt that our aggression would have justified theirs – and they surely hoped to teach us a lesson in good socialist behaviour.

The most aggressive was a local unemployed small-time thief and drunk called Zac. He was a skinny, tall fellow who kept jumping at me – the tallest in the group – wanting to get a reaction and use it to accelerate his anger. He certainly didn't get any.

Sarajevo's Elusive Spring

We managed to maintain a compact group, pushed them away, screamed, called for help, and held together as a pack – like buffaloes fighting back hyenas. By the time we walked out into the lights of the main street, Zac was virtually hanging on my back, completely out of control and furious.

I was trying to shake him off when a uniformed Militia man popped out of nowhere and ordered those who were obviously involved in the scuffle to produce IDs and explain what was going on. Most of those responsible slipped back into the darkness, but Zac couldn't. He was spotted "riding" me – a defenceless, pacifist victim. I placed the complaint, produced my ID, and he had to do the same.

Zac tried to pass some blame onto me. My friends all supported my statement defiantly. The officer clearly saw the last bits of aggression and could easily imagine what had been going on in the dark before he turned up. The Militia man wrote it all in his small notebook, issued him with a strong verbal warning and promised to take my complaint to the Local Court.

I did get a letter to appear as a witness. I went to the hearing at the Local Court. It was a farce and a waste of time. The judge knew Zac well as he was a repeat offender. I told them the details of the event. He got away with another verbal warning.

I don't know what I was hoping for. It was so naïve to think they would prosecute him for such a minor act of violence. Perhaps if they did, it would have sent a strong message to the gang culture ruling the Town.

However, Zac never laid hands on me again. Every time I'd seen him since, I could sense cold hatred in his bloodshot eyes as a warning. It was obvious that I had danced my last dance in the local Club.

It turned out to be the best thing that happened to me at the time. I was unofficially expelled from the "swamp" where I clearly never belonged. The mini metropolis of Sarajevo appeared open and welcoming.

Sami Tischler

Slav

In 1972, as a fifteen-year-old, I started a course in Electrical Engineering. In a single day, the destinies of thirty people my age were linked together for a period of four years. They were all exceptionally bright students. Enrolment criteria for the college filtered in only the top students.

Slav appeared very young and looked like an overgrown child who had accidentally enrolled in the wrong course. Small, thin, with his face hidden under a wild bunch of hair, he radiated feminine, fragile features. Very pretty for a boy, and immediately a target of harassment by Sarajevo thugs, already grown big, strong, and aggressive at that age. I couldn't resist taking his side and stood firmly in his defence. We had so much in common and formed a strong bond through our love for music, literature, and Eastern mysticism. We gravitated naturally towards each other. He was the only son in his family, and so was I. We both smoked and had the occasional drink.

Soon, he came over and spent a weekend in my neighbourhood, and I was invited to visit him in Vareš. There were six people from Vareš in our class, including Slav. Some travelled back and forth daily on a slow and unreliable rail network. Vareš wasn't far, but you had to change two "local" trains to get there. Faster links were direct bus lines, but they were generally more expensive and often overcrowded and unreliable. Once full, they left surplus passengers behind. If you missed an early bus, you'd be stuck in the city after school, hungry, with nowhere to do your homework or study.

Slav's elder sister Slava studied at the university. Their parents paid for a privately rented room near the school. They both commuted home on weekends. In those early days, Slav went home frequently. Later, he would spend most of his time in Sarajevo's suburban periphery, near the school, and rarely wandered into the city for entertainment.

My early days were similar. I travelled and walked for kilometres before, between, and after my bus and tram rides to get from "Joša" to the college on the other side of the ridge dividing the two. The peculiar network of roads and tramlines made this trip an adventure. I rode overcrowded public transport to school and back, as well as walked a total of 10 km in between. It was a shocking adventure when it rained for days in autumn or during the bitterly cold winters. You depended on good waterproof shoes, dry socks, a proper raincoat, and a warm cap. I'd get out of the house at 6.00 am to get to school by 8.00 am, returning home by 5.00 pm after a full class schedule. I had to carry textbooks, notebooks, technical drawings hand-drawn in ink, and sports gear for PE. I felt like a donkey at times and still have a crooked back from dragging shoulder bags filled with dead weight.

Slav walked across the paddock, and he was at school. His trips home and back to the city on Monday morning were a different story. He got up at 4.00 am on Mondays to catch a train and make it to school on time.

However, our trips to Vareš were unforgettable. We would go out to their community hall in the Old Town and dance to a local band formed by students of the Academy of Music in Sarajevo. They played covers of progressive Western bands but played them well and to an amazingly appreciative crowd. The whole town was there. I'd meet up with my school friends and be introduced to their local friends and girls. Although underage, they all drank freely. I never had to deal with aggressive thugs there.

I met a guy who had my name and surname. We were the same age, and he even looked a bit like me, except that everyone called him Dado. After being called Krupatz, Fetty, Bambalo, I acquired a new nickname: UFO. My cousin Gev had painted an image from an LP cover by the band UFO on the back of my Super Rifle jacket. It was a weird feeling every time we met, Dado and I. Girls were mad about him, but he appeared so unhappy and drunk every time I saw him. Within a year of our first meeting, he committed suicide. Apparently, one of his girls drove him mad and finally deserted him. Dado just couldn't take it.

Sami Tischler

I pondered my own bad luck with girls and the feelings they left me with every time I had to deal with rejection. If I had known that the trend was going to continue for a long time, I might have considered the same solution, perhaps. However, without a crystal ball in my hand, I was safe for the time being. Later, I took every single rejection bravely on the chin and kept walking. I understood the simple truth about luck and the fact that things can only improve once you've hit rock bottom, sitting in the gutter.

Slav came to stay with me over the weekend several times. My parents, for some strange reason, never objected to that. We only ever had family staying with us overnight. My friend Tzar, an older boy, was about to do his National Service in the Yugoslav Army. In those days, families organized send-off parties. The table was loaded with food and drinks. Nobody objected to us underage youth drinking. We were strongly encouraged by some older guests as a challenge and a proof of manhood.

This time, Slav was with me, and we started drinking together. I held back and watched him get drunk too fast. We stayed until late, and he refused to go home. He hardly ate, mixed his drinks, and talked nonsense. A large quantity of alcohol sent him almost under the table. Most of my friends from the neighbourhood got drunk too. We sang farewell songs appropriate for the occasion. Slav joined in, and so did I. The sessions went on forever.

Bosnian music heritage is all about loss, misunderstanding, emotional pain, and tragedy. The repertoire is inexhaustible. Once infused with alcohol, tragedy, poetry of longing and loss, and collective sadness can be overwhelming. Slav was its main victim that night. I had to drag him to my place, carried him part of the way. He was so drunk he couldn't stand on his feet any longer. Somehow, we got there, and I tucked him into bed.

After a while, he was desperate to visit the loo. I thought it wise to chaperone him there. As soon as we got in, he threw up across the small bathroom and splashed his vomit onto the wall. Fortunately, we had a squatting toilet set in the concrete floor with a tap and a short hose attached. He made a proper mess. I hosed most of it into the sewer drain, opened the window, and went back to finish the clean-up after settling him back to sleep. My parents heard the commotion but left it to me to sort out. Things didn't look too bad by morning, apart from the sickly stench that lingered on for a long time.

When I stayed in Vareš, we slept in the attic. It was a large space with exposed beams, a couple of beds, and a couch for furniture. Slavko owned the legendary YU-made gramophone Tosca and a decent collection of records we would listen to late into the night. We both loved Pink Floyd and The Doors, played with the lights turned off. Their psychedelic mood transported us to another world with the gorgeous sounds of Wish You Were Here, Dark Side of the Moon, or Absolutely Live by The Doors. Unbelievably, all those albums were released in Yugoslavia by our own record companies under licence as soon as they came out.

Sami Tischler

Sam

Sometime around that time, I met a boy of similar age. Sam was a local lad who mixed with freaks and thugs. He never really figured out what he was. He had crudely done tattoos all over his arms, crosses, "Peace" signs, and names. One time, in his girlfriend's bedroom, he tattooed a small "Peace" sign on my arm which, over time, transformed into a large dot. Every time I was arrested, I had to declare it to the cops. During my hitchhiking days in Yugoslavia, this happened a lot. I didn't get jailed every time I was arrested, of course. I was often held at some random police station for an identity check, while policemen asked questions and wrote down my answers, including a description of my pathetic tattoo. It would've taken some time to get Sam's tattoos down in an arrest report.

I took my first hitchhiking trip with him. We travelled to Konjic, 70 km south across the range, hoping to reach Mostar in the middle of a freezing cold winter. By late afternoon, we made it to Konjic and started looking for a place to sneak into and spend the night. We found an unlocked shed by the lake and froze our arses off trying to sleep there. The sleeping bags we had didn't offer much protection in the damp, foggy night, just beside a huge man-made lake on the River Neretva. We made it back home by sneaking through a semi-open sliding door on an empty goods train carriage.

Another time, I got invited to visit his grandfather in the village of Okruglica, high above the city of Vareš. We made it there on a local bus through deep snowdrifts and spent a couple of nights drinking homebrew, playing cards, and listening to his grandfather's wartime stories. During WWII the whole area was held by *Četniks*. When they weren't pillaging and slaughtering, they were drinking and quarrelling among themselves. "If you pillage and slaughter extensively, you run out of victims and end up finding them amongst your own population," the old man said. He told us about the time one of their leaders got "nailed" by an axe to a barn door.

Sarajevo's Elusive Spring

Sima's Grandpa drank like a skunk. He treated us like royals, generously pouring big glasses of his homebrew and filling our plates with smoked meat, cheese and chopped onions for *mezze*. At the time, we were considered underage kids. He drank methylated spirits, 90% alcohol, bought at the agricultural supplies' depot in Vareš. Anything weaker didn't do it for him anymore. Sima was so proud of his grandpa's drinking abilities.

My grandfather, hero of the battle of Dujmovići, had never tasted alcohol in his life. That battle was held against *Četnik* bands, at a time when communist rebels and *Četniks* operated together in an uneasy alliance.

My friendship with Sima didn't last long. He was too wild for my taste and treated his girlfriend Vera badly.

"I've had enough of her. If you want her, just take over. She's all yours. I'm done with her," he said as we were lounging at Vera's parents' place.

We would hang around her apartment during cold winter days. Centrally heated, stocked with food and alcohol, combined with Vera's hospitality, it was a perfect hangout. I had no intention of taking him up on his offer, as tempting as it was. I thought it was the work of an immature little bastard.

"Bugger off, you need to grow up and start behaving like a man. You don't deserve her. Is this what you think you need a friend for? Someone to take over your girlfriend once you've had enough of her?"

He laughed my comments off. "She was good for the winter; the spring is coming soon, and I need something fresh in my life."

Vera didn't usually go out in the city, but one odd time she turned up at Club Cactus. It was a bitterly cold winter evening, and she wanted to talk to me. We were outside in a sheltered corner of the modern concrete complex, and she spilled her heart out to me.

Sami Tischler

By the end of it, I wasn't sure if she was making a move or genuinely suffering a break-up. I was so uncomfortable with her hanging onto me, shivering, crying, and wiping her face and nose with a soiled hanky. I soon realised she was overdoing it.

Vera was an attractive girl with long black hair and a generously curved, voluptuous body. I was tempted to embrace her large breasts and get her warm curves against my freezing body, but that soaked hanky put me off. I had a feeling she was disappointed with my lack of enthusiasm.

She tried all those moves that could've led to intimacy, crying on my shoulder with her lips on my neck, her tears soaking my collar, her big boobs pressing and rubbing against the winter layers I was wearing. She was a tall girl. I didn't realize that was a rare privilege at the time. For some reason, I rarely got the chance to be intimate with tall girls ever since.

If only this had happened in summer, I probably would've fallen for it, no doubt. Just imagining our hot flesh so close and so fired up. But a bitterly cold Sarajevo night and the sand blasted brutalist architecture around us killed it in its cradle. I was never an opportunist and still had some respect for my mate Sam.

Besides, while I had to listen to the moaning and groaning about her irresponsible boyfriend, they were playing the most amazing music sets in Club Cactus, just behind the wall. My ears were there the whole time. I escorted her to the bus, back to the Township, and never said a word about it to Sam.

The thing that impressed me most about him was his careless and uncompromising attitude. He walked around like he owned the shitty little Township we lived in.

If I was walking through town with him, I shook off all those anxieties about small-time thugs and their potential to hurt me.

When I met my special friend Chuck, Sam and I were already falling out with each other. Sam couldn't get out of his past associations with

Sarajevo's Elusive Spring

neighbouring gangs, and I always felt uncomfortable in their vicinity. They dragged him down, and I was looking for a way up and away from that constricting environment, their narrow borders, and even narrower minds.

Sami Tischler

Chuck

Chuck came like herb on a wound (Bosnian proverb). I needed a friend who was looking for new ways to live, someone with an expanding mind who could see beyond the borders of his street. His sister Jad met Chief at our disco club, and on her next visit to Joša, she brought her brother along. They were twins. I liked him right away. He was straightforward, happy to share his cigarettes, a great quality in a penniless youth. He wore an oversized winter coat known as a garbage collector's cape. His sister looked gorgeous, and Chief appeared smitten by her.

Chuck and I agreed to meet again. He was born into a large family. His father worked on the railways, and they lived in a cottage beside the Podlugovi Train Station. When he was very young, Chuck was adopted by a family member with his parents' consent. His childless aunt and uncle who lived 70 km away in Zenica became his new parents. Later, they moved closer to his original family and siblings. As a boy, he was restless and disliked school or authority. He must have missed his original family a lot. Virtually born beside the tracks, Chuck knew trains and railway workers well. He'd sneak into an empty rail carriage and travel long distances on goods trains.

Many years later, when he had already disappeared in India, I found out his family were Roma Gypsies, which explained many aspects of his character. Wanting to show off his world and his skills with trains, he invited me on a trip to Zenica, something he'd clearly done many times before. I followed his masterful routine, which got us easily into the guards' cabin between wagons. Unfortunately, we were caught by an unfriendly, overzealous guard. He gave us a strong verbal warning, mentioned police and jail, and insisted what we were doing was both illegal and dangerous. Worst of all, we were kicked off the train at a station on the wrong side of the Bosna River. There were no connections to the main road on the opposite bank where we needed to be to continue our trip. A 5 km walk took us to a suspended pedestrian bridge, where we crossed the river and hitched a ride to Zenica.

Sarajevo's Elusive Spring

It was my first visit to the second largest city in central Bosnia. It was the centre of the Bosnian steel industry, as well as home to the notorious high-security state prison. It was obvious Chuck had friends among the street kids and gypsy beggars there. He casually greeted cops, a few passers-by he knew and asked people for small change. That was something I'd never done before. Out of the proceeds, we bought food, cigarettes, and went to the movies. There was hardly anyone there. By the time we came out, night had already fallen. He returned to his familiar routine of asking for money. Soon we had enough for tickets back home. Tickets in hand, comfortably lounging on the express train, we laughed our heads off as we recalled and reenacted scenes from the comedy, we'd seen that afternoon. From then on, our friendship grew stronger by the day, and we met often in the city.

Chuck always made time to see me. He travelled 30 km using all his tricks to meet in Sarajevo, whether for a night at Club Cactus, a concert, or a movie. I visited Ilijaš, his nearest town, frequently and got to know his mates. They held discos there on weekends. We danced in a half empty hall to great music played from records brought by our friends. Chuck was always lucky with girls; they swarmed around him. I was awkward and shy with them. He was likeable, funny, played childish games, and the girls loved it.

Our friendship grew quickly, but one event almost cut it short. It happened on one of those weekends when I had to stay home to study. I was a good student, and my parents gave me a lot of freedom. If I had schoolwork to do, I'd refuse to wander around and waste time. Chuck had enrolled in a government-sponsored apprenticeship at the Ilijaš steelworks foundry. He hated it, wasn't built for hard work and hadn't developed a sense of responsibility, then or ever. The pay was miserable, the work was dangerous and unhealthy, and he wasn't going to work or school regularly. Eventually, he dropped out.

On days when I was busy with school, he spent time with two brothers, Ziyo and Budo. One night, Chuck and Ziyo snuck into their old primary school through an open window, planning to spend the night there. Both lived within a few kilometres of the school. Bored out of their minds, they were craving adventure. Sleeping on school benches was rough, and when they couldn't sleep, they began rummaging through the classrooms and offices. They found class roll books and couldn't resist burning a few. They kicked a ball inside, smashed vases and light fittings, knocked Marshall Tito's compulsory picture off the wall, destroying the frame and the glass front. Eventually, they realized how reckless it all was and slipped back into the night.

I don't know if they bragged to their mates or someone had seen them leaving, but the local cops had ears everywhere. Within days, they were both arrested and jailed. Ziyo was under 18, so he was sent to a juvenile correction facility for 12 months. Chuck was over 18 and got sentenced to 9 months in a low-security jail just outside Sarajevo's airport.

While he was away, I did errands and small jobs for his ageing aunt, "his mother." She was heartbroken and critical of his behaviour, deeply worried about his long-term future. She genuinely hoped my influence might help him change his ways.

Hardi

When I was ten, my father, the baker, worked in the bakery shop and at a small production plant on the opposite side of the township, just a stone's throw from our house. I went to school at a temporary location near the fresh food markets, where my father was working at the time. I used to drop by on my way to school, and my father would give me a couple of croissant-like pastries, which I'd eat on the way to school nearby.

The baby boomer generation was ready for school, and the authorities were running out of space to educate us. The government was building a new school, but in the meantime, they housed two Year 3 classes in a small gym hall.

One morning, I walked out of the bakery through the market hall, navigating the usual morning crowd, when I was surrounded by a small gang led by a boy barely older than me. They took my croissants in full view of the morning crowd. I ran back to the shop and alerted my father. He came out straight away and saw the group of kids as they fled. I pointed out the one who took my croissants. My father couldn't leave the shop to chase after unruly kids, naturally, but he must have taken a good mental image of the culprit.

Seven years later, I started going out to the local disco, got into rock music, started smoking, and hung around with like-minded local youth. Hardi was one of the boys I was mixing with, and I particularly liked him. He wasn't pretentious and accepted me straight away. He was very funny and had a laid-back, free-spirited nature.

One day, my father saw me with Hardi in the street. We were both smoking, and I quickly hid my cigarette behind my back as soon as I spotted him. But it was too late, he had already seen me. At home, my father offered me a cigarette. I refused, but he knew now that I was a smoker. From then on, I felt OK to pinch cigarettes from him when desperate.

He also asked, "Do you know who the young man I saw you with earlier is?"

I tried to search my memory and solve this puzzle for a moment. "I have no idea, Dad," I said.

"Remember the boy who stole your croissants when you were about ten years old? That's him! I thought you should know," he said.

That certainly had no impact on our relationship. When I questioned Hardi about it one day, he laughed.

"How could I possibly remember all the kids I stole croissants from in my life?"

We had a great laugh about it, and our friendship grew stronger. The travelling and endless hours spent on the road chatting while hitchhiking made our friendship deep and intimate. On top of that, we became business partners and came up with the idea of selling Christmas cards door to door. We earned enough money to travel as far as India, Morocco, and Australia (in my case) from the proceeds.

Professor Philip

My friendship with Slav continued throughout our four years at college. Although we were studying electrical engineering, we had other nontechnical compulsory subjects such as a foreign language, French in my case, and German in Slav's. On top of that, we studied our own Serbo-Croatian language, as well as progressive contemporary socialist and Western literature, Marxism, social science, and civil defence.

Both of us read progressive contemporary and classic Yugoslav, European, American, and Russian literature, and we exchanged the books we liked. At school, we studied revolutionary writers and, to be honest, we read and admired them, but we had our own views on their messages, political morals, and philosophies.

Our professor, Philip, wouldn't let anyone interpret the revolutionary rhetoric in any way other than the "correct" official version. He also had a habit of terrorizing weak and insecure students. His methods were torturous. He would raise a question and expect a precisely formulated answer; one he hadn't disclosed to anyone. As a result, he would call on most of us, one by one, to respond and keep us all standing. You were usually called to stand in front of the class at the blackboard, where you had to discuss, answer, explain, and demonstrate knowledge across various topics. In this way, he assessed a whole bunch of us at once.

I handled his methods well because I read a lot and had the ability to argue and verbalize my opinions without fear. But those who were insecure, or too afraid to stand up for themselves and their views, were scrutinized to tears or into a complete mental block. It was sad, frightening, and frustrating to watch, but none of us had the courage to confront him.

There was one exception to his method, and at first, none of us understood what was behind it. Goddess, who also came from Vareš, drove a car, an unimaginable phenomenon for someone our age. Her father was a wealthy butcher, and she was his only daughter.

Philip would get her to stand and ask her a question, just as he did with any other student. But while he would usually throw in sub-questions as soon as he sensed someone knew their stuff, grilling them for "correct and specific" answers and terms, like an interrogation, he treated Goddess differently. You felt humiliated all the way through those sessions, even when you knew the material. He never let you conclude an argument without interruption or provocation. Yet Goddess was the only one allowed to recite a well-rehearsed response in total silence, uninterrupted.

Slav and I became suspicious, but our thoughts were too bold, and too dangerous, to voice. One Sunday, we were hitchhiking by the roadside and weren't entirely surprised when we saw our professor and Goddess drive past in his Ford Escort. He was married, a member of the Communist Party, and pushed political correctness in class to the point of terror. They both clearly saw us.

We decided to keep this knowledge to ourselves. From then on, the professor was noticeably less aggressive during our oral exams. This came in very handy when I wrote an essay in which I expressed concerns about the hypocrisy and fragile future of our socialism. I was especially critical of those preaching revolution and equality while living lives of wealth and privilege.

"I cannot show this to anyone," he warned during a private meeting in his office. I felt things could have gone very differently for me, but he knew what I knew. He was sleeping with a student in secret and had been doing so since she was sixteen. My essay was a parabola of his behaviour and hypocrisy. He was a respected, well-paid psychopath breaking the law, while my friend Chuck, a Romani boy, sat in jail for nine months over a trivial offence by comparison.

My professor's crime certainly caused widespread emotional, moral, and political damage among the new generation of young socialists. There was a rumour that he'd been sacked from an all-female admin college previously for the same offence. Many of my female friends, university students, spoke about being molested, blackmailed, or failed in exams for refusing to submit to professors with a taste for young female flesh.

Slav and I had our way of playing the system, practising a quiet conspiracy as a form of rebellion. We sat in the front bench, middle row, right in front of the blackboard. Most of our oral exams were held at the blackboard, where we had to explain the laws of physics and those relevant to the generation, distribution, and use of electrical energy. Everything was expressed through graphs and formulas. Memorising them and working them out wasn't easy and doing it in front of the whole class made it even harder.

We came up with a strategy. Those who weren't sure of themselves and lacked confidence prepared mini cheat sheets on specific topics they struggled with. They handed over their miniature notes to us before class began. Gradually, we built up a considerable collection and kept them with us. If a student needed help with a question, they would leave the sponge on the edge of our desk. We would then find the relevant mini card and place it discreetly under the sponge. They'd grab the sponge off the desk, with the card tucked underneath.

Though they barely used the cards, just having them gave a sense of confidence and an easy refresher before presenting a set of formulas or working through laws of physics. As obvious as it might have been, we never got caught. Maybe our professors knew but couldn't imagine we were that cunning. We'll never know.

I didn't need the cards for my exams, but I found them incredibly helpful when studying those multiple formulas, laws, and principles. The cards were the simplest possible extractions of the complex theories we studied, easy to memorize in such a compressed format.

For some reason, I took the risk for others, as I often did, and usually suffered the consequences. This time, though, luck was on my side.

Sami Tischler

Dumped by Imam's Daughter and the Moonlight Beauty

I wore long hair, unofficially banned in schools, and dressed in clothes from old family collections or government-issued workers' uniforms. I frequently visited my uncle, who had built his house illegally on the edge of the city, overlooking the airport. I smoked contraband tobacco, buying it through my uncle's connections from a woman who lived near my school. I was reluctant to spend the whole summer holiday in the village because there were things I'd miss out on in the city. Besides, they expected me to work in the fields like my cousin Asim did. My father had left the village after a disagreement with his brother, giving away his share of land to him. I didn't feel responsible for farming it. I never refused to help, but as I grew up, they expected more from me, and I had other interests.

One year, I happened to be there during the largest festival in the region. It's called *Aliđun* or *Ilindan* by the Muslim and Orthodox populations of Bosnia, respectively. Bosnians say, "Some of us celebrate Aliya, and others celebrate Iliya." They fall on the same day in the calendar, though. This is a two-day festival, and people come from far and wide to meet, dance, and eat lamb from the spit. Alcohol was sold, but its consumption wasn't seen as appropriate for Muslims. As a result, these festivals were generally peaceful and trouble-free. Muslim and Christian crowds celebrated within a short but welldefined distance. Young unmarried girls were free to court more than one suitor, and the suitors could challenge each other. The final decision was in the girls' hands. Young women danced and used the chance to choose their marriage partners. Older family members kept an eye on morality and family trees, advising on appropriate matches. Although Muslims and Orthodox gathered in sight of each other, mixed-religion marriages and courting were taboo and not possible in this location.

That year, I met a young girl, just finishing her primary school. We walked up and down the stretch of grass provided for young couples.

Sarajevo's Elusive Spring

We even sat on a grassy slope and chatted about life in the city, where she lived with her parents. It turned out that her father was an Imam. I really liked her. She had a small, fragile figure and long, thick black hair. She was extremely beautiful, with pale skin and a pair of dark, black eyes. She gave me her address and said she would love to see me in the city. I was a year or two older and thought about looking her up when school returned.

That same summer, within days, I courted a girl in my village the way my ancestors and villagers had done for hundreds of years. This girl came to visit her relatives in the village. She lived in Sarajevo, too. We met at the evening gathering around the village spring, where everyone came to fetch drinking water before dinner. It was a time to socialise and sing. They danced if there was anyone playing music. In those days, they had battery-powered gramophones, and they used them on occasions. Also, a local boy, Hakiya, played dancing jigs on a pan flute. We started talking, and I got an invite to come to her window after dinner. She gave me the exact time and coordinates.

"I'll be fine and don't need anyone," I said to my cousins when they offered to come and support my first courting at the window, Bosnian style. I'd already witnessed my cousin Asim's shy, word-poor approach and style. One winter, we walked for two hours on frozen snow crust to get to the village of Godinja, where he couldn't gather enough courage to court a girl. We spent hours in a barn while our local cousins worked on him. Eventually, he went there, and within 15 minutes, the girl's father woke up and chased him away. The story kept us amused on our way back across the frozen countryside, lit by the full moon. We laughed loudly in the moonlight like horny wolves, repeating the old man's curses and threats. His conversation with the girl had been so uninspired and boring. No wonder the old peasant found him a bad choice for his giggling daughter.

I went to meet the chosen one by myself, found the window in the basement, and knocked gently at the windowpane, trying to alert only the one expecting me. All the lights were out, and they had no dogs. Everything was perfect. She came to the window, and we were chatting quietly. Girls weren't allowed to open the window. It was considered immoral. She decided to break the rule. "This is boring and awkward," she declared, opening the window. She wore her pyjamas, and her top buttons were undone. She was 16, the same age as me.

There was no light other than the natural summer night light coming from the star-speckled sky. I could see enough, and she wasn't trying to hide anything. "Aren't you going to kiss me?" she asked cheekily. "I didn't know you'd like me to," I responded shyly, as I moved closer to her. The window height was perfect. We kissed badly but didn't give up, improving in minutes. I couldn't believe it was happening. She took my hand and placed it over her small, firm breast. I could feel her hard, swollen nipples like cherries. She wanted me to play with them and held my hand there. We were both getting very excited and gradually deeper into trouble. A door opened somewhere in the house, and floorboards squeaked. It could have been someone going to the outhouse. She quickly closed the window, buttoned up her blouse in panic, and walked away into the darkness of the house. I sat on the grass under the window with a hard-on, listening. A few minutes later, she came back. The magic of the moment was broken. She had no courage or permission to continue talking to me and certainly not to continue where we were heading earlier. We hastily arranged to meet in the city at her college on a certain date in September.

On my return from summer break, I had something to look forward to in September. I even had a photograph of the Imam's daughter to look at. It was one of those professionally done portraits for a document. She was very pretty, and the photo was touched up by hand, as was fashionable at the time. Considering the religious ban from mine and my first girlfriend's parents, and another imposed by a small-time gang, I wasn't feeling very optimistic about the future of either one of the two possibilities. As time went by, the excitement wore thin, and doubt crept in. At one point, I wasn't sure if any of it had ever happened. I was back at school and tested the window princess first.

Sarajevo's Elusive Spring

I went to her school at the time we had arranged to meet. I waited in the street, covered by fallen leaves, looking for her in the crowd leaving the school in the afternoon, but she wasn't there. I felt like a loser, depressed for days, stood up by a girl I thought would have happily jumped into my arms. Eventually, I accepted that the night of erotic touches in the moonless night had been pure luck and something she would have seen as a thrill, a thing to do under the nose of her conservative village family. "I'll go and see Imam's daughter," I decided.

Imam's daughter lived in an industrial township built around a large factory. They made truck engines and employed thousands, much like the one at the end of my street. Most of the workers lived nearby in the government-built township housing. The Imam lived in his own house, not far from a new mosque built on the edge of the city. I wrote her a couple of letters beforehand. She responded with one, and when I suggested that we could meet up, she went silent. I was annoyed and decided to pay her a visit. It was one of those freezing cold winter days. The snow was old and grey from the pollution in the city. Hard layers had turned into ice, making walking on it hazardous. After a tram ride, I boarded a local bus and was driven into the suburbs. I found her house by asking local kids for directions. Once I was in her street, I sent a kid with a message that I was waiting for her at the nearby corner. It took a long time before the kid returned. "Her father told me to tell you to leave her alone and not to contact her again." The young boy delivered his message and went away. He turned around a few times and looked at me, wondering what I was going to do. I stood there for a bit longer, smoked another cigarette, and watched passersby as they stared and walked away. "What the hell are you doing here in this shithole?" I asked myself. None of them would let their daughters have a chat with a guy like me. I had long hair, wore a building workers' jacket I'd scored from my uncle, and hung around notorious dives like club "Cactus."

Club "Cactus" was the place where a new breed of youth gathered to dance to Western rock and smoke hashish. They branded us with a name that had Turkish origins. They called us "Hashish-ari," those consuming hashish. The jacket I wore was meant to be a statement and a symbol of protest. It was directed towards the new breed of well-to do career politicians and their worn-out revolutionary rhetoric. China was going through the end of the Cultural Revolution, and Mao was using his last breath to warn his revolutionary comrades against hypocrisy, abuse of power, and the devaluation of revolutionary ideals. Our own ageing revolutionaries, army officers, and managers of public companies lived in luxury, completely isolated from the working-class population, students, and the youth. If they were forced back into industry, mines, wheat fields, and farmyards, most of them wouldn't last a week. Even our President Tito, who travelled extensively around the world, kept away from Mao. They must have known what was going on there: government-issued blue pyjamas, a one-child policy, and everyone on a bicycle. Anyone looking, thinking or behaving like an intellectual or upper class had to experience the rice fields again.

There was nothing wrong with my jacket. It was a great jacket, worn by government employees as outdoor working gear. None of my peers would have worn anything like it. They all wore clothes smuggled from Trieste, Italy, and sold illegally in the markets of the Old City. I understood that these townships surrounding Sarajevo had no place for an avant-garde youth like me. A lot of my distant relatives and immigrants from the mountains of my birth lived in these suburbs, but they had no intention of letting their children get corrupted by urban culture and emerging Western trends. I realised that I was exactly the kind of young man they wouldn't like to see their daughters with.

Funnily enough, my mother warned me about Imam's daughter: "Dearest son, her family aren't going to be happy about seeing the two of you together."

"Mum, she likes me, and I like her too, she is very nice," I defended our naïve courtship at the time. "I'm sure she likes you, but her father, the Imam, will be the one to decide." Sure enough, that's exactly how it was. The Imam had the last word. The word was a definite NO!

Sarajevo's Elusive Spring

With Chief in Dubrovnik

Chief, my unofficial mentor/guru, invited me and my new friend Slav to join him on a trip to Dubrovnik for the long weekend holiday on the 1st of May. Sarajevo can be cold at that time of the year. Snow is visible on distant mountaintops, and chilly winds come down over the blooms in the hillside orchards. We travelled as a trio. Slav almost looked like a young girl, and we believed his appearance helped us get good and fast lifts. We made 120 km to the coastal highway by the afternoon. Bathing in the warm spring sun while trying to hitch rides south to Dubrovnik felt like carefree fun. Luck wasn't on our side, and as the day came to an end, the sun was setting, and it started to get dark. We hopped on a bus. By dinnertime, we walked on the marble cobblestones of Stradun. Notoriously short of funds, we ate a quarter of a loaf of bread and yoghurt for dinner.

We found a park above a monastery housing a community of Catholic nuns as our base. It was a top-notch residence and a hideout for our sleeping bags during the day. In those days, the early '70s, Dubrovnik looked empty on the 1st of May. Tourists came much later, and penniless hippies like us stood out. We were forced to leave if spotted by the cops. Leaving our luggage and sleeping bags in hiding proved to be the best strategy and the only way to avoid getting evicted from the city. We came to the city to eat and sit on the ancient marble steps in front of St. Vlaho's statue and church. From there, we walked to the port through the old gates. We sat on bench seats, enjoyed the view across to the small island of Lokrum, a stone's throw away, and listened to the church bells tolling every quarter hour, half hour, and full hour. The water was too cold for a swim.

Access to the ramparts wasn't restricted as much as it is these days, and the tickets were cheap. On a nice day in May, walking around the old city on top of its defensive walls was a great pastime. You could see all its corners, little terraces, gardens, inner courtyards of monasteries, government-owned buildings, villas, churches, cathedrals, and residences. Dubrovnik is an oasis of well-preserved layers of history, medieval architecture, ancient urban planning, and self-sustainable infrastructure. From its ramparts, you could read it like an open book. Besides, a major part of its structure faces the sea. However, there aren't windows in its walls. The walls were built as massive defensive barriers, with the only view towards the sea from their defensive walkways, platforms, and guard shelters. Every time I walked on the ramparts, I'd discover something new, understand another intricacy of this city so connected to the history of Bosnia as its trading and export agent. Dubrovnik maintained its limited trading independence throughout the 500 years of Ottoman rule and remained a major link with the international markets and trade routes, as far as China in the East and the Americas in the West.

We walked back to the park wall overlooking the monastery and sat there, trying to make eye contact with the nuns. Most of them were barely older than us. We watched them working in the immaculately kept garden, hanging their washing, sitting on garden benches, and reading. We exchanged little hand gestures here and there and picked on those who had responded to our signals. We bought bottles of wine, and Chief played his guitar. It was the end of a lonely, long winter for them too. We couldn't understand why a young girl would waste her life as a bride of Christ and deny herself family, sex, music, travel, and general fun available to the rest of us. Our socialist government never banned religious institutions and religious practices amongst its population, but we weren't encouraged to follow them. Our education openly referred to religion as "opium for the masses" and promoted atheism as an alternative.

Slav mimed to a couple of sympathetic nuns how poor and hungry we were and asked them for a food donation. He must have figured out that his request fitted into a category of charity. Two nuns went away and came back after a while, asking someone to come down to the gate where they were going to hand us some food. They may have mistaken him for a girl, as some of the drivers did on the road. So, he went down on a steep footpath all the way to the gate. We could see him coming back with a big plastic bag full of goods, slowly ascending the rocky track until he disappeared at the edge of the park.

Sarajevo's Elusive Spring

Shortly after, he presented the bag for inspection. There was a fresh loaf of bread, cheese, olives, spring onions, raisins, and dried figs. It was everything they produced in the monastery: their gardens and orchards. We had a feast and plenty of leftovers for the next meal. While chewing on these delicacies, I marvelled at the magical possibilities that communal living could nurture in an organised, disciplined system, rewarding self-sufficiency with the best produce imaginable.

Chief told us stories of spending a winter in a commune in Germany a couple of years earlier. He certainly wasn't its most productive member, considering his disability, but he raved about jam sessions, hashish they smoked, parties they had, and the music they listened to. Yugoslav media published articles damning Western youth, its culture, music, drugs, sexual promiscuity, communes, warning us about its destructive and immoral aspects. On the contrary, I read every word with deep interest and became more attracted to the positive side of what was happening in the West. I was already hooked on music and travel. Being penniless on the road seemed like so much fun. Becoming an object of police harassment frequently wasn't something to brag about, but I had no access to drugs, no criminal record, and always had my ID and some cash on me. There wasn't much they could slap me with. I learned to keep my tongue in my mouth much longer than I liked, fake some respect, and be patient. The militia was easy to provoke, and they didn't hesitate to use truncheons. I remember the late '60s when militia officers chased young men in the "Corso." Their only crime was the long hair they wore. Once caught, they were taken to the station and given a military-style haircut. In 1968, when all of Europe boiled under the student rebellion, there was an open confrontation between militia troops and students in the Capital. President Tito stepped in and managed to defuse tensions while allowing more civil freedom, culminating in giving Yugoslav citizens the right to hold a passport and travel abroad freely. Six years later, in 1974, I was only 17 when I got my passport.

Sami Tischler

There was another significant aspect of our trip to Dubrovnik. Slav and I got introduced to Sarajevo's legendary freak, a guy called Zizi. Everybody knew Zizi. I had seen him before. He was easy to recognise. He wore long hair, a beard, beads, and a headband, often walking wrapped in a colourful bedspread, like an Indian chief. He was about 15 years older and known as one of the first hippies in the city. It was his idea, at least 10 years earlier, to come to Dubrovnik for the 1st of May. Zizi was a working-class socialist, an automotive spray painter, working in the VW/TAS car factory at the end of my street. He was self-educated, active in the Socialist Worker's Union, and wrote mad poetry. He was an outspoken critic of the Yugoslav political scene and a passionate supporter of the Palestinian PLO "Al Fatah." He rented a room in his apartment to foreign students: Palestinians and Iraqis. They flooded Sarajevo universities at the time. Zizi snubbed off our existence arrogantly by labelling us "weekend hippies." Little did he know at the time that his comments were completely out of place and that our stars were about to align. Our destinies took both of us across the Great Ocean. Our lives realigned and stayed close together, reconnecting in crucial moments for years. However, it was so important to have met him in the company of someone like Chief, an "Old Folk," because Zizi paid attention from then on. It was tough to break into these avant-garde circles. They (Stara Raja/Old Folk) had a big fanbase. However, they appreciated and needed inspiration, which could only come with new people and from younger generations. By the time Zizi died in Melbourne, I was one of the few people in Australia who knew what we had lost and how significant his life and contribution were to what we may call Sarajevo's elusive Spring.

Sarajevo's Elusive Spring

Travel, Travel, Travel, Everybody Travels to the Coast!

I bought my first sleeping bag from Chief, of course. When I brought it home, my parents were in shock. They'd never seen anything like that and couldn't understand why I would need one. The previous summer, we went together to the Adriatic Coast for a two-week holiday. My father owned a Fiat 750 at the time. We packed a tent, camp cooker, blankets, linen, cushions, groceries, inflatable mattresses, fold-up chairs, towels, food for the road, my parents, my two younger sisters, and me. We had a roof rack loaded with stuff, and every bit of space between us had bags, boxes, and canisters in it. The little Fiat 750 did great, and we made it into a camping park in Podgorica.

I had already been to the coast twice through a subsidy by the Socialist Workers' Union. Both times, we were housed military-style in temporarily converted primary schools on metal bunk beds, eating, bathing, and sleeping on tight schedules supervised by our schoolteachers. It was a great experience and excellent preparation for the future National Service. We travelled on a narrow-gauge railway line all the way to Dubrovnik. By the time I evolved into a serious traveller, all these narrow-gauge railway lines built by the Austro-Hungarian Empire were dismantled. These small carriages with wooden interiors, drawn by steam-powered engines, had that unmistakable charm and grandeur of the past. The new socialist society, obsessed with erasing the past, travelled fast into prosperity on wide-gauge electrified railways through industrialisation, urbanisation, deforestation, pollution, and environmental degradation. Small villages on the coast were fast becoming tourist centres with hotels, camping parks, private rooms, and seasonal entertainment.

My parents did it on a small budget, paid the camp fees, and cooked food at the site. We bought milk, bread, meat, some veggies, ice cream, and cold drinks. Our days were spent at the beach, where we befriended a Czech family with a son and daughter our age. My parents couldn't speak Czech, but the oldies had a great time, and so did we. Czech and Bosnian languages are both of Slavic origin. It doesn't take much to find a common core and use it in communication. To my parents, it would have been a linguistic adventure, but nothing too foreign to them. My father read, recited Arabic from his memory, and used both Roman and Cyrillic alphabets. Both of my folks prayed in Arabic. Their vocabulary was loaded with Turkish, German, and Arabic terminology. I'm sure they somehow used it all in their communication. The Czechs even came for a visit to Sarajevo on their way back home. I slept with my legs out of the tent while on holiday. There wasn't enough space inside for all of us. This was the first and last time I went to the Adriatic Coast with my parents.

In the Scrap Yard

The following summer, a cousin arranged a summer job for me in a scrap yard. I had already held short-term summer jobs. The previous summer, I worked in a mini concrete block "factory" for a pittance. I worked for days on an open slab, mixing concrete, filling formers, cleaning up, dismantling, and again pouring, cleaning up, and dismantling. My final pay could hardly cover the price of shoes and clothes I had destroyed in the process. The scrap yard job seemed promising. It was a government yard, and I was going to get paid the wage of a full-time labourer who took his annual leave. I was the lucky winner. It's true, I was the lucky winner. Seasonal work was hard to find, and when you did, you usually got screwed.

I started the work early, travelled on public transport, and came back home dirty, covered in sweat, tired like a dog and hungry like a wolf. I could hardly last an hour watching TV before I fell asleep. My father laughed: "That's why you need to study and go to school. Now you can see what the real job is like. Hope you appreciate the food on the table. You have no idea how much everything costs," he raved on. He was right. I couldn't imagine doing this for a living and was hoping not to have to. I didn't mind school and studied out of habit and interest. I hated the embarrassment at the blackboard if I couldn't respond to questions and solve problems during my oral exams at college. Studying was easy for me. It was unfortunate that electrical engineering wasn't exactly my favourite topic. What worried me was full-time work afterwards and the routine I was watching from my house, the one followed by millions in this Workers' Paradise. Get up in the morning, go to work, come back home, eat dinner, watch TV, go to bed, get up in the morning... You were meant to feel lucky to have a job, a roof over your head, food on the table... So basic, so boring, and so depressing.

My father asked: "What are you going to do with the money? You should help us out a bit, times are hard." I realised; he had already spent the money I hadn't even received yet. I knew that I must contribute some funds into the house budget. It was only fair. My father worked hard, rolling shifts in the government bakery, and the pay wasn't that great. My mum knitted by hand and worked on a knitting machine at home. She did custom-made garments for men and women using her traditional skills, as well as all the cooking, cleaning, and shopping for the family. She grew veggies in the small garden, made jam, pickles, and preserves in winter.

"No worries, Dad, I'll help out, but I'd like to keep some money and travel to the Coast for a couple of weeks," I declared. "You can have half of whatever I make." My father was a hard man, but my offer must have impressed him, and he had questions about my trip and my travel plans. "I have a sleeping bag and plan to sleep on the beach. I'll hitch rides along the Coast and try to meet others who are doing the same thing." He was shaking his head, unsure of my plans and the legality of it. I wasn't too sure if it was going to work either, but I had no alternatives, especially now that I had promised half of my pay to the family.

I kept going to work, sifting through piles of aluminium scrap, pipes of various sizes, twisted lengths of rusted reinforcement rod, engine parts, and wire coils. One afternoon, cleaning myself up took some time. I was trying to look decent on public transport among other passengers going back home from work. Most of them looked quite presentable, beside me, who was sunburnt, sporting cuts on my hands and arms, and wearing stained clothes. Occasionally, a Gypsy trader returning home from the street stall looked puzzled and wondered how it was that he or she didn't know me. I could have easily passed for one of their own. I wished I knew a few greetings or phrases in Romani. Always fascinated by Gypsies, I could have befriended someone from that unique tribe.

I managed to clean up mostly, which wasn't that easy, considering the garbage and waste materials I handled every day. On that day, it took some time to make myself look decent enough for the trip on public transport. I started chatting with the night watchman who had just arrived for his night shift. He was a young man from my region in the

Sarajevo's Elusive Spring

mountains near Sarajevo, and we shared a few cigarettes while talking.

Everyone had gone by then, and I offered to get us a six-pack of beers from the shop nearby. When I came back, he showed me a spot on the bank of the river behind the perimeter fence of the scrap yard. Right on the opposite side of the river, as we enjoyed our beer, we could see a temporary Gypsy camp. There were tents, vans, and horses in the paddock. Just another levelled area earmarked for industrial development. There were smoking fires, people around them, and kids everywhere.

"They have the best life," he said. "Every night, you can hear music playing, you can see them dance around the fire, and then I get here the following day, and they're all gone." Seeing that I was interested, he continued, "Such a mobile lot. They set up and dismantle camp in no time. Everything fits on the cart, inside the van. They're the last real nomads!"

I had seen them often when they came to drop off scrap metal and negotiated the price and weight with my bosses. Their bony horses, covered with flies, looked almost apocalyptic. The men were something else, their golden teeth showing under a curled-up moustache, dark-skinned, dirty men, wearing well-weathered clothes and shoes. They always showed off bundles of worn-out money, their cocky wives, poorly dressed, and neglected children in tow. Women, in the habit of breastfeeding uncovered, always attracted my attention. As a child, I had watched a family of Gypsy coppersmiths at work in the village of my birth, and their women breastfeeding uncovered around the fire. I saw it later in the city markets and on public transport. This was so different from the conservative society of mixed religions and ethnicities in Bosnia.

"It would be great to spend some time with them, travelling and hanging around," I said.

"C'mon, you wouldn't do that. Imagine eating on the ground, everything is dirty, dogs, horses, everything open, no privacy..." he was trying to bring it back to the raw reality and away from the romanticism of a free spirit and a non-conventional, carefree lifestyle.

We were on our second beer when we spotted a group of Gypsy youth approaching the opposite riverbank, only about 100 metres away. The river was low, and sandbars stretched along its length. Apart from the polluted water, the gentle shallow stream provided a perfect swimming beach and a magic spot to wash and cool down at the end of a hot summer's day. Small kids ran into the shallows, splashed, and dived into the stream, remaining cautious and keeping close to the shore. We sat in the shade of a long wall, partially screened by the greenery of the neglected industrial site. Two young girls followed the kids to the water and sat on the bank. They appeared to be keeping watch. After a while, one of them pulled out a couple of cigarettes and they lit up. We could see them puffing out small clouds of smoke at the short distance. They talked and laughed, puffed on their cigarettes, pushed, and touched each other playfully, unaware of our presence across the river. Gypsies in Bosnia speak a mix of Bosnian, Turkish, and Romani. You could understand words they used as substitutes for the ones they had lost from their original language. Both of us remained silent, carefully watching the scene, and sucking on our beers. The children came out of the water and walked across the paddock back towards the tents. The girls stayed on the bank. I could hear the murmur of the water and a few words from the camp breaking the silence. We watched them as they stripped off their long skirts and jumped into the stream. They played and splashed each other, proceeding with washing themselves as if they were in their own bathroom. I couldn't see every detail of their semi naked bodies. Both kept their shirts and underpants on as they went through their routine. It was so erotic and intimate, watching them expose small sections of their breasts, thighs, buttocks, and nipples while swinging their charcoal black hair and flashing sections of skin rarely seen by anyone. The industrial wasteland surrounding the scene provided a great backdrop for two gorgeous young girls, barely women, getting themselves washed as if they were in a mountain creek well hidden among willows and reeds. I couldn't say a word, completely absorbed

Sarajevo's Elusive Spring

in my privileged, coincidental, and unexpected gift. Young breasts, similar to those I had touched the previous summer while courting a young girl from the city at the village window and had hardly seen in the faint night light. There they were in full view, on display for our secret enjoyment. Bouncing firmly, dark, swollen teenage nipples, erect and proud, hiding and disappearing behind the wet fabric of their loose, half-buttoned shirts.

I looked at the guardsman sitting beside me, his gaze glued across the stream. He had forgotten about my existence, just as I wasn't aware of his for a moment. I pulled out my cigarette packet and nudged his shoulder. "You want to light one up?" He turned towards me, his eyes dreamy and glazed. I could almost see those bouncing tits there like on a TV screen. "Yeah, why not?" he swung his head back as he grabbed a cigarette and stuck it into his salivating mouth. He would've forgotten to light it up if I hadn't brought a match to his cigarette. Within seconds, we were puffing on our smokes, forgetting that we were in a virtual hiding spot. The cloud of smoke rising up against the dark wall of the shed must've given our observation spot away. One girl pulled the ends of her shirt tightly over her chest and whispered something to the other girl. They both looked in our direction briefly and started moving towards the safety of the opposite bank. In their careless play, they had moved so close to our hiding spot, close enough to hear their excited breathing and fully enjoy their facial and body features. We both knew that we had been discovered. I felt a bit embarrassed, like a thief who had been caught, but there was no point in jumping out of hiding and giving myself away unprovoked. Just before the girls ascended the bank and still in clear view, they stood with their backs to us and for a minute, took off their wet underpants. They both bent forward as if bowing to the audience in front of them, fully exposing their beautifully shaped naked bum cheeks with a small bushy area between their legs for our last assessment. In unison, they slapped their arses for our pleasure and slipped their skirts back on. They climbed the bank, turned towards us one more time, and made another clear gesture by raising their middle fingers high in the air before walking with exaggerated hip movements back towards the camp. It was an exhilarating experience, and I spontaneously clapped as I watched the grand finale. "Stop it, you fool! Now they know we've been watching; they won't come again!" he said disappointedly. "Don't worry, my friend, they'll be here next year, but they'll be married by then and won't be showing it all off to the world. They'll keep it exclusive to their men." I was silent for a moment and remembered my fetish. "If you're lucky, they won't hesitate to show you a glimpse of this erotica while they feed their snotty babies one day." This must've erased any romanticism he would've kept about the event in his memory. He had the whole night ahead of him to deal with it in the loneliness of his job as a scrap yard watchman.

I went home on public transport and looked at the tired faces and exhausted bodies of the socialist working class returning home after a hard day's work in factories, shops, and offices. A few women appeared talkative and full of life. Most couldn't wait to dump their tired bodies into worn-out bus seats. Their hairdos couldn't last all day in crowded transport, bad ventilation. Synthetic clothing they wore couldn't subsidize the energy they left behind feeding the big administrative and industrial City monsters. The memory of those energetic, carefree, homeless girls in the river lingered in my mind all the way home and much further. I desperately wanted to avoid the working-class slavery but had no skills or traditions that would provide me with the solution. I naively believed that Gypsies had it all worked out. Living on the fringes of society, outside of its norms, limitations, rules, and predictability could be the answer, I thought at the time.

Adriatic Coast

The day I got paid, the Gypsy camp was empty, deserted, with lonely piles of garbage left behind. They would've moved on, either of their own accord or by a government order enforced by the police. Within days, I had given half of my pay to Mum, the family treasurer, and packed my sleeping bag, swimmers, spare socks, underwear, and went on the road. My pack weighed around 5 kg. I spent around 40 days travelling up and down the Dalmatian Coast. Picking up rides wasn't as smooth as you might think. Considering the volume of traffic in summer, it was depressing. You'd stand there in the hot sun while single-driver cars casually went by. On a lucky day, some lone foreign tourist would pick you up and drive for 150 km in barely more than an hour. One time, I sat beside a tiny Italian driver in a two-seater, open top Lamborghini as he drove his beast along the steep slopes of Biokovo mountain, pushing the speed to suicidal limits, overtaking semitrailers on blind corners, cutting across sharp bends in the road while blasting the wildest bands on his stereo at full volume. I spoke school-learned French at the time, and we exchanged a few words here and there, but he was too busy enjoying his own mind trip. Thinking back, he could've been riding out an LSD trip or been high on any drug completely unknown to me and the naïve Yugoslav Road patrols in their Fiat 1300. This guy was just flying his Lamborghini in midair, hardly touching the ground while I pretended to be too cool to show how terrified and concerned for my life I was. Other times, I'd be sitting at the back of a Ford Transit, Citroen, or VW minibus with a young couple up front, trying to have a conversation in a mix of French, basic English learnt from John Wayne and Clint Eastwood Westerns, and some German picked up from Yugoslav-produced wartime films. They all played great music on their stereos and had a lot of questions about life and politics in Yugoslavia. I could've told them a lot, but my foreign language skills were limited, and we never had much time. Most of them were using the picturesque route along the coast, following lesser-known paths through Montenegro, Kosovo, and Macedonia on their way to Greece. Some talked about going further to Turkey. The Middle East was risky, with the endless war in Lebanon raging on throughout my youth, and most Western travellers avoided it. I met a lot of young Yugoslavs who dressed like hippies and freaks, who shared tents in camping grounds, cooked their own food, and spent their holidays on a small budget, often financed by their parents. I did it my way. I lived off my earnings from the scrap yard, ate simply, and slept in my sleeping bag in various places. Olive groves, remote beaches, coastal rock shelters and caves, grounds of public buildings, secluded corners of public parks, and graveyards made great places to crash for the night.

Dumped in Drvenik

My first destination was the small town of Drvenik. I wanted to visit my former girlfriend. She'd told me while we were together the previous winter that her parents owned a house there. This was a place where she spent her summers. She was one of those girls who did all the work. She came to me during a wild concert in the city and told me that she wanted to kiss me, which she proceeded to do right away. She decided that she liked me and wouldn't leave after that. We started dating. We met a few times, kissed, and fondled each other in the dark corners of the club, in the stairwell leading to her parents' apartment, and a little more. I wasn't really into her and her forwardness. I saw love as something more subtle, intimate, and unspoken. She introduced me to her best friend, a tall, gorgeous older girl. She had long black curly hair and the shapes of a woman, including her sizable backside and generous breasts. She never said much, and I never had much of an opportunity to develop a closer connection with her. All three of us went to a grand concert hall in Skenderija with a capacity of 20,000 in the stands. It was a hall designed for large indoor sports events. In a concert, when the grounds turned into a massive dance floor, it catered for an additional 10,000. Large spacious hallways surrounded the auditorium. Everyone between the ages of 16 and 25 would've been there on that night. I went to get us drinks and left my girlfriend on the dance floor with her school friends. I made my way through the huge crowd and ended up in a massive queue at the bar.

I waited for a bit, and suddenly someone placed soft female hands over my eyes from behind. I felt warm breasts touching my back and a wiggly pelvis against my backside. A sexy fragrance reached my nostrils. I figured out I was in good hands but wasn't sure whose. It wasn't my girlfriend. Her perfume and body shape I knew well by now. I struggled to turn around in the tight, crowded space we were in and straight into a passionate kiss with my girlfriend's best friend. She held my head and gave me her tongue shamelessly in the middle of the crowd and in full light. I had nothing against it. She took my hand and dragged me away into a secluded space, away from the bar and the passing crowd. I was about to receive a full treatment. We were squeezed behind a large concrete column, pretending we were invisible. She was picking my pocket for a growing fish while I had my hand under her blouse, polishing rockmelons and starting to work my way further below. I was eating her ears, tongue, neck like a beast at a wild feast. We were so lost in our passion that we didn't realise my girlfriend was standing with an open mouth, watching our act. When we stopped, I was embarrassed but had nothing to say. Neither gave me a chance. They both stormed off together in silence. Her busty girlfriend would have a lot to explain.

I've hardly seen her since. I thought that 5 months could've given her time to heal, recover, and reconsider our unfortunate history. I know, it sounds low, but before I dived fully into my newly discovered Gypsy lifestyle, it could've been great to enjoy some homely treats from my old sweetheart. Drvenik was a small village back then. A significant aspect of it was that the ferry to the island of Korčula operated from its tiny port. Cars, trucks, and people moved through its tiny streets all day long. They all disappeared into the belly of an enormous ship, and as soon as one left, more cars and people arrived and lined up for the next one. Other than that, many Bosnians bought blocks and built holiday homes there. Rome wasn't built in a day, nor was Drvenik. One summer they prepared the block, dug footings, poured the concrete slab, and the next year they bricked up one level and formed up for the slab. They poured the slab using a gang of friends and relatives who camped on the block while doing it. They mixed concrete in one small mixer or by using the two-shovel hand method. All of it was carried on top of the wall in buckets manually. They would roast a lamb or a piglet for the day's meal and hydrate the crew with warm beer. At night, after the evening shower at the beach, they'd party until late and continue the next day. On the hillsides, around the port, you could see permanent building sites with houses at different stages of development for years. The only sound, once the ferry had gone, was the cicadas, the rattle of cement mixers, and the faint sound of waves moving the gravel at the small beach back and forth.

Sarajevo's Elusive Spring

I Met my Ex at the Beach.

It was easy; the beach is the only one, about 100 metres long. She turned up with a bunch of young men, suntanned, relaxed, and trendy. She looked great, suntanned in her bikini. Her generous, voluptuous body somehow dropped the innocence of a girl. I felt it matured, became inviting, sexy, and womanly. Summer suited her well. She'd lost a bit of weight, and her figure flourished once the winter layers of clothes and jumpers were gone. She was surprised and appeared flattered by my visit at first. "Here is something good about to happen," I thought. When I told her that I was sleeping outside, hoping that she might offer a better alternative, she just looked away and changed the subject. She went off with her crowd and hardly paid attention to me while there. I couldn't see that she was intimate with any of the boys around her. Perhaps she was too smart, didn't trust me, and couldn't afford to give me another chance. She may have wanted to see me crawling, begging, humiliated, and asking for forgiveness. At the time, I had no wisdom or experience to find or try a strategy that could've led to a conciliatory outcome. When the sun went down, I was alone on the beach, feeling like an abandoned dog. The atmosphere was idyllic, the last ferry left an hour ago, the sun had settled behind tall trees, and the sandy beach appeared cool and breezy.

I felt like I got what I deserved. It felt like torture, and I knew that she hadn't forgiven my betrayal. That night I slept in an olive grove above the village. The sky went black and thunderous over the nearby islands, but it remained dry over the mainland. I woke up early, before the first ferry or the shops, walked to the main road above the village, and caught a ride to Makarska. There was nothing in Drvenik for me other than the regrets of the past and the cold shoulder of that summer day. That wasn't what I had slaved for in the scrap yard for a month. As I was driven by a vegetable delivery boy for the following 50-odd kilometres along the glorious coast of Dalmatia, I understood that the time is now, life is this moment, the past doesn't exist, and the future is uncertain, but what a moment that was. Small villages hanging on

Sami Tischler

steep cliffs or nestled in small bays among olive groves looked like Biblical towns, and nothing less than scenes of Heaven, including fig trees loaded with fruit. Why worry? Life is to be lived, and regrets are to be buried away.

Sarajevo's Elusive Spring

Wandering, Foraging, Partying

In hindsight, it was lucky the way things turned out. She pushed me off the cliff and away from the safety of the familiar, supportive, and reliable. I had to learn to fly, and this was the time to break away from any fears and inhibitions. In the following 6 weeks, I travelled up and down the coast without a major plan. I kept an eye on venues and visits by bands from large continental cities. There was no internet and no tour dates online. I'd listen to transistor radios played by holidaymakers at the beach, look systematically through discarded or borrowed newspapers on the beach or in parks, and study public notice boards for information regarding concerts. Frequently, I'd meet someone who was a genuine freak and exchange information on where to go, where to sleep, how to avoid police night patrols, where there was a mulberry or fig tree in full fruit and easy to pick without trespassing. Any fruit with overhanging branches above a public road was fair game, according to Yugoslav traditional law. I certainly exploited the custom. I'd never heard of foraging as a term, but that's clearly what I was practising. It was a formula for survival on a small budget. Ever observant, I paid attention to a fig tree growing in the wild. When harvested in the cool of the morning, like those in the Havens, chilled perfectly ripened figs... Is there anything like it in the world? Juicy, sweet, loaded with the secrets of the Earth, life, pleasure. It offers the sense of instant intimacy as you open it and discharge all the goodness into your mouth, on your tongue, and down in your belly.

Coastal villages organised "Fishermen's Nights." Locals offered their day's catch, barbecued and with unlimited cheap wine, to tourists and locals alike. Using a newspaper cutout with dates and places in my notebook, I tried to incorporate such events into my travel plans. I passed them on to grateful others and met them again on specific dates. After a couple of weeks, my hair was bleached, as well as my clothes. I looked as suntanned as the locals and blended in well with the tourist crowd and foreigners. At night, I kept my travel pack hidden, as I had already tested in Dubrovnik. That way, you looked like someone accommodated in a camping park or a private room, not much different from anyone else. Disco clubs were super expensive, which kept bums like me out, but beaches were full of young people gathered around someone playing guitar or sitting around a cassette player with bottles of cheap wine in hand. I spent many nights on the beach and met people from everywhere. I was often alone and enjoyed the sound of the waves on the gravel. Reflections of moonlight on the moving water or streetlights on the opposite shore of a bay created fascinating images on the surface. On a moonless night, fishermen were out casting nets using acetylene lamps on their boats to attract the fish. Being someone born in the high mountains and living among them, the sea fascinated and inspired me. My mind would catch the wave pattern and fly with it if I was alone.

People often got on my nerves, especially those who worked hard to attract female attention. Summer holidays were a paradise for them. Young provincial beauties fell for those handsome entertainers who spouted grand statements, comments with no sense of humour, and uninspired compliments. Girls loved them, not realising that any success they had with them was shared with anyone who wanted to listen the next day. However, in a week or two, they'd all go back to their little provincial towns, continue with their little conservative lives, and throw themselves into the arms of their little conservative girlfriend or boyfriend. The whole thing was so pathetic. Perhaps the only reason my ex gave me the cold shoulder was the fact that she wanted freedom and space for a good, saucy summer thrill. I certainly didn't have, and wasn't planning to acquire, the skills of a gigolo. I wanted to talk to girls about literature, history, philosophy, travel, progressive music, and politics, but that wasn't necessarily what they wanted to hear, and I know now that my approach was very pretentious. After all, most of these people studied various areas of human knowledge, but they all wanted to forget about it for a while. Unfortunately, I studied electrical engineering, hardly a great seduction topic. Other areas of my interest were generally outside of school, and I genuinely enjoyed talking about them with others. I

Sarajevo's Elusive Spring

knew that my time would come, and my misfortune with women was inevitably going to change.

Sami Tischler

Mitzy

I came back home. Neither my parents nor my friends in the street could recognize me. I looked and behaved differently, according to them. I was more self-confident and richer for the experiences of that summer. I felt a new sense of awareness and strength as a result. I had no intimate or romantic memory with the taste of salt, the smell of olive or coconut oil to reflect on. I had no active romance to return to. Emotionally, I felt wide open and hungry for intimacy.

The city was filling up again with students from small towns and rural areas for another academic year. Mitzy was studying to become a nurse and had come from her village to live with her Aunt Kate, our neighbour. Her straight blonde hair was cut short, trendy at the time. Her strong, solid legs marched in leather boots that reached her knees. Her well-defined wiggly round bottom struggled to remain covered beneath an extremely short miniskirt, which she wore regardless of the season.

She was a peasant girl, no doubt, and you could tell by the way she walked. But she never tried to hide it. The confidence and freedom she felt in this new world, walking on bitumen streets, far from the watchful eyes of her village, was evident in her every movement.

I watched her quietly from a distance, holding my breath as her full breasts or her bouncy bottom, shook and pulsated, threatening to escape flimsy constrains of her half-unbuttoned blouse and tight mini skirt stretching at the seams. She moved with a rhythm all her own. She reminded me of an overloaded sailing boat gliding over a rough sea, moving in a slow, deliberate *tempo*, sails full, her sides brushing the waves as she rolled up and down, in slow motion. She was three years older than me and looked like an abundant fruit tree, ready to be harvested. Just the sight of her exhilarated me. I didn't believe I'd be lucky enough to taste any of her fruit.

One evening at Crook's, we started watching a movie on TV and I decided to stay until the end. Kate, Crook's mother, had gone out. His father was drunk and asleep in their bedroom. Crook's tenant, a young

Sarajevo's Elusive Spring

factory worker who shared a room with Crook's younger brother Joseph, was sitting in an armchair. Joseph was stretched out comfortably on a couch beside it. I sat on the second couch, behind the armchair. Crook had already left, claiming the film was stupid.

I could see the back of the factory worker's head bouncing from left to right as he struggled to stay awake after a long day. Joseph and I kept watching the film, occasionally laughing as we heard the tenant snoring. The main light was off, and a small, shaded lamp cast a faint glow across the room, competing with the soft blue hue from the black and white TV screen.

Mitzy came in as quietly as a cat and sat beside me. I greeted her with a shy naive grin. I felt that having her on the couch next to me was already a dream come through. She had just walked out of the shower and my nostrils filled with the freshness of shampoo and a feminine aroma of soap on her skin. She was wrapped into a pale blue dressing gown and just kept looking at me with a strange expectation in her eyes. I realized that she did not come to watch TV. "I hate German movies, don't you?" she said with a cheeky undertone. I wanted to say that I liked Swedish sex comedies but went on defending Germans and their experiments on the screen instead. "You have to pay attention and be patient to get something out of a German film." I wrapped up philosophically. "Patience is not my *forte* and you should pay more attention to what I have on offer and wait for you." the last sentence she whispered. I turned sideways, blocking the view of Joseph, and reached across under her bathrobe searching for those big floating breasts. I was hoping that this was what she wanted me to do. I had nothing to lose anyway. I discovered a hot, solidly swollen nipple and gently squeezed, turned, and played with it. I was relieved to see her half-closed eyes and noticed a change in her breathing pattern.

The movie went on and so did my right hand. She moved a bit closer, rested her head sideways on the back of the couch, and caught the bottom of my earlobe between her teeth. She responded to my playful touches with gentle bites, licks, and low guttural sounds of approval.

Sami Tischler

All I could hear from the armchair was snoring and decided to ignore Joseph whose full view of the action was well-blocked. He kept quiet and must have hoped to remain invisible. Mitzy had her bathrobe tied over the waist and by now I had both of her round pinkie blue tits with dark swollen nipples uncovered and in full view lit by the shimmering blue light from the screen.

They looked delicious and inviting. I had to get my teeth and lips into their soft flesh. She kept hanging onto my ear and gave me small bites on the neck as I was messing up her boobs with my both hands now. Tails of her dressing gown opened, and her full round thighs flushed. I did not waste any time and reached between her legs. I was surprised how the whole thing was going so smoothly. Have I fallen asleep while watching a piece of contemporary European cinema?
Something in me said: "This is the reality you have been dreaming of, do not be afraid, show the girl what you know and if you don't know what you are doing, just go with the flow and enjoy what comes. It is your lucky night," I said to myself, half aloud, and in response, I heard a faint groan of pleasure coming from her mouth sucking on the back of my neck.

She parted her muscly legs and offered her wet lips to my fingers. I did not know at first what I was going to do or find. In my first encounter with this alien female feature, I was expecting to discover a lidded well like muscle or something complex and mysterious. I went to explore its position, her slippery folds, and the direction of the slit. She felt my hesitation, took my hand licked my fingers for a while, and placed them carefully between her moist lips gently guiding my fingers to a nipplelike part, and whispered: "Here is the lid to my honey pot, touch it and treat it gently". I was so relieved that it wasn't the mysterious lid I had nightmares about, touched its silky wet surface and kept exploring.

My fingers were so happy there, entranced by the warmth of her depths, and its pulsating movements. She appeared to be floating on my fingers as my salivating mouth attached to her swollen nipples. I could not believe it when I felt her hand squeezing over my swollen dick which was bulging under my loose shorts. She worked my rhythm for a bit, let go of it, slipped her hand along my leg, under my shorts, and reached for his throbbing body and his bold head with her warm soft fingers. I gave her all I had in a couple of sequences spilling it through an ecstatic spasm while she extracted worm wetness of her boiling honey pot into my hand.

We sat there entangled, sweaty, breathing heavily into each other's necks, completely motionless and, in my case, liberated, from a world where the physical experience of a woman and her magical secrets had long tormented my mind. It took a while before we became aware of the world around us again. The TV screen was showing the dancing eruption of black-and-white static. The movie was over, the young factory worker mumbled something in his sleep, and Joseph was sound asleep on the second couch.

Mitzy eventually pulled a pair of clean panties from the pocket of her dressing gown, used them discreetly over my fading erection and her small hand, then led me gently to the door. She kissed me again and said, "My sweet boy, it is time to take your leave, and you will have to promise me one thing," she whispered. "You will not talk about this to any of your wanker mates, and you will remember me and my gift to you forever."

She led me out and let me walk into the fresh summer night. I walked, when I said walked, I levitated around the deserted streets of the small township for hours, with no desire to go home or sleep. My hands were in my pockets, holding on to the memory of the magical evening. I had known something like this was going to happen, and now, it had.

Sami Tischler

Passport

The summer was over, and I was going back to school. My parents listened to my stories about the summer's adventures, and my sisters were impressed by my courage and ability to break out of our parents' tight control and strict upbringing. Even our relatives wanted to know how it went and where exactly I had been. Some of the villagers had never even seen the sea in real life.

I couldn't be bothered to tell them much about how I travelled. I remember my uncle asking, "Did you go there to work? I heard there's good money to be made on building sites over there." Most of my relatives travelled for their National Army Service, worked on infrastructure projects, or, in the case of the more adventurous, got involved in black-market business in Trieste. I mumbled something about how work and money aren't everything in life, and he left me alone, possibly shocked by such a naïve response and attitude.

My father, however, must have seen an opportunity in my newly developed desire to travel. He came up with a plan:

"What do you think, my son, about going to Trieste and buying some clothes for yourself and your sisters? We can add a few more things for the household. Now that you've seen the world, I reckon we could send you on a train, you'll find your way with all the other folks heading there for shopping."

I was surprised by the offer, and the fact that I'd be making a trip outside of Yugoslavia (barely, but still), and at their expense. I understood his motivation. We all wore jeans bought on the black market from professional smugglers at outrageous prices. Even if I paid customs duty on three or four pairs, plus the train fare, we'd still come out ahead.

"Sure, Dad, that'd be great, I'd love to do it!" I was so excited at the prospect of travelling across the country on my own. But there was one catch: I didn't have a passport.

Sarajevo's Elusive Spring

It turned out I could get one at 17, provided I registered for my National Army Service. I went to the Department of Defence and registered. With the copy of my registration, my ID, birth certificate, and a couple of photos, I applied for a passport at the Department of the Interior. One month later, I had my red Yugoslav passport, with six burning torches embossed in gold on its cover. I was so proud of it.

I flipped through its empty pages, fantasizing about getting them stamped in exotic countries around the world. The first one would be Trieste, just across the border.

"You've got to start somewhere," I thought.

I had no idea at the time that Trieste was a grand city, an ancient Roman port further developed by the Austro-Hungarian Empire as its main international port and naval base.

Mum baked *maslanica*. There was a rumour that bread and any other food in Trieste was extremely expensive. I was going to bring my own. *Maslanica* is perfect food to take on a trip. Layers of homemade pastry are brushed with a mixture of cream, butter, and eggs. Once baked, it looks like a savoury baklava and gets wrapped in brown paper for the journey. The paper turns oily and transparent after a while, and you must keep it in a plastic bag or risk staining your luggage and clothes. You eat your pieces straight out of the bag, placed on your knees in a train compartment amongst mixed second-class travellers.

On a long train trip, it was common to see a variety of foods and delicacies, homemade brew included, on display at mealtimes and shared around. Yugoslavs readily shared food, jokes, stories, drinks, and cigarettes. Train buffets were poorly stocked and couldn't compete with the variety passengers carried in their bags.

I left Sarajevo in the evening and headed to Zagreb, where I had to change trains. I boarded the train to Trieste sometime after midnight. It carried a massive crowd heading in that direction. I kept walking through the carriages, hoping to find a seat. Most compartments were already occupied by groups of travellers from all over the country.

Sami Tischler

Their gestures and body language made it clear they didn't want a single outsider joining them. Many carried money, and most of them looked like genuine crooks.

I had some money myself, much more than I usually had in my wallet. I'd been warned to keep my cash and passport in a safe place. Black market business attracted small-time thieves, pickpockets, and gamblers. I moved through carriage after carriage, slowly, hoping to find a friendly coupé with a spare seat.

Suddenly, I found myself in a half-empty carriage and walked into an empty coupé. I ate a piece of *maslanica* and the train took off. The heating was on. I took my shoes off and placed my bag between my head and the armrest. It felt so comfy lying there. I wondered briefly why the other cars were packed, while there was so much space in this one. I was exhausted and fell asleep before I could figure out a logical explanation.

Later, in a semi-sleep, I felt that we were stationery at a random station for a long time. In that strange drowsy state, I noticed the train had taken off again before I'd had a chance, or the wits, to investigate. I drifted off again. When I woke, I was still alone in the *coupé*.

A uniformed ticket inspector entered and asked to check my ticket.

"You're on the wrong train, my boy," he said with a smirk.

"What do you mean, comrade?" I asked, shocked. I'd only just woken up. After travelling all night, I felt dazed and confused.

He explained what had happened. I had failed to return to the overcrowded carriages heading to Trieste when they disconnected the last four cars at a junction and hooked them to another train coming from the north, bound for the port of Rijeka.

"You'll need to get off at Divača, the next station, catch a local train and return to the junction at Zidani Most."

I had no idea where these places were or how long it would take to get back on the main line and catch the next train to Trieste.

Sarajevo's Elusive Spring

"You should be able to get there before lunch on the Belgrade–Trieste express," he said, sounding slightly irritated. His moustache jerked as he spoke.

"You're not the first one this has happened to. Happens all the time. Thousands are rushing to get their jeans in Trieste. I don't understand what the fuss is. I've never worn them, and I never will. I swear, I'll never wear that capitalist rubbish. We fought so hard for our independence, and now we're throwing it away for a pair of jeans. Super rifle, Super rifle, everyone wants a pair! Let them! I don't need any!"

"You'd better get ready, Divača is coming up in a few minutes." His moustache settled again, and he seemed calm after that short, fiery outburst. He must have seen straight through my thin disguise, just a greenhorn smuggler, a black marketeer who couldn't even get to Trieste without losing his way.

I did feel a little embarrassed. I couldn't quite understand the connection between cheap Western goods in Trieste and the loss of revolutionary values and ideals. To me, it was just a matter of fashion. The truth was, everyone wanted to wear jeans. What really irritated me was that our mighty domestic industry couldn't make them, saving us all the trouble and embarrassment of trying to get a pair from abroad.

The train barely stopped at the next station. I managed to get off into a freezing, foggy morning. The platform hung over the edge of a canyon, with an angry river raging below in the darkness. I couldn't see it, only hear it crashing against its narrow boundaries. No one boarded eery ghost train. One more person disembarked at Divača.

The poorly lit platform and small station building showed no signs of life. We both stood there, looking lost and miserable.

"Where are you off to?" I asked, pulling out my packet of Blue Morava and offering him one.

Sami Tischler

He took a deep drag from my freshly lit cigarette and yawned sleepily, "I'm on my way to Trieste, same as half this bloody country. I've no idea how I ended up in this shithole. I just hope I can get back to the main line in time, sort out my purchases, and be back in Belgrade before the Sunday flea markets."

I felt relieved we were both up the same creek without a paddle, and that I was now in the company of an experienced smuggler. We looked over the timetable display and worked out that there was no reason to rush. The next local train heading back to the main line was scheduled in two hours. It was one of those that stopped at every house and stable, picking up early risers heading to work in the great socialist collective machine.

The waiting room was locked. We stood in the fog, smoking my cigarettes. I felt okay about it; I still had six packets left. I'd stocked up on cigarettes. I'd been told a packet of Marlboro cost as much as a dozen Blue Morava.

The old-time smuggler from Belgrade gave me no credit for anything I said. He was full of himself and talked about big-time purchases and the large amounts of goods he'd taken across the border. He mentioned warehouses and a sliding price scale he'd be negotiating as a bulk buyer. I listened, hoping to learn something. After all, I was only buying a few items for my sisters, my parents, and myself. You could hardly call it smuggling, or even illegal.

"If you've given me a passport and I want to spend a bit of money in Italy, I should be entitled to do so," I thought.

The fact that our own ideology couldn't justify producing jeans domestically, as a smart business move, remains a mystery to me. The country was run by men raised in a self-sufficient society, where people only wore clothes, they made themselves, and who had fought Germans, Italians, and an assortment of Nazi-inspired nationalists for five years.

They couldn't approve or support this obsession with Western goods, consumerism, or the corporate control of the human mind and

Sarajevo's Elusive Spring

behaviour through fashion and trends. They gave us passports thinking the gesture would release some social pressure, but all it did was open a can of worms.

Finally, the waiting room opened as the day was breaking. By that time, we were both frozen to the bone, sheltering on the protected side of the station building. There was a pile of firewood beside the stove, and we got the fire going. We had just managed to warm up when a two-car *Šinobus* arrived. We boarded the small composition and joined fifty odd working-class folks on their way to work. We sat together and remained quiet for the length of the trip.

We eventually got onto the overcrowded Belgrade train, packed with a colourful smuggler mix of shy amateurs and boastful professionals.

Gypsies stood out and made up a large section of the crowd. We crossed the border and arrived in Trieste in the late morning. The whole city looked like a flea market as we exited the train station. My newly acquired friend had business to attend to and left me at the markets. The opportunity to test sliding price scale was gone.

I managed to buy what I wanted. It was easy. They accepted our money, YU dinars, and most of the vendors spoke some basic Serbo-Croatian. I was given plastic bags along with my purchases. Knowing that my train was due in the late afternoon, I decided to explore the port city on foot. I browsed record shops, amazed by the range available, walked into boutiques untouched by the Yugoslav crowd, and bought myself a cool jacket, not made of denim. I did pay a handsome amount for it, but it was a great one and worth it.

I stumbled across a well-preserved Roman Colosseum in the middle of the city. Trieste looked beautiful, with its hillside villas and old working port. No wonder Tito occupied it at the end of WWII. Unfortunately, it was now an Italian city, but he had managed to keep the whole Istrian peninsula instead. What a great strategist he was, he managed to expand Yugoslavia beyond its pre-war borders into the territories of the defeated fascist states of Italy, Austria, and Hungary. He had to withdraw from Trieste, but we were taking it over now on his behalf. We came in packs, heavily concentrated around the flea market.

Trieste citizens wanted our money but hated our presence, you could tell. Keeping us hoarded around the markets must've seemed the best way to minimize our impact and reduce cultural damage. We were harmless, with our bundles of near-worthless dinars, humiliated by the fact that our system couldn't provide basic commodities so common in Western European countries.

The whole shopping experience wore me out. I sat down on a bench at the port, ate another piece of *maslanica*, drank some water from a tap, and returned to the railway station. I had spent all my money and bought everything I needed.

The station was full of Yugoslav traders. The most obvious ones were Bosnian old ladies wearing traditional Turkish style *shalvare*. They were perfectly designed to hide jeans underneath and avoid import tax at the border. I watched them trying to pull on multiple pairs of jeans under their *shalvare*, right there in the middle of the train station.

The contrast between seeing fashionably dressed Italian travellers casually walking in and out of the station and my people desperately preparing for customs inspections, working out ways to evade the inevitable taxes, made me feel sad, humiliated, and downgraded. I felt it was our government's fault that people had been pushed into such a miserable position. Everyone was just trying to survive and make a buck out of a need that the government had created through its failure to respond to economic and cultural shifts in society.

Once we'd all boarded the train and neared the border, Gypsies came into the coupés with bags of goods, plastic slippers and nylon underwear, which they threw under our seats.

"If anyone asks, tell them you don't know whose it is," one Gypsy smuggler told us before disappearing, leaving no chance to protest.

Customs officers came by but paid no attention to what I had. They removed a few passengers, searched their bundles, and held the train for a while, but eventually, everyone returned, and we continued. I had no idea who paid what or how the whole thing worked, but all the goods made it back and into the country. All the smugglers claimed it "wasn't too bad this time".

I came home the next morning, completely exhausted. I'd been on the road for two days and two nights. My parents were impressed. I bought everything on my list and came back safely. They had no idea what I'd gone through, none of them had seen these places or the whole misery of the black-market phenomenon.

Strangely enough, it was a challenge and an adventure, nevertheless.

"Any time you'd like me to do this again, I'd be happy to. It's hard work, but I've enjoyed it," I said.

My father was impressed.

"Sure, son, we'll do it again. There's no need to pay those prices in the flea market when you can do it for us. Well done!"

Sami Tischler

Third Time Lucky

My travels took me to the city of Trieste many times again. The next two times, I took the trip to buy goods for the family. One of these two trips turned out to be a memorable experience. By the time I did my third shopping trip to Trieste, it felt very casual and effortless. I'd learnt the ropes and knew my train schedule as well as the important junctions where I had to remain in the correct section or change trains. I travelled with my freshly baked maslenica again and felt its warmth in the shoulder bag beside me for a while.

My mother was an old school woman and never failed to do something special for each one of us children, showing her love through personal commitment and sacrifice. All throughout my schooling, she would get up long before me, start the fire, cook breakfast, feed me, and see me off to school. In winter, she would have my boots sitting beside the wood-fired stove to ensure they were dry and warm before I went out in the rain or snow. She gave me pocket money out of her own earnings, and when she learnt that I'd become a smoker, she gave me money for cigarettes.

"I don't like doing this at all, but I'd hate to see you begging people for cigarettes. Here's money, and make sure to buy your lunch first," she would say with an expression of serious concern on her face.

"Of course, Mum, you know me! I cannot function without food."

This time around, she timed her baking like Mao timed his troops' movements in the Long March. *Maslanica* hardly had time to cool down before she had it packed for the trip.

I boarded the train and, before we left the station, two elderly gentlemen joined me in my compartment. Shortly after, we started a casual three-way conversation. One of them appeared knowledgeable about all things agricultural and very interested in traditional, self-sufficient Balkan family communes. This tradition was slowly disappearing, and the traditional agricultural methods, free of artificial fertilizers and genetically modified crops, were on their last legs.

Sarajevo's Elusive Spring

I was the first generation in my family growing up in the city and away from the village, but I was someone who was searching through my heritage and the useful information in it for future reference. I was fascinated by communal living and the ability of my ancestors to survive in the harsh mountainous environment of Bosnia while being more than 90% self-sufficient.

Before I was born in 1957, my family members sourced all their needs for food, clothes, shelter, and entertainment within their community. They bought sugar, tobacco, copper vessels and containers, gold, petroleum for lamps and lanterns, and a small range of tools. Most of their farming tools made of metal were manufactured by the local blacksmith.

They were true mixed farmers. They milled their own grain, kept bees, distilled alcohol, foraged forest fruits, fermented and preserved vegetables, slaughtered their animals, smoked and cured meat, processed wool and leather, built their own houses, furniture, farming tools and accessories out of wood, and made rugs, floor coverings, cloth and footwear.

The train was half full, and once ticket control was over, we were starting to relax.

The train stopped in Zenica, and as it slowed to a standstill, I spotted a gorgeous young woman in a fashionably cut long green coat. Her beautiful pale face was framed by short black hair and a black fur collar. She had a small black leather suitcase beside her as she perched on high heeled black lacquered boots. It was lucky my mouth was closed at the time. I noticed she was alone.

She climbed in and appeared at the door of our compartment. She looked unreal under the dimmed interior light of the train. We were all stunned.

"Do you gentlemen have a spare seat?" she asked in a soft, clear and uncompromising voice.

"Of course, we do. Please come in and take the window seat here," I offered her a seat beside me as I moved away to create a comfortable space for her.

"Thank you, you are so kind."

She moved through the space like a breeze. We all welcomed the exotic scent of her foreign perfume into our nostrils, and the exquisite freshness of her body brought a new energy into the space. She slipped off her coat as I lifted the suitcase onto the rack.

She turned towards me in the tight space we were stuck in, and suddenly almost touched my face with her small breasts, dressed in a thin white woollen jumper that clearly suggested the silhouette of her minimal bra below. She wasn't showing much. She wore a low-neck jumper complementing her small head mounted on a long, beautifully curved neck. A tight skirt covered her knees, and as she settled into the seat, her fine legs, her knees and below, flashed out impressively.

The two older gentlemen couldn't hide their excitement at having this beautiful creature in our midst, but they didn't know how to deal with such a special gift. So, they decided to ignore it. They wanted me with them. We returned to our agricultural topics, and the two oldies fought for the floor, lecturing me on everything they knew. I kept asking questions just to show interest, and they kept going with what I already knew but still enjoyed listening to from yet another human perspective.

One of them was a war veteran, a partisan fighter, and he certainly saw things the way they were decades ago. It wasn't only courtesy; it was genuinely becoming more interesting.

The young lady beside me took an illustrated fashion magazine out of her bag and appeared uninterested in any of it. Hours went by, and we all settled into that tired state where conversation gets hard going and the enthusiasm dies down. The oldies were nodding off, and the old guerilla fighter started dribbling at the corner of his mouth as his head collapsed into a worn-out, half-drawn curtain.

Sarajevo's Elusive Spring

I noticed a small smirk on her face, and I had to respond with a quiet laugh. We made eye contact, and I discovered her hazelnut-coloured dreamy eyes. She looked at me for a few seconds and winked as she moved her head towards the empty hallway.

"Let's get out of this coffin before we all decompose," she whispered close to my ear in that melodic, soft voice of hers.

She wrapped the coat over her shoulders and walked out. I slipped my jacket on and followed her. She stopped by the window a few compartments away and turned around to see if I'd followed. That wasn't necessary. I was there like a puppy dog, of course.

"Fuck, man, you can listen to some nonsense. I've been waiting for more than an hour to get your attention. Those fucking agricultural topics, what's the crop going to be like this year? What's the current price of a live yearling this summer? Is the government going to approve keeping goats again?"

She laughed big, loud, and childishly, exposing her beautiful teeth behind burgundy-coloured lips. I saw her tongue, nostrils, that Modigliani curve of her neck as she slapped her thighs like a kid. She was laughing over the grinding noise of wheels on tracks, and her coat almost fell off her shaking shoulders.

I caught it by grabbing for its shoulders and lifting it back. I held both of my hands there for a bit longer than necessary. She took its folds and wrapped herself into it, showing no visible objection to my misplaced hands.

"Who gives a fuck about the crops and the potato harvest this year? Do you?"

I only laughed, pulled out a packet of my Blue Morava and asked, "Do you smoke?"

She looked at me, she was cheeky, very cheeky.

"I smoke, but not your brand. I'm not going to offend you, so I'll smoke one this time. Next time we'll smoke mine. Is that a deal?" I licked the side of my cigarette, lit it up and handed it to her.

"You'll have to do the same for me when I smoke yours," I was trying to take this into the erotic sphere, and she went for it.

"I will, I will," she said as she took the cigarette and sucked big puffs out of it, looking at me shamelessly.

She was older than me, but I couldn't figure out what was so different about her. I didn't want to be too direct and ask questions. My short life experience had taught me that people loved talking about themselves anyway, you just had to wait and create space for it. You had to learn to listen.

She told me she was going back home to Italy, where she'd married three years ago, worked in fashion, grew up in Zenica, and studied in Sarajevo. She didn't really like Italians, but she hated the Bosnian mentality, Yugoslav politics, and couldn't stand Zenica, its small-town culture, pollution, and lack of opportunities.

"I love glamour, fast cars. Milano is the place for me. Zenica is a hole," she was transported somewhere else for a moment. The shape of her mouth changed from relaxed and beautiful to grotesque as she gave her town its place in the world.

We both looked through the window as we flew through the flats of northern Bosnia. The ground was covered in snow, almost black and white in the bright silver moonlight. Dark silhouettes of lifeless trees, shadows of small houses with the occasional light shooting past, almost romantic in its simplicity.

"It isn't too bad here; I like it, I must admit. It's a messy place, but it can only get better," I was saying it more for my own sake than in hope of convincing her. At that time, I hadn't seen any other Western places but Trieste and had nothing to compare my reality with, but I did believe my country was on its way to greatness.

The hallway was deserted and drafty.

Sarajevo's Elusive Spring

"My name is Lucia. And what is yours?"

"They call me UFO."

"What a name, my boy. I'm impressed. Let's go inside. I'm freezing." We went back to our seats. The oldies had turned the lights off while we were away, and we could hear them snoring and mumbling in their sleep.

This time we sat half facing each other, made ourselves comfortable against the headrests and continued talking. It was more like whispering. Instant sense of intimacy, sitting close in semi-darkness, whispering to each other.

"That's what you do in bed," I said to myself.

She was wrapped in her coat but left one arm out, with her hand casually placed on the seat between us. Our knees were almost touching. We were both starting to nod off. A few times I felt our hands touching and our knees clashing gently.

I fell asleep.

Some commotion woke me up and Lucia was leaning against my body, her head cushioned comfortably on my shoulder. She was still asleep as the two oldies left the compartment as quietly as they could.

"Let's leave the lovebirds to their romance," the old partisan commented in the hallway.

"I wish I was young again. I can tell you; I would have done the same. Grabbed the opportunity! Good boy! I wouldn't let this one get away!" They never turned the lights back on.

The next stop was Zagreb. Lucia woke up but snuggled against my torso and pretended there wasn't anything unusual about it. I loved her unconventional, no-shit attitude. All the girls I'd been dating were robbed of their freedom by restrictions, had to do this, couldn't do that, had to get home at a certain time, rules and conventions denying us so much enjoyment we could be having.

This was a train ride in no man's land for both of us.

Sami Tischler

"We could be heroes just for one day." Why not?

It felt so natural to let her rest on my shoulder while I held her hand.

She was awake now and showed no discomfort.

The train was getting new cars connected and we were going to spend some time waiting.

"I'll get out and get us some drinks."

She looked at me with her sleepy eyes.

"Don't you dare leave me. Make sure you come back fast. I can't live without you!" she said, laughing as her shoulders shook like those of a little child.

I stepped out onto the freezing platform and found a kiosk selling hot dogs and beer. I grabbed four longnecks and went back inside.

Lucia was there all fixed up, her hair spotlessly combed. A freshly drawn, shiny, precise lipstick line adorned her face. Both her clothes and her face looked as if she'd just ironed them.

I pulled my *maslanica* out and spread it on my shoulder bag in its greasy brown paper wrapping. I opened the beer bottles, and we sat there like two bricklayers gorging on *maslanica* and washing it down with bottled beer. Every now and then I had to hold back my burps out of respect for the gorgeous company.

Eventually, she couldn't hold it any longer. She fired out the loudest one I'd heard in a long time. We broke into laughter like two proper peasants lunching on bags of potatoes in the markets. We were having so much fun.

"Your mum makes the greatest *maslanica* I've ever tried. It puts all Italian cuisine to shame. Fuck it, that's what I'm missing the most over there. Hence the great figure I have."

She stood up and spun around in front of me, showing her best features, great line, finely shaped little boobs, tight compact arse, Modigliani neck and the head of an angel.

Sarajevo's Elusive Spring

"Where is motherfucker Modigliani to paint you!" I screamed as she kept spinning and lifting her skirt higher to expose more of her exquisite features.

"Motherfucker has been dead for 55 years unfortunately! He should have lived just to see this!" she screamed.

She was so proud of her looks, and she had nothing to be ashamed of. She was showing them off for me, a young, lucky bastard on the way to Trieste, hoping to save some pennies on cheap Western goods.

I was so proud of her and so wanting to have a woman like her. We still had hours to travel together, and I had no idea where this game could lead us. It felt like a space capsule, an insulated, compressed time and space where anything was possible.

The new carriages got connected and the crowd spilled into the hallways and compartments. They were workers returning to Austria and Germany after Christmas holidays, loud, drunk, and rowdy, travelling in packs.

By the time we had new company, our *maslanica* was neatly packed away, we were finishing off our first longneck and ready to get out for a smoke. Lucia took her handbag, and we went out to try her brand.

"Before I let you try my brand, I have to warn you of a few things," she restarted the flirting.

"My brand is soft, clean, sensitive, aromatic, likes to be licked before it lights up…" she stopped and took a swig from the longneck, holding the end much longer than decent, exaggerating the in and out sequence of it. She was acting the whore, and I loved it.

"I know, I know, I'll suck on it, and I can lick and get her fired up without the lighter, I promise," I got back into the game myself.

"What are you waiting for, give it to me," I was acting desperate.

Sami Tischler

She pulled out a pack of long Pall Mall and teased out a long piece ever so slowly, back and forth, before she took it out, licked it, lit it up, and handed it to me.

As I started puffing my cigarette, she performed the extended version of the routine before lighting hers.

It almost felt like a cigarette after sex. We were relaxing after a tense performance and enjoying each other's presence and our newfound intimacy. I was certainly charmed, inexperienced, easy to charm. Hadn't had full-on intercourse with a woman, craved it, easy to be teased, naïve, young, and harmless. Still, I couldn't have imagined a more adventurous train journey, and I enjoyed every moment of it.

I thought of it as a good dream, one where good, unreal, almost impossible turn of events take place and you know it's only a dream, but you wouldn't want it to end. So, you'd dive back into it if you could. That was exactly what I did.

I knew that the magic of that moment could disappear as soon as we walked back into the crowded compartment. They were all strangers, dressed in the cheap German fashion common for Yugoslav guest workers. The men wore pepita-patterned, small badly fitting hats, large multicoloured, almost psychedelic neckties, nylon shirts and patterned tight pants. In their conversation they mixed common German words with the rural Croatian dialect, and "Deutscher Marks" were mentioned all too often.

I walked in for a moment and took my two beer bottles. Not a very arousing ambience, as I expected. I always hated German fashion sense anyway.

I gave Lucia a wink and a nod of the head, as she had done earlier in the evening, reached for her hand, which she squeezed tightly around mine. I led her through the narrow corridor, Lucia in one hand and two longneck beer bottles in the other.

The corridors appeared empty, and compartments were full along the way. Many had drawn curtains across the glass doors already. It was the early hours of the morning, the train was gliding through the night driven by powerful electric engines at the front, and I was looking for a secluded corner.

I remembered a small entrance hallway that made a nice alcove behind the toilet wall. I was hoping the toilets weren't going to spoil it. We were in luck. There was a small wooden crate placed against the wall.

I took my woollen shawl and made a handsome seat for us on its rough lid.

Lucia had her coat over her shoulders and once settled on the crate, she looked like a film star waiting to shoot the next scene. We had our beer bottles on the crate, and I stood against the locked entrance door. She lit up a fresh cigarette; I opened one bottle and offered it to her. She took a swig out of it with gusto and passed it back to me while she licked her lips. Her tongue was so inviting, her lips like fresh cherries.

She still looked immaculate as I sat down beside her with the beer bottle in my hand. She leaned towards me and brought her cigarette gently to my mouth. She smelled of exotic fruit, and I dragged a long smoke with my lips on her fingers. We were so close to each other; I felt her warm, excited breath on my face.

Her majestic body with open arms appeared to be welcoming me. I couldn't think what to do with the bottle in my hand and the smoke in my lungs, but I knew this was the moment when our innocent flirting game became serious business.

I held her hand and kissed her beautifully manicured fingers, holding her middle finger between my lips for a moment. She placed her burning cigarette on the metal frame of the window ledge carefully and rested her hand on my head, ruffling my hair for a bit before pulling it gently towards her into a hungry, passionate, endless kiss.

We both wanted it, and I managed to place the bottle safely on the floor as I went on exploring her Modigliani neck with my lips. For a while we weren't aware of our surroundings at all and went on exploring our passion and desire for each other.

Although we weren't doing anything more than what I'd done with my girlfriends in the darkness of a stairwell, we were reckless and exposed. I never had my hands anywhere under her clothes, nor did she ever reach for my crotch. I wished she had, and if she did, she would have found an erect, mighty muscle craving for attention. "Tickets please!" the call reached our ears almost too late.

We pulled ourselves together, laughing our heads off, and both reached for the bottle. That's how the uniformed ticket controller found us, laughing and fighting for the bottle like two cheap drunks on a park bench.

I could see in his eyes how surprised and shocked he was. It wasn't me who puzzled him. I looked like someone of that sort, the sort that hung around long-distance trains, drinking cheap beer, hunting. He couldn't fit Lucia, the lady with a tramp, this weird combo into his conservative mind.

Working on this section of the Yugoslav National Railway network, he would have seen all sorts of people in all sorts of situations, but this one was a strange one.

I showed him my ticket and wasn't going to explain anything. He pierced it with his little pliers and took Lucia's ticket. His brain was struggling.

"Madame is off to Milan? That is a bit unusual. Everyone is going to Trieste like him." He pointed towards me with his tool and a certain amount of disgust, expecting some sort of sympathy or alliance from her.

Lucia took her ticket back, placed it safely in her handbag, fixed a strand of hair that had fallen over her forehead and said:

"Perhaps you should take a trip to Trieste sometime, comrade. After all, you have your discounted travel with your K15 card. There's so much to learn out there, and the world is changing continually with or without revolutions."

She lifted the bottle in her elegant fingers, took a long swig out of it and let out the biggest burp from her beautiful mouth, with no lipstick left on it whatsoever.

The ticket controller, lost for words, left aimlessly, trying to process what he had just seen and heard.

Once he was at a safe distance she stood up, took her coat off her shoulders, and slung her bag across her chest, exposing the shapes of two beautiful tits with the strap running between them. She pulled out small scissors and asked:

"Tickets please!"

She pretended to be inspecting my ticket with a serious expression on her face:

"Young man, why are you going to Trieste when your whore is travelling to Milan? There's something very suspicious about that, don't you think? It's something I'll have to report to the Ministry of Fear."

Then she broke into laughter, threw herself into my arms and we danced in a close embrace to the rhythm of the train wheels hitting the joints on the tracks.

"Chakka, Chakku, Chakka, Chakku, Chakka, Chakku…"

She was so sweet, unpredictable, reckless, smart, sexy and beautiful. Every step and every beat on the tracks were bringing us closer to Trieste, where this dream was going to end. I held Lucia in my arms like a treasure I had found and was about to lose.

"I know, my love, I know, such is life, we meet and we part. Let's enjoy this as if it were forever," she whispered into my ear and placed her lips on my neck.

We stayed like that for a long time, like two enchanted moonwalkers bound together by some invisible thread, fused forever by a moon ray coming through the amazing frost patterns in the window. We danced our own Last Tango in Zidani Most, enchanted by the aroma of tobacco and beer like they would have been in the tango bars of Buenos Aires once. Bitter taste of beer and sweet taste of tobacco fused together and about to get pulled apart.

The train stopped in Ljubljana, where we got out and changed trains. I went back into the compartment and took her suitcase down. We walked out into the freezing night and changed trains. We soon found an empty compartment and settled in for the last leg of the trip. We took the full bench on one side. I sat at the end, and she stretched across the whole bench, placing her head in my lap. I threw the green coat over her beautiful curves, and we fell asleep…

I walked through a narrow street in the port of Trieste. Small bars and brothels lined its sides. There was a woman in the doorway dressed in green lingerie. "I could show you a good time, my boy, if you can handle it." I looked at her and she looked familiar, hidden behind dark sunglasses. She fixed a strand of hair fallen across her forehead; she had perfectly drawn lips in burgundy, a Modigliani neck… I felt in my pocket, looking for my wallet before giving her an answer… but my wallet was gone.

I stood on the footpath searching my pockets and couldn't find the wallet anywhere. I looked at the pavement and the discarded cigarette butts on it and then at the woman. She held my wallet in her long, fine fingers and asked:

"If this is what you're looking for, you won't need it. This time will be on the house!"

"Passports, control!", a command-like shout woke me up. Lucia's head was nestled in my lap; she was sleeping like a child. They came in like in a raid, Yugoslavs and, shortly after, Italians. We both looked as if we'd been woken up from a dream, but on the way to the gallows.

Reality was shocking, uniformed, cold-faced men parading through the train. I wondered if she had dreamt, and what it was.

Sarajevo's Elusive Spring

The train descended into Trieste railway station before we could say long goodbyes and farewells. She had to go to the loo, came back wearing a beautiful silk tunic, neatly combed hair, worked on her makeup fast, and looked at me in intense silence as if she had to memorize my features and I did the same.

They were desperate moments. The train stopped, my mind was in a panic about what I had to do: "Walk to the flea markets, haggle, buy some goods, walk around, come back to the miserable world of smugglers at the railway station, go through customs, travel day and night, get back to foggy Sarajevo, never see Lucia again."

"Never see Lucia again," spoke reality in panic as we hugged one last time. I was trying to archive her curves, eyes, hair, suddenly so foreign in the daylight.

I walked out and waved to her as the train slowly took off. I saw her waving back but couldn't see clearly if she had any tears or if they had ruined her perfect make-up. I stood on the platform crying as her image and the train slipped away.

The fogged-up scene I was looking at, so desolate and sad, had no train or Lucia's face in it anymore.

I wasn't in a state to deal with the markets right away. I walked all the way to the port and watched big ships leaving the tight channel, heading to distant lands. I wanted to be on one of them so much.

It felt too painful to remain abandoned on the shore. I wished I could at least fly and get away from these hills, borders, tickets, cheap goods dealers, smugglers and customs controls.

All I wanted were her arms, her warmth, and her nonchalant presence with me, near me. But there I was, abandoned, miserable and alone again. The money I had in my wallet wasn't mine, and if it was, I would be searching for that narrow street with small bars and brothels lining its sides, my watery eyes scanning for a woman with short black hair and hazelnut-coloured eyes.

Sami Tischler

School is Over

Graduating from the electrical engineering course wasn't easy, considering that my interests were elsewhere. Fear of failure and respect for authority had faded away over the previous four years.

Thirty years have passed since the end of WWII. I was 19 years of age, held a passport, had developed a passion for travel and figured out ways of doing it on minimal funds.

The graduation project involved a complete design for an industrial electrical transformer. I had to calculate and figure out all its elements and detailed wiring specifications based on a set of given requirements.

Digital calculators were still rare. Slav and I managed to borrow one for a couple of days, just long enough to cross-check our calculations done with the *"Shibber"*, a sliding rule calculator. You had to be excellent in mathematics and trigonometry if you were to get your complex calculations right.

The ruler device gave you numbers, but you had to figure out the decimal points. It was so easy to make massive errors. Luckily, both of us were good at mathematics and managed to present our engineering designs at the open forum to a committee of professors at the end of our fourth year. We both passed. It was a great relief.

We celebrated our graduation in a brand-new hotel, built in the middle of a forest on the plateau above Sarajevo near the small town of Pale.

A narrow-gauge railway operated at the time, and the whole class piled into a small train made up of old Austrian-built carriages. We were all so happy and felt on top of the world.

Some of our female classmates were going to spend their first night away from home as grown-up young women. All of them came from respectable Muslim families, except for Goddess, the "secret lover" of our professor Philip. By that time, he'd been our Head Educator for four years and was responsible for organizing the event. Dinner, the graduation party, and the overnight accommodation afterwards were all part of the deal.

We certainly knew the whole thing was his idea and just another opportunity to spend the night with Goddess. I didn't really care; I'd already written what I thought about it and made it obvious to him in my essay. It was the end of the saga for me, and I was looking forward to wrapping up the school business.

As much as my ability to deal with complex problems in science, physics, math and engineering led me to college and helped me get through it successfully, my heart wasn't in it anymore. In the meantime, literature, music, travel and art have become the focus of my intellectual interests.

There was a party to get through. The girls withdrew to their quarters to dress up and do their make-up. I was with the boys who hung around in the garden, smoking and starting to drink. Drinks at the bar were quite expensive and most of us had our own stash of alcohol. I bought Coca Cola at the bar and mixed it with rum from a small flask.

By the time the girls came out in the evening, most of us were at various stages of drunkenness. We had never seen any of them dressed up for a fancy party like this one. I had only seen a few of my male school friends out in the city, mainly at concerts and clubs.

We wore compulsory blue overcoats in class, and the girls couldn't wear make-up at school. I got kicked out of class in my last year of college for letting my hair grow past the officially approved length. I decided to get my head shaved as a protest against the way our personal freedom was suppressed by those in authority. The professor who ordered the haircut didn't appreciate my gesture, couldn't hide his shock, and was clearly pissed off.

Our five girls left us speechless and in awe when they turned up in the garden looking gorgeous in their short summer dresses, showing off young, fully developed curves and shapes. They only displayed as much as our conservative society considered appropriate.

Sami Tischler

As a rule, girls our age weren't really interested in us. Most of us boys were immature, fun as friends, and great company at school. We smoked cigarettes together in the male toilets. This was the most popular spot where we could have fun together. That's where we laughed about what happened in class, gossiped about our professors, relived exam traumas, openly criticized our leaders, dissected politics, told rude and risky jokes, shared our last cigarettes, built friendships and grew into adulthood.

Straight out of smoky toilets into adulthood. Sounds scary, doesn't it?

This time our girls came out to impress us immature boys, and they certainly did. I was sitting next to Layla at the dinner table. I was dressed in a creamy set, pants and a collarless jacket. My hair was only just growing back, thick and charcoal black. I was one of the tallest in class, and Layla was always my favourite. She wore a pink dress, showing off the contours of her nicely shaped boobs. Her hair was styled in an Afro.

I was in heaven, next to her cute face with a few tiny freckles on a long, naked, elegant, unrestrained neck, just beside me, talking fast as she always did. Layla had a few glasses of wine with dinner, and we all sat around the table singing afterwards. Many had their arms around the shoulders of those sitting beside them as we sang popular pop and folk songs.

Layla's left arm rested against my right shoulder and her fingers wrapped around my neck. When we sang, we looked at each other, and she was the one who started playing with my prickly short hair. I just had to return the favour.

"Your hair is so fine and smooth, I love it," she whispered as the loud, drunken voices filled the dining hall. I nestled my head on her fingers to show her how much I was enjoying it and continued singing.

Slav was sitting on my left and understood exactly what was going on. He was a clever boy and paid no visible attention to the small acts of intimacy taking place.

Sarajevo's Elusive Spring

The bar at the end of the room had a jukebox right beside it, and some of our friends got it to play dance tunes.

"Let's dance, Layla." I took her hand, and she jumped up onto her stilettos and sped with me to the dance floor. I had never seen her wearing a pair of those before.

"Let's do it, Layla. This might be the first and last time for us." She came close and looked at me with real sadness in her eyes.

"Why did you have to say that? Don't ruin this for me. That would be so tragic. I want to savour this memory and hope, at least pretend that you and I could be more than school friends." She stood there looking up at me.

"Come to me. I'm not going anywhere, and I'll take you out any time if you'd like me to, I promise." I really meant it.

She came close against me, holding both of my arms. Her Afro was in my face and her small body pressed against mine as we started moving with the music.

This wasn't a time for intimacy though. We were already in the middle of a small crowd, surrounded by friends keen to have a good time. They were drunk enough to drop all their insecurities and inhibitions.

We hadn't really partied as a class before. Both of us joined in the wild dancing in groups, hugged together in a circle, moving without any coordination. Some tried to continue the singalong, while others stomped around like they were performing some unknown tribal dance.

The uncoordinated groups eventually merged into a train where we all moved in a line, holding the person in front of us around the waist. That went on forever with 30-odd students weaving between chairs, tables, the bar and the toilets.

Occasionally, someone would drop out and run to the toilet to empty their guts, stop at the table for a refill, or light up a cigarette and join back in as soon as they were done, hoping not to miss any of the fun.

It was a wild night. Layla, Slav and I managed to make it through and stick together for most of the collective fun. You could tell Layla knew how to have fun. She danced, laughed, hugged the boys, had a great voice, knew popular songs and sang them loud.

She seemed happiest when she was near me and didn't hesitate to show her affection and warmth in the total mayhem of the party. I got kissed, "accidentally" touched, and casually pinched on my arse and belly.

Slav and I had run out of our stash. She went to the bar and came back with a bottle of red wine and three glasses.

"Boys, why don't you take me out for a smoke? I need to get out of this party before things get totally out of control. Hahaha, they already have!"

Right at that moment, one of the boys, completely wobbly on his feet, fell over the table and on his way down pulled the tablecloth and everything on it with him. Luckily, he landed on the floor first. Glasses and bottles followed a fraction of a second later.

"Layla, you're a genius, your timing is immaculate. Let's get out of here!" I approved. Slav took the glasses from her, I took her hand, and we walked out into the freshness of the mountain night air.

There was enough light coming from the restaurant to find our way around. We found a long table with two bench seats on either side and settled in there. She never let go of my hand and sat right beside me, snuggled in, looking for warmth and intimacy.

We could hear the noise that followed the accident, then the quick return to the sounds of the party. Music from the jukebox, drunken collective singing, screams and laughter, the sounds of alcohol-fuelled happiness went on and on. Slav put the glasses in front of us, poured the wine, offered cigarettes, lit one for Layla and me, then finally lit his own.

Sarajevo's Elusive Spring

We sat there quietly smoking; fragmented moonlight sneaked through the thick canopy above us. We looked like three ghosts in the patchy light, hardly visible until we dragged smoke from our cigarettes.

Someone walked over from the restaurant towards us.

"It's Goddess coming to join us. Must have had enough of that psychopath and coming over to regain her sanity," Layla whispered.

I realized then that she knew what was going on between Phillip, our Guardian, and Goddess.

"It's about time to have a chat with her alone. I've had it with that overinflated hero. I'd be happy never to see his face again. Must admit, he's only reinforced my interest in literature. I've realized how powerful but dangerous and misleading it can be in the hands of deviants like him," I managed to wrap up before Goddess came close.

She asked quietly, "Can I bum a ciggie off someone?" Slav was the fastest and lit one up for her. As the flame lit her face, we could see how upset she was. Her make-up was a mess, and she must have cried. She sucked on the cigarette in desperation.

"That swine Phillip, you have no idea what he did. He insisted on taking me to his room in front of everyone. I really am a goose, getting mixed up with a pig."

Slav was always fond of her. She could have been his much older sister, with her motherly instinct and generous, womanly figure. He wrapped his boyish, thin body around her, trying to console her.

"Why worry, dear? The sooner you get away from him, the sooner your life's going to flourish. School's over! Who gives a shit about maniacs who taught us and manipulated us? You've got to stand up on your own feet. You must liberate yourself, no one else will do it.

You've got your diploma and your whole life ahead of you. Fuck him! What do you say, UFO?"

I grabbed the bottle, handed it to Goddess and said, "Fuck him from me too. Let's drink to that."

Goddess took a big swig from the bottle, and we each took one from our glasses. Like the rest of them, we were drowning our disappointments and anxieties about growing up and facing responsibilities ahead.

At the same time, strangely enough, I felt completely free. I wasn't sure if I'd continue studies at university or what that would be. I had no girlfriend and no defined plans but felt very comfortable with the sense of freedom this position promised. There was an open door and a clear field in front of me. It was so vivid and real in my mind. I was afraid of losing sight of it as I felt ready to jump.

"Can you guys come back in there with me? I've got to try to get him to bed. He was completely wiped out when I left."

We all got up with drinks in hand. Goddess walked with the bottle, face like a bandit with smeared make-up all over it. As we stepped back into the light, we looked at each other, stopped and laughed.

"Let's get the swine to bed and he can fuck himself."

Goddess was truly funny, and we stood there in agreement, laughing and sipping our drinks.

Inside, the party looked dead. We could barely recognize the place. Furniture was scattered all over the large room. Small, random groups sat around tables.

In the middle of the room was Phillip, slumped on a chair, his body practically "hanging" off it, completely wasted. His tie was undone, shirt half unbuttoned showing thick black chest hair. The thick mop of hair, usually combed to perfection, covered most of his fallen face. It was unclear if he was a victim of some collective punishment or if this state was the product of his own overindulgent personality.

Slav and I took him away towards the motel section, still in the chair as we found him. The girls held his arms and kept him steady. He was a chubby, small, insignificant man, especially now. In this state, his power was gone, evaporated like air from a half-depleted balloon.

Sarajevo's Elusive Spring

We tipped him sideways out of the chair. I took his shoes off and Goddess tucked him in.

"He'll be fine. Let's get out of here before I start feeling sympathy for the bastard. He is pathetic."

We soon piled onto two single beds in our room. I spent the night with Layla in one. She was a small girl and fit well into the empty space left by my long body frame.

It was a tough night; we only whispered sweet nothings to each other and kissed in silence for a long time.

"That's enough, you two," Slav finally voiced his protest. "You're making me horny, and Goddess isn't into it tonight." She couldn't resist:

"What would you like, my little child? Boobie? Wouldn't that be nice? Sorry, it'll be a dry night for you, and no wet dreams, thanks." Slav sounded disappointed.

"OK, mummy. I'll be a good boy and sleep."

Layla and I turned around restlessly until we found one of those impossible positions for sleep. By that time, we'd all had enough.

Her small, curved body and round little bum felt as if they were moulded to my chest, belly and bent leg muscles. I was tempted to place my hands in all her warm, secret little places. I had her virtually on a plate but wasn't keen on pushing the limits of what had evolved between us during the evening. I felt her trust was more precious and worth preserving.

We'd known each other for four years, and although there was a sense of intimacy between us, I was aware of her strict upbringing and her Muslim background. She had probably gone as far as she felt comfortable with already and was genuinely embarrassed by Slav's comments in the dark.

Sami Tischler

The fact she'd spent a night in bed with a boy might be the highlight and the pinnacle of her personal freedom and certainly not something she'd be telling anyone about.

The day was breaking when I had to get up. I went to the loo, washed my face, drank a load of water from the tap and went out into the garden. I lit a cigarette and listened to the sounds of the forest. Birds were already up, playing their morning symphony, perfect therapy for my hangover.

I wasn't going back to the room out of respect for the girls. I wanted to give them time to sort themselves out before facing the day and returning to the city.

Slav came out next, his face barely visible through the mess of his hair. He grabbed one of my cigarettes.

"What a night, my friend. I'm so glad it's over."

He was holding the side of his head, which must have been splitting as badly as mine.

"If we stayed together for another year, we'd self-destruct. That's how I feel. We must get away from each other and face the world. I'll have to make some serious decisions myself. The smart thing would be to go to university and ride out my parents' generosity and patience, but I doubt this system has anything to teach me without annoying the shit out of me. My parents can't support me for another four years, I reckon, and I've got unbearably itchy feet. I'm afraid it'll be so easy to find myself in the trap of work, annual leave, marriage, kids, career, and retirement. The whole thing scares me." I went silent, exhausted, with no energy to say more.

Slav came closer and gave me a big hug.

"Don't worry, big fella. I know you'll find a way out of the One flew over Cuckoo's Nest."

Sarajevo's Elusive Spring

I pictured the Big Chief breaking the glass window in the movie we'd seen recently. I felt so proud of his metaphor, and a sense of hope washed over me.

Tears came to my eyes when Layla arrived and wrapped her arms around me, kissing my wet mouth. She looked great, smelled fresh, her hair still wet but in fine black curls. Her warm eyes looked at me.

"What's going on? Why is my boy sad this morning? Mummy's here. Tell me if anyone's been bothering you."

She clung to me and wouldn't let go until she saw a small, faint smile on my lips.

"I'm good, babe. I'm just paranoid about the future, boredom, old age and death."

She started laughing and kept kissing me warmly.

"There's a whole life ahead of you, and you're a man, free to do whatever you want. Imagine my future and my opportunities as a woman, with everyone having expectations, prepared plans and restrictions for me. You should be laughing."

She made complete sense, and I remembered my thoughts as I was lying next to her gorgeous body last night. I felt so proud of her and her courage to take risks and explore her moral restrictions within the boundaries she had to live with.

Goddess went to check on her "secret lover", Phillip. When she came out, she looked determined, made-up and ready to go. She was travelling in her own car and offered us a lift to the city.

"How's the prof doing?" Slav asked as we took off.

"He survived last night. He's a swine and a liar. I'm not sure I want to see him anymore. I feel strangely relieved. I feel free, and what a feeling."

She chucked a cassette into the player, and a folk song came on. We sang the old, sad tune about unfulfilled love and a tragic death. The words were sad, but the melody and our voices together were so healing. There was no reason to fear.

The pine forest on either side of the road looked ancient and untouched by human hands. Life ahead of us was waiting to be lived, and we were free to do what we wanted with it. I was glad we left before the rest of our classmates and our Guardian emerged from their drunken stupor.

Layla had cushioned her little body against mine on the back seat, my arm wrapped around her, calm under my big hand, protecting and covering her warm belly. Both our heads faced the road ahead, winding its way between giant walls of forest on either side.

Before she left the car, I felt her arms wrap around my torso, her fingers digging into my ribs, refusing to let go, clinging to the experience and a missed love, an impossible love. I couldn't believe she was already going. These separations from women I loved were starting to feel strangely the same.

I did promise we'd see each other again, but I wasn't sure about that anymore. Her desperate grip before she stepped out of the car wasn't promising. I watched her slip behind a small wooden gate in the wall, and we drove down a dangerously steep lane into the abyss of the Old Town.

Where to Go, the Question is Now

At the end of our college, Slav and I decided to study language and literature at Sarajevo University. He passed the entry exam, and I didn't. At the exam, I wrote about the violence and bullying among the youth in our society. I wrote it in the form of a psychedelic experience, more like a piece of poetry in prose. I didn't really expect anyone to understand or appreciate my text or my experience.

My father refused to support my further education. I tried to test my endurance as a paper delivery boy and couldn't see myself slaving my life away for a pittance. I wrote what came to mind and in a style of my own, as I always did. It was a raging torrent of words, emotions, political and social criticism, and a chaotic stream of images and references. What did they know about our lives at school and the violence in the streets?

Most of these educated academics had it too good and enjoyed a range of privileges that our generation never would. Some of them were responsible for setting those squeaky-clean socialist morals we had studied at school but were already plotting divisions in society based on ethnic intolerance and grand nationalist dreams.

By that time, I had already become a full-time traveller and craved to see what was going on outside of our "Land of Milk and Honey". Part of that summer I took my friend Isac to the coast. We were thinking of forming a band and had some original ideas about the style, instruments we wanted to play and introduce, as well as the message we were working on. We were on a great track, but it wasn't meant to happen.

Everyone leaves Sarajevo in summer. I was delivering papers in Joša for a month. The only thing I got out of it was a miserable commission and a stronger desire to get out of there. My father suggested another family-sponsored shopping trip to Trieste in Italy. Lucia's beautiful features almost materialized in front of me when he said it. As I was preparing for the trip, I understood that the chances of seeing her ever again were zilch.

Sami Tischler

Isac was keen to go to the Adriatic, and we devised a different travel route and strategy. We packed our sleeping bags and hit the road. Two men on the side of the road never get anywhere fast. The trend continued as we followed the coastline travelling north. We enjoyed the beaches, swimming, and the little company of other youth on holidays. He was missing his guitar, felt hopeless and socially inadequate without it. I found it ridiculous to be so dependent on a simple device. It confirmed my views on summer affairs fuelled by the sound of waves across a pebbly beach accompanied by the sound of a guitar playing popular tunes.

We made it inland across Plitvice Lakes, where we sneaked into an official National Park zone and spent an enjoyable night camping in the forest. The next morning, we were found by a ranger who charged us for camping as well as issued a hefty fine for illegally entering the Park.

Zagreb, capital of Croatia, looked as deserted as Sarajevo in summer. We camped in the big town park the first night, and I took the train to Trieste the next evening while Isac stayed in Zagreb the next 24 hours on his own. I was riding the train and Lucia was on my mind.

Trieste appeared gloomy and depressing, crowds of smugglers looked as desperate as ever before with their bags, layers of jeans under their bulky clothes, crying to customs officers about the poverty that forced them to smuggle goods when discovered. I was disgusted with their official attitude and merciless decisions to confiscate goods or issue disproportionate fines at times. It wasn't the time or place to fight for social justice, since I was doing the same thing, just on a smaller scale.

A young gypsy girl brought a bag of slippers and asked if she could place them under my seat. "Go for it, love!" I didn't mind. I'd seen it done before. During the control at customs, no one bothered with it in the mayhem of desperate pleas to the Yugoslav officers, issuing fines to the unfortunate ones getting caught. Once we got through the control, she came in loaded with another two bags of slippers.

Sarajevo's Elusive Spring

As I offered to help her lift them up onto the luggage rack, she told me in confidence that she'd smuggled 300 pairs without paying any import tax. She must have said it to impress the big Bosnian bloke I was, and she did. No doubt she had mastered her little trick of dumping goods across different compartments and letting them make their own way across the border tax free.

She smuggled cheap plastic slippers. She would have made fivefold on their resale price somewhere on the street. I was impressed by the young gypsy and her ability to find ways to survive, bypass rules and regulations and make a living out of a risky activity outside of well-established norms and conventions not many would dare to explore.

She sat beside me in the seat. I started observing her features secretly. She sat there totally relaxed, looking sleepily through the window. She kept her legs apart, both hands on the seat between them, calm, widespread across the red and yellow floral pattern of her long skirt. She had worn-out sneakers on her small feet just reaching the ground. Beside my long legs and big feet, she looked like a not fully developed child.

The only thing giving her away were beautifully presented small round breasts nesting in a partially unbuttoned blouse, with no bra in sight. From my perspective above they hung unsupported, defiant of gravity for my enjoyment, assessment and viewing. I struggled to do it with discretion. After all, I was still a very inexperienced and sexually deprived, overgrown young boy.

There were times when all I thought of was sex, erotic zones of the female body, moments of past intimacies and craved for opportunities where my sexual experience would expand and ultimately lead to intercourse. The night was creeping into the hills the train was advancing through, and the mysterious light of a summer dusk filtered in.

A string of fine amber beads on a short necklace adorned the dark bronze-like skin of her neck. She resembled a princess child from an ancient culture. I looked around and across the faces of the overcrowded compartment, faces of smugglers, little crooks, street vendors and stall holders. Pale, exhausted, tired, unkempt and unshaven men mostly. An old Bosnian Muslim lady leant against the headrest with her toothless mouth half open, most of her face and torso covered under a large headscarf, perfectly comfortable in layers of jeans under her traditional dress. She was perched on the seat like a chook on her nest.

My trips home from the scrapyard the previous summer came to mind. Working class in motion is a powerful image. Yet you looked at each individual and their personal burden they carried, engraved in their faces was their life, hardships, disappointments, and tragedies. I couldn't take it anymore and turned back to the face exalting hope and beauty in its raw form, belonging to the gypsy girl beside me.

I met her gaze; she was already looking at me. She had a small trace of a smile on her face and didn't get embarrassed at all. I couldn't think of anything else to say but a phrase: "How about you tell me your name and introduce yourself?" It sounded almost aggressive, unintentionally.

She kept that faint, mysterious smile. "As far as I know, we have already met. All that is left to do is exchange our names. My name is Jamilla. What is yours, handsome?" she responded in a tone and volume just loud enough that I could hear it over the mechanical grinding, rolling, and squealing of steel rushing ahead on tracks.

"They call me UFO. And what is this about us having met before?" Jamilla brought her small head closer, looked at me through her amber coloured pupils intensely and continued, "If I stripped and showed you my backside, you would have linked it to the shape of my boobs you have been systematically observing and assessing."

She gave me a little giggle, just to confirm that she hadn't been offended by my inappropriate, but discreet, attention.

"Tell me if I'm wrong, but I saw your handsome face in the grass with another baboon watching me and my cousin bathing in Miljacka near the Sarajevo scrapyards last summer. You would have seen more of me than decent, and both of us gave you a good visual of our buttocks for a lasting memory."

I felt so embarrassed. The sight of their bums on the bank, the wiggly walk back to the camp, and bouncing young breasts, untamed, rebellious in unbuttoned wet shirts, had not disappeared from my memory yet. I had been caught twice by a girl, virtually a child, in a situation I wasn't so proud of.

"Look, I'm OK with that. I'm not that modest, if you really want to know. It's not a reason why we can't be friends. I'm very grateful for your unspoken assistance at the border. It is so interesting that we've met again. I'm not sure if you're aware that our elders don't approve of mixing with gadjos beyond friendship." She stopped and looked at me.

"Jamilla, I've already learnt what it means to get a broken heart out of a forbidden love. I hate this country where we're taught and encouraged to mix, while people themselves have no capacity for such a logical affair. I agree, there's no reason why we couldn't be friends. I sometimes feel that I was born into the wrong tribe. I should have been one of yours and I could go ahead with courting, loving, marrying, and children making with you."

I felt so happy and careless about this expression of sympathy for her and her people. I was genuine about it, and it came straight out of my heart.

"Shhhush, you handsome fool, someone could hear you." She slapped my thigh in a friendly gesture. "We are going to be friends, I can tell, in spite of the world and all hypocrites."

I'd learnt impressive details of Jamilla's life. She was studying music and planning to enrol at the Academy of Music in Sarajevo. She sang traditional and contemporary songs with a gypsy band from Gorica. Smuggling was going to support her education.

I didn't realize that anyone from the gypsy community pursued such an intensely progressive goal and had such a strong determination to achieve it. By the time we reached Zagreb, we had become great friends. I gave her my home phone number; she didn't have one. Nobody in Gorica did.

I helped her with her bags and settled her on the direct train to Sarajevo. I was puzzled, how had she got them from the market to the train station in Trieste? I recognized other gypsy smugglers filtering out in the same direction.

I was trying to be reserved and impersonal before leaving her behind, perfectly aware of members of her community watching and keeping an eye on her. We shook hands like soldiers do, and I walked off to look for my friend Isac in the city park.

I only met Isac in the morning at a bakery nearby, where we ate breakfast together.

"UFO, I swear, it was the worst 24 hours of my life. This Park where we'd slept is the gays' hunting ground. So many of them swarmed around and tried to get my arse. Going to the public toilet block was real hell. I had to go into the bushes instead. They came knocking on my door every time I went into a cubicle. I'm not staying here any longer. Let's get back on the road."

I felt sorry for him and couldn't tell him right away how excited I was about having met Jamilla on the train. I thought her to be a perfect addition to our future band, and somewhere around the city of Doboj in Bosnia, as we waited on the road for a lift, I told him about it.

It was hard to tell if he was excited at all. Isac sang hippy standards,

Simon and Garfunkel, Crosby, Stills, Nash and Young, Bob Dylan, The Rolling Stones, The Beatles…

I was interested in exploring music beyond what we knew so well and listened to too often.

I was hoping to find authentic folk instruments once played all around Bosnia and other Yu states and integrate them into modern sounds and styles. Jamilla was already doing that in a way, or that was what I thought she was doing or hoping to do once she "learnt" the music.

The sad thing was that I couldn't play a single instrument well, and my only musical skill was that I could keep a rhythm by tapping a tin, cardboard box or hitting a bottle with a drumstick.

Most of the friends I knew who could play an instrument were hopeless improvisers and had already been robbed of all creative power by endlessly practising learnt tunes or well-known popular standards. Sarajevo's pop scene was a disaster at the best of times: badly covered hard rock numbers screamed in a language only remotely sounding like English.

Few played guitars well and quickly gained legendary status by imitating Jimi Hendrix, playing guitar on their shoulders or destroying our hearing with pure noise at maximum volume and distortion. Isac was more interested in acoustic sound, and that was where I was hoping our band would stay. A gypsy singer interested in modern interpretation could be someone I would have liked to work with.

It wasn't the time to argue any of this since I hadn't spoken to Jamilla about it yet. She was too busy surviving in the real world and getting an education while fighting poverty and prejudice. My obsession with Bosnian traditional music, ancient instruments, gypsy music heritage and its potential for experimentation and exploration of its psychedelic elements would have sounded like pure indulgence to her.

She was already on the stage, making money as a singer, according to her. She told me about places her band played at. I'd never been to any of them. They sounded rough and dangerous, but she certainly had the passion for music. I promised myself to look her up. Well, she had to call me if that was ever to happen.

Sami Tischler

Boom Boom

Sarajevo was becoming "the centre of the world" in the mid-70s. Bijelo Dugme and Goran Bregović had certainly placed it on the map of Yugoslavia and its increasingly Western-oriented youth. Young freaks from Belgrade and Zagreb started turning up at our beloved Club Cactus, and at the Boom Festival in Zagreb in '76 we were present in force.

I managed to convince Jamilla to come with us. She called me, of course, and I went to a couple of "venues" she sang at. Her band was awesome, made up of her young relatives, it rocked these folk dives to the core. Punters, generally young drinkers, paid them handsomely to sing their favourite numbers.

It was folk genre, sung in smoke-filled would-be restaurants late at night to a rowdy young crowd. She wasn't sexy enough to attract arousal and the consequent follow-up. Jamilla sang in a sensual, strong voice which eventually took the audience with her into a trance.

She invited Iso and me to Gorica for a jam session. We found her house in a shanty town on top of the hill where we jammed with her band. It was an elevating experience. They had all the instruments. I played *darbuka* and *tapan* for the first time. They were more than impressed with Isac's technique and his shiny, expensive guitar.

The boys played several Beatles pieces as well as a few fresh folkie tunes by Bijelo Dugme. After the jam session we got drunk together and discussed music, fame, innovation, and tradition. They loved playing, but the fact that music provided a means of survival was an essential motivation. None of them were concerned with originality, authorship, or intellectual rights. Creativity wasn't pursued, they thought music should be played well and from the heart.

Three of us went to the biggest Yugoslav rock festival in Zagreb. We didn't play at the festival; it was reserved for the greats. Some of them certainly were the greats. We played in the street. Busking was banned by militia, but we ignored this rule as we had ignored many before and played unplugged at the fountain in front of the National Theatre.

Freaks and hippies from other cities joined in for a jam session. Jamilla sang a few contemporary standards, a bunch of Bosnian folk songs and some more gypsy tunes. Isac and I played basic rhythm, and others joined in with cello, flutes, more drums, and percussion.

There was a spontaneous street dance party on the go well before the festival doors opened. It certainly turned into a highlight of our trip.

We remembered the vibe of celebration and collective spirit inspired by our music for a long time.

Bijelo Dugme, in its original line-up and with only one album behind them, turned the place upside down with their original sound and trendy image. They brought the house down with a potent mix of folk and contemporary progressive rock.

Sami Tischler

Accidentally in Istanbul

By the end of summer 1976, already known as UFO, I took off with my friend Hardi with a plan to spend the winter in Amsterdam. In our pockets we had roughly 100 DM each, hoping naively to "impress" customs officers at Western borders with it.

Two penniless vagrants, Hardi and I, were to show it as proof of our capacity to survive in the streets of EU capitals without begging for meals. We believed that a hippy commune was waiting for us, with its doors wide open, somewhere in Germany, Amsterdam or ultimately at Christiania in Copenhagen.

For the start of this epic journey, we chose Belgrade. Bernarda was coming over from Zagreb to see us and her boyfriend Čičko before our departure. She turned up at the meeting place near "The Horse" with a long-haired German truck driver on his way to Istanbul.

We were sitting down at the bar and Gerhard generously offered to take us there. It didn't take much to modify our plan. The ride was worth 1000 km and neither of us had been to Istanbul before. Next morning, we jumped into his truck and drove east.

Gerhard smoked Drum and rolled his cigarettes one-handed. We spoke in fragments of French, English and German, mimed, drew sketches, and wrote phrases we couldn't pronounce. In Bulgaria, one of us had to hide in the mini bedroom at the back of the cabin. A third passenger was illegal, and hitchhiking was out of the question there.

We slept in the field near a truck stop, shared cigarettes with a Bulgarian farmer when we woke up and conversed in the common terminology used in both Bosnian and Bulgarian languages.

We were impressed by the tidy fields covered with crops, vineyards, and orchards along the highway. The little man we spoke to appeared happy, looked suntanned and healthy, and wore a blue working suit, like the workers' suits worn in Yugoslavia. He liked our cigarettes and was fascinated that we travelled and had passports at our age. I was nearly 19 and Hardi was one year older. We were virtually kids.

Sarajevo's Elusive Spring

At the Turkish border at Edirne, Gerhard was told that his papers weren't in order. He thought it was typical for a Turkish crossing and expected to pay *bakshish*, the traditional unofficial bribe. He was going to get in touch with his German company and expected to be held back for a day or two before he could enter Turkey.

We said our goodbyes and thank-yous, walked across the border, and hitchhiked the last 150 km into Istanbul.

We entered through the ancient Theodosian gate ruins into walled Constantinople on foot. They had simply demolished a whole section of the defensive wall structure, once 5 km wide, to fit a four-lane highway into the city. The wall stretched on both sides of the broken gate as high as a four-storey building.

Traffic appeared to be total chaos: a mix of American, English, and German trucks, limousines, vans, horse-and donkey-driven carts, bicycles, tricycles loaded with goods, motorbikes, and masses of people on foot, a river-like motion, colourful, loud, enveloped in fumes and dust.

We merged with the flow and walked into the dusk towards Bosporus with no map or any idea where we were going, how far the centre was, or what it was going to be like. What we knew was mainly Roman and Ottoman period history. We'd learnt a bit more from ancient Bosnian songs dating back to the Ottoman era and Orthodox Christian references to the famous 5th century church, Aya Sofia.

We didn't realize that in 1976 Turkey was facing massive civil unrest and edging towards civil war. We couldn't explain or understand the sounds of skirmishes around the centre, shots fired, sirens, fire trucks and ambulances all through the night.

The next morning, the city appeared calm. Business returned to normal. If it wasn't for army checkpoints at major intersections, armed guards at government buildings and trucks filled with heavily armed soldiers shifting across the city for the following night's action, you wouldn't know any different. Occasionally, a whole mass of people with banners shouting slogans would pop up from nowhere. The army would appear and disperse them with tear gas.

We would withdraw into mosques scattered around the old city everywhere. Within their courtyards, everything looked normal. The *muezzin* called from above; people washed at the fountains and entered the mosque for prayer. Pigeons flew around, ate seeds from the cobblestones, cats yawned out of boredom and lazed around along pavements and ancient stone walls. Real calm before the storm.

Out in the streets, tea shops lining major roads played Turkish music on black-and-white TV screens. Elderly men sat there with a tea glass before them, talked, played backgammon, smoked Samsun, caressed their curled-up moustaches, and laughed.

Often, a waiter brought Turkish tea on a tray in clear glasses shaped like a lady's body in a long dress upside down, just because we sat nearby. Some curled-up-moustached, welcoming, generous man had sent it across. When we asked for a cigarette, people often gave away the rest of their packet.

At the markets we were given cheese, fruit, and vegetables free of charge when we told stallholders that we had *"Yok pari"*. We didn't try to ask passers-by for money. We could both make up simple sentences from Turkish vocabulary we'd acquired from our Ottoman era heritage, and that was how we communicated in the street, markets, and shops.

Beggars on Istanbul's streets were numerous and looked desperate or disabled. We didn't feel it appropriate there. We'd come to Istanbul out of indulgence and quite unexpectedly. The little foreign currency we had we kept for our journey to the West. We bought bread and happily accepted people's generosity, which partially came out of their curiosity and partially from their ingrained traditional sense of hospitality and responsibility to assist travellers, ultimately, pilgrims.

I saw myself as a pilgrim. Istanbul had been the centre and root of my Islamic Bosnian heritage. None of my direct ancestors, Bosnian semi nomads and farmers, had been to Istanbul or Mecca. They had

Sarajevo's Elusive Spring

converted from their Bogomil Christian faith to Islam during the early days of Ottoman expansion in the 15th century.

All the big mosques, *Kapali Çarşi*, small shops, street vendors, the smell of food and sweets in the windows of cake shops were so familiar. Sarajevo was just like that, a small microcosm of the big Constantinople–Istanbul. However grand Sarajevo was, it was only a provincial centre of an enormous empire with borders as far as Saudi Arabia, Iraq, Libya, Sudan, Hungary, Armenia, Russia, and Austria.

This was a real pilgrimage for me, and I walked around places mentioned in songs, stories and books as if my feet were walking through the Holy Land. As we sat on enormous ancient rugs in the Blue Mosque under the universe-like mosaics and cupolas over our young heads, it wasn't hard to imagine generations of Ottoman Muslim subjects, humble or wealthy, noblemen and the poor, sitting under these miraculous domes and thanking God for their existence. It was fascinating to see that not much had changed.

The calm and the permanence of something eternal was an overwhelming and encompassing feeling. It prevailed within its courtyards, prayer halls, and around its perimeters. The trouble in the street appeared far off and unreal.

My friend Hardi, a Bosnian Orthodox by birth, a child of Socialist Yugoslavia, same as I was, walked into the Church of Aya Sofiya with awe and deep respect. In 1976, the church was open to visitors and functioned as a museum. We stood under its monumental dome on the worn-out marble floor, fascinated by its blinding opulent beauty and grandeur.

We touched columns recycled from monuments built by previous cultures, Greeks, Romans, Byzantines, and wondered if we were placing our hands on the same polished surfaces where Marco Polo or St. Sava once had. We went there every day.

Very few tourists came to Istanbul then. They may have been better informed about the political instability. Turkey was facing a Kurdish rebellion and their renewed struggle for independence, as well as a strong socialist movement in a united effort to overthrow a conservative, pro-military regime.

Many years later, as I was reading a book written by Orhan Pamuk, I realized how serious the conflict brewing in the streets had been, and how dangerous Istanbul was at the time. As the army managed to crush the rebellion, they jailed tens of thousands of young students, political activists, Turks and Kurds alike, for lengthy terms.

Kemal Atatürk kept his deadly gaze over the Turkey he had created out of the Ottoman's leftovers. His fragile creation had struggled to stay out of trouble and world politics through WWII. But at this time, ominously, the trouble came from within.

The end of August was a perfect time to visit Istanbul. The weather was warm, and we discovered a way into a gated park housing the university. Students hadn't returned from their summer break yet, and most of them would have been in the streets with the rebels and protesters.

We felt safe there in our sleeping bags at night amongst the trees and bushes. All that racket outside seemed to be safely away, and our days continued in reasonable calm. We explored the shore and watched big ships gliding in and out of the Black Sea through the Bosporus.

My eyes and thoughts caught glimpses of faraway places parading through this ancient waterway. On the way back, as we climbed the steep alleyways from the shore and into the old city on the hill, we walked into a skirmish taking place on the main street.

Military police in full riot gear, truncheons in hand, white-helmeted, in tight rows, were advancing towards the protesters a short distance away. We happened to emerge behind the police lines and realized that we were in a war zone.

Rocks and various objects thrown at the police flew over them frequently and rained onto the street, smashing into parked cars, shop windows, or anyone else who happened to be there. We retreated into

Sarajevo's Elusive Spring

the alleyway and crossed through the maze of dark, narrow streets to get away from the trouble.

That night, as I listened to the sounds of gunfire and sirens in the distance, I said to Hardi, "This is not safe. We were lucky to get away from trouble tonight. I have no idea what exactly is going on here. Let's leave before it's too late. What do you think, my friend?" Hardi, who virtually never panicked, sounded a bit shaken and responded instantly: "This is scary shit, UFO. I'm with you. Glad we came and saw Istanbul. I've got a feeling we'll be back here soon, but this is a bad time. I'll be missing Aya Sofiya, I tell you."

Neither of us slept well that night. We had a big journey ahead of us. The next morning, we were leaving, anxious about the trip and return to Yugoslavia. Gerhard had been a lucky dip, but now we had 1,000 km to hitch and make it across a country where "auto-stop" was officially banned.

Sami Tischler

Back on the Road Heading West

Back on the road and on the outskirts of Istanbul, we struggled to get rides. Multiple Ford Transit minivans operated on short routes. Owned by returned guest workers from Germany, they were run as unofficial suburban shuttle buses. Drivers stopped and offered lifts, expecting us to pay a fee. We were penniless, and they were wasting our time. We decided to walk on and out of their operational zone.

We walked for hours, started getting short lifts, made it into the fields and rural land, and fed on sunflower seeds piled up beside the road, harvested from adjoining fields and awaiting transport to the processing plant somewhere. While waiting for the next lift, we filled our pockets with tiny little black seeds, munched on the tiny contents, spitting the black shells out continuously – the way birds do.

It got to a point where this became an obsession, and we couldn't stop. I felt like a little bird fattening up on an unexpected feed.

"I cannot do this anymore," I said as I emptied my pockets. "This is driving me crazy." I spat the last bits out onto the road.

Hardi was sitting on his rolled sleeping bag, still munching.

"Stop it! I cannot watch you anymore – you look and sound like a mouse!" I was getting annoyed by our obsession.

"OK, I'll stop for your sake." He got up and emptied his pockets right there and then on the side of the road.

We got another short 50 km lift, and they dropped us off at an intersection. A short walk along the road brought us to yet another small hill of sunflower seeds piled up there. First thing we did, we both walked over and filled up our pockets again. We looked at each other and laughed like maniacs, losing our minds.

Shortly after, a Land Rover with European rego plates stopped. We grabbed our small travel packs, ran, and opened the door. They were two young French travellers inviting us in.

"Where are you off to?" we asked.

Sarajevo's Elusive Spring

"Back to France through Northern Greece and Yugoslavia. What about you? Where are you headed?" they asked.

"Well, we are trying to make it back to Belgrade at this stage. We were planning to travel through Bulgaria, but we'd happily change our route if you could take us along with you."

I was trying to sound as if we had already booked a luxury trip in a coach and not like a desperado who felt this to be one of the luckiest days of his life.

"Bien sûr," the long-haired driver responded without hesitation. "We'd love to offer you a lift with us. It could be fun having you along as we cross into Yugoslavia. We normally drive through, unsure if we should stop and explore places there."

They told us about their trip in Turkey, where they drove around the Black Sea shore in the north, camped in remote locations, smoked hash with local youth, and generally had a fantastic trip. On the way to Turkey, somewhere in Kosovo, their diff got busted on some rough roads they took.

Broken down near a small town with little hope of getting the Land Rover repaired, they walked on foot to an improvised mechanic's shop on the side of the road. A kid who studied French at school explained to the mechanic what their problem was. He took them to the wrecker yard out back, where he had a perfectly functioning diff on a half-dismantled Land Rover.

He towed their Rover to the village. His wife fed them an unforgettable dinner and set them up for the night in their guest room. The Albanian mechanic worked on their car through the night. By the end of the next day, they were back on the road.

"We've done a couple of thousand km with it, no worries."

They were so excited about the experience and couldn't stop talking, adding more details to the story. I felt so proud as we travelled closer to the border with Greece, near the Hebros (Marica) River. Most of the time, Westerners avoided travelling behind our Adriatic coast, concerned about safety, ruggedness, and unsure of the cultural mix of our people and their capacity for hospitality.

I started feeling more comfortable about the deal we'd negotiated with the French. We drove through the Turkish customs gate onto a long bridge, high above the river in a desert-like landscape. On the Greek side, Hardi and I were told we couldn't enter Greece without a visa and that we could get one back in Istanbul. I suddenly recalled that I had heard about this before. It was a measure introduced to stop the Greek Macedonian population from returning to their homes from the exile they were forced into to avoid genocide. A great example of ethnic cleansing, masterfully perpetrated by Greek royalists and their British allies during the Civil War in 1946.

Our French hosts couldn't believe we had to disembark and march back across the bridge. The Turkish officers were surprised and offered us cigarettes as a sign of sympathy. The day was coming to an end, and we figured out that Edirne and the border crossing to Bulgaria were a couple of hundred kilometres away. We walked for kilometres to an intersection with the road that followed the Turkish western border. We managed to get a few rides on the backs of tractor trailers loaded with people or crops. This was a rural area, and the road carried local agricultural traffic.

It was starting to get dark when we reached the outskirts of a village in the distance. A bunch of kids started talking to us. They were shepherds, returning cows and sheep to the village after a day of grazing in the open country. The kids were so friendly, spoke bits of European languages, and promised to bring us food once they returned to the village.

We found a spot to spend the night on the edge of the forest, beside the road, and started a small fire. We had nothing to cook and just a few cigarettes. We didn't think the kids were serious about their promise and had almost forgotten about it when a couple of young boys came to us with a range of delicacies, neatly packed and ready to serve. It was the same arrangement as if I was working in the fields

Sarajevo's Elusive Spring

in Bosnia and my female relatives had brought us cooked lunch. Everything was wrapped in cloth: warm, clean spoons, homemade fresh bread, salad, pastries, chunks of meat, baked potatoes, yoghurt.

The kids stayed and watched us eat. They were curious and had to return the pots, spoons, and tablecloth. They walked away into the dark, heading back to the village, and we were both anxious about the next day.

"It will take forever to get back on the main highway. Nobody travels far on this road, and very few own private cars." I was analysing our position pessimistically.

"Don't worry about it. You can't explain luck, as you know. Auto stop is like playing roulette. When your number comes up, you've got to be there to collect the jackpot." He laughed madly, his face lit by the flickering flames in the fire. "We'll get there, where else would you rather be?"

That was so true. We were free to do what we'd always wanted to do. This unexpected turn of events didn't mean the game was over. The roulette was spinning all the time, and our bets had been placed.

"You're right, my friend. Why worry about trivialities when the world has opened its arms and is welcoming us on the secret roads and to the magical valleys. Look at this moment. We have no Turkish money left; we've hardly had any for the last ten days. Yet we just had the most delicious meal and the company of friendly children. This food was sent to us by their families. There's no way they did this in secret. We are being looked after. What a grace for a troubadour on the road to Bombay."

Soon the fire was dying. We curled up in our sleeping bags with a mattress of dry hay beneath us. The smell of grass and earth all around, a clear sky splashed with stars across its enormous indigo depth, and a complete absence of moonlight brought a sense of safety, warmth, and belonging to this cosmic womb. The barking of dogs in the distance reminded me we weren't alone on this planet and sent me to sleep.

Sami Tischler

Through the Dust & Across Borders in the Company of Brothers

The following 100 km we travelled on a full variety of village transport: tractors with trailers, small trucks and large trucks, horse- and donkey-drawn carts, and a few cars on short trips. There was a Ford Transit taxi trip where we travelled free of charge between two villages.

By the afternoon, we were hitching rides before the border crossing at Edirne. Anyone who's done it knows how impossible that is. Who in their right mind crosses the border from Turkey into a totalitarian regime of the Eastern Bloc with two freaks on board, picked up just before customs?

We stood there in a car park covered in five centimetres of fine dust. Occasionally, a truck would stop for a few minutes while drivers looked over their paperwork or stashed some unwanted items out of sight. Private cars and truck drivers clearly ignored our existence and avoided eye contact. We were starting to look like dust-covered statues, miserable, abandoned, and a little offensive with our desperate pleas in mime.

A truck with YU rego stopped nearby. Hardi ran over, and I could see him talking to someone behind the open window. He was gesticulating humbly, using his hands, head, whole body. I couldn't hear him over the traffic noise, with trucks and cars passing constantly. But I saw him change into a happy man, so happy he was jumping and running towards me.

"UFO, they'll take us! They'll take us, imagine, they'll take us!" He was breathless.

The truck was taking off. I didn't understand.

"They're not waiting for us. They're pissing off! They just fooled around with you, got rid of you!" I shouted over the traffic noise. "They've asked me to walk across the border and wait for them on the Bulgarian side. They promised to take us. Can't have passengers through customs, but they'll sneak us in on the other side. We'll have to sit behind the curtain in the sleeping compartment. It won't be first class travel, but it'll have to do." He was excitedly explaining and calming me down at the same time.

We tried to tidy up a bit and clean the dust from our bags, shoes, and pants. Fine dust had penetrated everything. Everywhere you looked, a grey, depressing layer had conquered trees, roofs, cars, trucks, and people.

I was still suspicious of the promise made to Hardi, but I couldn't stand another minute in this hopeless situation. However, walking into Bulgaria penniless and without a ride, knowing that hitchhiking was officially banned there, didn't seem like a real solution.

Customs were packed with cars and people. International lorries used separate gates. We left Turkey after our passports were checked and stamped. Bulgarian officials did the same, and we walked out onto the road and away from customs.

We found a shady spot at a small car park where we sat and scanned the road for the red truck with the YU insignia on it. We were only one kilometre from the dusty hell we had just left. The trees around us were clean and healthy, the road surface dust-free. The traffic intensity and noise remained, but the feeling inside had changed. We could even hear birds again.

Auto stop offered options, unexpected, surprising sometimes, unbelievable at times. There weren't any options this time. We had only one, as uncertain and as unbelievable as it was, intensely waiting for it, straining our eyes for the red semi-trailer.

A few times we almost jumped for joy, seeing what we believed to be the one, but to no avail, it wasn't the right one. We were sure it couldn't have slipped by unnoticed. We kept looking, checking, and yet the truck wasn't materializing.

I even started projecting quick, hardly noticeable head gestures at those who acknowledged our existence, hoping to attract attention, generate someone's sympathy, and produce a lift offer. It wasn't working. We couldn't openly hitchhike, and a sense of depression was settling in.

The afternoon was coming to an end, and the daylight was getting to that dangerous point where drivers no longer felt safe picking up a stranger from the side of the road.

Our cigarette reserves were almost gone. The food leftovers we'd brought with us after the previous night's feast were finished. The sunflower seed piles were far behind us on the Turkish side of the border, and still, no red truck in sight.

"They're coming! They're coming! UFO, here it is, our truck is coming!"

Hardi was holding back and rising to his feet, barely keeping himself from running towards it with open arms or jumping up and down. The truck was rattling along towards us, speeding up in the distance. It didn't look like it was stopping or even planning to.

I could see two rugged, unshaven faces behind the dusty windscreen staring at us as they got close.

"They're not going to stop, no way!"

My heart had almost stopped in anticipation when I heard the screaming sound of braking, and with my mouth open, I watched the truck slow down and stop on the long parking lane behind us, engulfed in dust and diesel fumes.

It was the most glorious sight I had witnessed in a while.

We both grabbed our small travel packs and ran to the cabin at the front.

"Jump in, boys! We can't leave you this far from home. It'll be tight in the cabin," the dark, unshaven, rugged-looking man yelled over the rattle of the engine as he came down to let us climb up and settle behind the two front seats on the narrow shelf made as a bed.

Sarajevo's Elusive Spring

They were apologetic about the situation. As for us, we were the happiest two boys on the planet.

It was uncomfortable, I must admit, but they made up for it with loud, straightforward interest and fascination with what we were doing. We asked about their trips to Iraq and Syria and listened with utmost interest and awe as they spoke of dangers, treacherous roads, risky cargo, and the smuggling schemes they'd devised.

They were coming back from Iraq empty. In Iraq, they had bought barrels of diesel dirt cheap and loaded them into the back of the trailer. The difference between the price they would've paid and saved on the way back was their bonus and unofficial earnings. It amounted to a small fortune and paid for the risks and additional bribes they paid in Western goods, cigarettes, and hard cash to ensure safe passage across borders and deserted roads.

Both lived in the south of Serbia, supporting young families, building a house each, all very typical aspects of a working-class existence in Socialist Yugoslavia.

I listened and thanked God for my uncertain future and the open road ahead of me, although I was very grateful for their generosity and the fact, they'd taken a professional risk to get us out of self-inflicted trouble.

The trouble wasn't over.

Bulgarian police patrolled every major intersection on the East–West highway. Most of the time, international trucks passed through uninterrupted. Our hosts warned us to keep the curtain closed and hide behind the seats as we passed through the checkpoints, and we did.

For some reason, that wasn't enough. We got pulled over. They specifically wanted to check the number of passengers in the truck. Someone may have dobbed us in.

Our generous drivers had clearly broken traffic regulations, and the police argued they had to let us out.

Sami Tischler

The drivers pleaded for compassion.

"Brothers..." our driver said. Generally, we addressed our Slavic neighbours as Bros.

The fact we'd fought for territories and nationalist interests for centuries, killing each other in the tens of thousands, hadn't divorced us from belonging to a great Slavic nation. After all, our languages, smoking and drinking habits, obsessions with sex, religion, history, and politics were so similar, we couldn't ignore those commonalities.

"Bro, we couldn't leave these boys behind. They're like family, you must understand. What would you do if you were in our shoes?" he asked the cold-faced policeman, who wasn't budging.

"Regulations are regulations. You know that. We must respect them. I'm sorry, but you cannot continue your journey as you are." He was determined to uphold the law of the land.

The other driver pulled out a box of Marlboro from the stash at the back and casually flashed it in front of the policeman's face.

"C'mon, Bro, we've got something you can remember us by. Let us get back on our way. Let us help our young boys learn about life and the world, something we can't do. Look at us, caught in the regulations, strapped in the uniform and behind the wheel. I wish I could be on the road, free and careless like they are."

The sight of Western cigarettes in a box of 12 certainly changed the mood and tone of the officer, who began apologizing as he reached for the box.

"Have a safe journey and keep an eye on the patrol checkpoint at the next city. Turn off to Burgas, they're known as baksheesh collectors. Thanks for the smokes. You shouldn't have, but thanks anyway. I really appreciate it!"

He waved us on and directed us back to the road.

They drove deep into the night, stopped, and let us out to find a spot in the field beside the road to sleep.

Sarajevo's Elusive Spring

We slept under a tree and woke with the first light, had grapes for breakfast, fresh and cold from the vines stretching forever in the distance.

The land in Bulgaria belonged to the collective farms. They grew crops and fruit on a large scale. Their produce fed the populations of Russia and other countries of the Eastern Bloc with foods not suitable for cultivation in its northern regions.

We walked into Yugoslavia and continued in the Serbian truck for another 100 km.

We parted at an intersection somewhere between two cities with a genuine sense of sadness and admiration for their formidable gesture. We promised to look them up if we ever made it to Ćuprija, and we knew the roads would lead us there one day.

Of course, they did.

Sami Tischler

Go, Go, West!

By the end of the day, we made it to Belgrade. The fine weather was holding, and the end of August felt like summer was never going to end. We stayed on the highway, aware of the approaching autumn and the urgency of our mission. We didn't contact friends like Čičko or Zuba, had no time to waste. As exciting as it was, our trip to Istanbul had to stay and ferment with us for a while.

Oak forests stretch along the highway at the western exit from Belgrade. They are a standard feature of the region between Belgrade, Zagreb, the northern Bosnian border, and the flat lands to the north between the big rivers, Sava, Drava, Tisa and Danube. We found a good spot in a small clearing, started a fire, and ate a poor travellers' dinner of chicken pâté from a tin and a quarter of a loaf of white bread.

Two nights ago, on the outskirts of a Turkish village, we'd eaten dinner around the fire, and its delicate aromas still haunted my senses.

This was a heavily urbanized part of the world, and people couldn't be bothered with two freaks in the forest, unless they were working for the militia, responsible for keeping the place squeaky clean. We were safe here. The militia ruled the evolving metropolis in the distance and wouldn't want any roadside dust on their immaculate government issue footwear.

We woke up early and emerged from the forest looking like rebels who'd been hiding there for days, ready to liberate the world. The stopping lane was full of parked lorries, and most drivers were asleep inside.

"Let's walk to some empty car park further up and see if we can catch a ride," I suggested.

Hardi followed silently, looking lost in his thoughts as always.

We walked for a bit along the edge of the road when we spotted a man squatting between two trucks. He had long, straight black hair, a dirt covered, deeply suntanned body, and his whole skeleton was visible, he wasn't wearing anything above the waist. He had a light cotton waistcloth and no shoes.

When my eyes met his, I noticed a faint smile behind a thin beard, and from his deeply set eyes shone a warmth and friendly vibe. I stopped. "Hi, how are you going, my friend?" I asked.

He responded in Slovenian, and as Hardi caught up, we started chatting.

This man had travelled for hundreds of kilometres in the back of an empty lorry. He was coming home after spending two years on the streets of Calcutta and six months wandering penniless along the northern Turkish shore on the Black Sea.

"Calcutta was tough. Sleeping in the streets was dangerous, a great experience though. But the Turkish Black Sea was something else," he said to our gaping faces. "People were generous and treated me like a saint. They brought food, gave me space to camp and sleep, brought hashish and wine to share."

Our jaws were still hanging.

"We've just come back from Istanbul and had a similar experience there, and in the villages along the Bulgarian border. It was great!" I was sharing my excitement about our "little" trip.

"Where are you off to now?" he appeared interested.

"We're going to Amsterdam," Hardi exclaimed proudly.

"Amsterdam, Amsterdam..." he sounded like he was wondering what it was, or where the fuck it was. "Why would you go to Amsterdam, or any western shithole like that? Most of the good people from there have already gone East, India, Afghanistan, Turkey... Well, you're young, and you need to see the West. I did that too, many years ago. I won't be going there again anytime soon, I know that much."

We gave him half a packet of Blue Morava to last him to Slovenia, and some leftover bread for breakfast. He clasped his hands together and bowed down out of habit.

Sami Tischler

As we walked away, I turned back, and he'd almost disappeared on the dusty pavement, between two dusty trucks like a lizard in the desert. All I could still see with certainty were his clear, warm, friendly eyes, saying a farewell to us naïve, road-hungry, and green travellers.

We were lucky with auto-stop for a change and made it down to the Dalmatian Coast within a couple of days. Zadar was the last great city we visited. The end of the tourist season brought a sense of normality back to the city. We managed to get enough money in the street for a feed and supplies for the trip further into Italy. People were friendly and relaxed for a change. No one commented on our Bosnian dialect, something that normally annoyed the daylights out of me.

We crossed the Istrian Peninsula, the Italian border, and made it to Trieste in a day

It was late evening when we found a small, covered shelter by the piers. We slept undisturbed. It was a foggy morning; the air was fresh and cold. Two female lookalikes stood a few steps away, smoking. Their laughter and chatter in Italian woke me up. The smell of good tobacco filled the air. They smiled and watched me peeling my sleeping bag away. Their body language suggested frivolous observation and judgement. I looked down at the front of my jeans and noticed that the hard-on which had woken me up was shamelessly visible. There was no point trying to reset it now, right in front of their faces. I walked closer to them barefoot and mimed a request for a cigarette. They both offered, and that's when I realized they were cross-dressed men. It was too late to be shy. I took one from each, gestured towards Hardi still asleep, and let one of them give me a light.

He/she had beautiful, elegant fingers; nails polished to perfection. The smell of expensive perfume floated around them, and I felt like I was inside Scheherazade's tent, standing between the two of them. They were both giggling in their fake female voices and gestures as we puffed and smiled at each other. Lucy came to mind. There was something superficial in their happiness, something I'd felt in my dream as we were parting, still embraced on the train bound for Trieste the previous winter.

I almost wanted to ask about the "red district" of Trieste, but I held tightly onto the urge. "What would I do if I found her? What would I tell her? I'm broke and planning to join a commune in Amsterdam or Copenhagen? Would my plan to visit Morrison's grave excite her? How impressive would all this madness sound to her?"

I looked at the two immaculately made-up faces, quite strange, bony male features telegraphing through, two handsome, happy faces for sale at the pier. "All for a few trendy and expensive rags, a grand address above the harbour, snorts of cocaine, shots of heroin, a great sports car... what else?"

Hardi was still asleep, only meters away in a messy pile of travel gear and sleeping bags, happy *"clochard"*, sleeping on layers of dry cardboard below. A pitiful sight indeed, and a courageous, risky philosophy behind it: "You can be free when you have nothing to lose." We certainly had nothing to lose. We wanted so much, but not at the cost of our freedom.

"This is the West. It starts with Trieste and continues in different manifestations from here. This is hard capitalist territory, confronting in many ways. People sell. People buy. Sometimes they sell their bodies, and others buy them to use. At the end of the day, everybody goes home and watches illusions on the screen like everybody else. Is it avoidable?"

The dream with Lucy in the brothel haunted me for a long time. "Maybe it was just a dream," I kept telling myself. I missed that woman so much on that pier.

One of the two giggling, handsome, flavoursome she-males pulled out a fresh packet of long, filtered cigarettes and handed it to me before they left, possibly to a dingy little cellar for some beauty sleep. I watched them walk away so elegantly on their high heels, their half bare behinds wiggling. As they turned the corner, the street was empty, grey, lifeless, depressing, and I realized I still had my hard-on. "World of illusions, here I come!"

Venice

We caught a trip on the Italian Autostrada to Venice in one single hit. I had never seen a four-lane highway or such a variety of cars as I did then. We were driven at a mindboggling speed all the way. You couldn't tell that the driver ever eased off the accelerator of his small Italian made car. He drove through the smallest and riskiest gaps in traffic at unbelievable speed, while everyone else seemed to be doing the same.

The craziest part was the causeway between the mainland and Venice. It was overcrowded to the tilt, but that didn't slow anyone down. Everyone seemed desperate to get somewhere before everyone else.

We got dropped off at the main railway station, a grand modern building. We went in and checked out the interior. This was clearly our best chance for a safe night somewhere warm and dry. It looked promising, there were homeless alcoholics and random people in questionable mental condition camped in the corners and on various benches. It was too early and depressing to settle for the night.

We only knew Venice from pictures, movies, and documentaries. None ever mentioned the stench. The place really stank. We got lost quickly, narrow streets, small bridges over dirty canals, crumbling mouldy facades of ancient buildings, most of them dilapidated and neglected. Amongst all that, charming mini plazas, grand villas with geraniums in their windows, tourists with cameras...

We were freaking out, had no map of the city, until we found one posted on a wall and figured out that the train station was called Santa Lucia.

"Lucia, Lucia, mi amore!" It was my favourite female name at the time. "Easy," I said, "we'll know how to get back to our free accommodation."

Eventually we stumbled into the Piazza San Marco. The cathedral stood there like a mirage, white, brilliant, fascinating, and enormous in the middle of a vast open space, with rocking gondolas along the shore. People in droves walked, photographed, paraded in their trendy clothes, amazing footwear, watches, jewellery, handbags. You could tell who had come from faraway lands.

There were a few freak-like characters mixed amongst the crowd, but they wore trendy Afghani boots, expensive jeans, original Indian cotton tunics and Eastern jewellery. Hardly anyone was without a camera. We were the only ones lugging our full mobile existence on our backs. We found some clean steps. Pigeons were everywhere, and clean steps were in high demand. We sat there and I almost felt like we'd never left Istanbul.

There's a fine connection between the two, as strange as it sounds. A long period of their history has roots in the Roman Empire. The grandeur of their layout, architectural aesthetics and building techniques come from the same tradition, born in the eastern Mediterranean. Tourism had evolved further here, and that was something I didn't like much. We weren't partaking in it anyway, and that felt liberating. We couldn't afford to dine on seafood at a white tablecloth-covered table with a view across the piazza. That was a shame, but we pretended our growing hunger wasn't disrupting our experience.

We had some leftover bread from Trieste and salami bought from a supermarket in Slovenia for our dinars. It was sweet and tasty, and the ambience was grand, beyond belief. Light reflections in wet marble pavements, the movement of liquid colour on the dark water surface of the harbour created a grand pulsating illusion. Neon signs, shop windows full of objects made of Murano glass, completely foreign and new to me, fascinated my senses with their elegant grandeur and indulgence.

We took our time walking back to Santa Lucia. The small alleyways were deserted by then. All the tourists with their cameras, watches, jewellery, and fat wallets wouldn't have felt safe anymore. The only people we expected to see were small-time criminals from our township who were said to make fast illegal crossings into Italy to rob and steal.

As we approached the station, a Polizia Alfa Romeo materialized and two black-clad officers, strapped in white leather, jumped out. *"Passaporto, per favore."* We handed over our passports, were properly searched, and had to show our foreign currency. They asked many questions we didn't understand.

Hardi started acting up and swearing in the Bosnian dialect. One police officer shouted *"Come?"*, which has a similar meaning in Bosnian, and for a moment we thought he understood the obscenities directed at them. Fortunately, that wasn't the case. He was just trying to understand our responses, while we'd already given up on being understood. There was nothing they could pin on us, and eventually they had to let us go.

We walked into the safety of the massive station and found a spot in the half-abandoned waiting halls, joining other Venice desperados with the same intention. Smoking was allowed. We lit up and were swarmed by the homeless and penniless, bludging a freebie. We decided to share our last reserves of cheap Blue Morava and kept the long-filtered variety, a gift from the she-males in Trieste, for ourselves.

We were soon rewarded for our generosity when an old man, with skin like a dry fig, arrived with a bottle of wine wrapped in a brown paper bag. We wiped the tip of the bottle neck with our sleeves and took long swigs. *"Grazie"* was one of the few words we knew, and so we said it. We handed out more cigarettes shortly after. They were clearly in high demand in these parts.

We repeated the routine a few more times before we ran out of spare cigarettes, and they ran out of wine. By that time, people around us had turned in, sleeping in various contorted poses and makeshift bed arrangements. It would have made a great study for a painting of Exodus by someone like Titian or Tintoretto. Their paintings already adorned museums, villas, cathedrals, and chapels across the floating city. My knowledge of the Italian Renaissance wasn't at the level where I'd have any chance of recognizing their work anyway. Our budget couldn't afford museum or gallery tickets.

We stretched our sleeping bags across the floor beside the hydronic wall heaters and spent the night in reasonable comfort. Certainly, safer than many exodus victims from Palestine, scattered across Lebanon, Egypt, Syria, and Jordan on the other side of the Adriatic.

The rest of the homeless crew scattered across the vast marble floor, shamelessly enjoying the benefits of the old Venetian Empire. We guessed the authorities wouldn't tolerate a second night of camping next to the heaters for us Yugoslav vagrants. It was still early when we packed up and walked across the causeway back to the main highway.

We had no proper road map and used tourist brochures to plan the next stage of our trip. We didn't choose the ride we picked later that morning. It felt more like one that chose us.

Driven Up the Alpine Wall

The driver in a small, beaten-up sedan turned out to be our first ride that morning. He spoke German and told us he was heading back home through Austria. Combining everything I could scramble together from German war films, American Westerns, and sign language, I asked, *"We come Deutschland, OK?"* He didn't seem thrilled by the idea, but he never said No or Nein in response. That was good enough for us as we ignored his grumpiness.

He turned off towards Treviso onto regional roads, gradually climbing hillsides covered with clusters of houses and villages, barely anchored against increasingly steep slopes. We seemed to be ejected towards peaks wrapped in clouds and morning fog. The road we were travelling couldn't be found on our map. The map had been torn out of a tourist brochure, and most of the small towns and villages weren't even listed.

Neither of us had ever crossed the Alps. Bosnian mountains are rugged and run in continuous ranges across the country, but the Alps of northern Italy looked like a wall disappearing into the heavens. "Poor Hannibal and the poor elephants he brought on his campaign," I thought as we climbed and zigzagged up the hillsides, the scenery changing every few minutes, my ears popping as I tried to equalize the pressure.

"UFO, where is this guy taking us? I don't know if this is the right road," panicked Hardi. Many years later, I researched the area in the Road Book of Europe. We had travelled through Conegliano, Vittorio, Belluno towards Dobbiaco. "It's freaking me out!" he kept saying. He couldn't relax.

By that time, the driver was focused solely on the road, still grumpy and chain-smoking. He didn't have time to entertain us. His hands were too busy between the steering wheel and the gear stick to use sign language anyway. The road was treacherously narrow, steep, wet in places, and didn't offer a straight section for kilometres. I tried to brace myself between our luggage and the window in the back seat, a heavy nausea sitting in my stomach. We had been travelling for hours and had no idea how much longer we'd be heading in this direction, up the Wall.

There was no point breaking the trip. As we climbed higher, traffic dwindled to just the occasional passing car, and there was no easy way out of this predicament. We passed the last houses and entered a forested section high up in the hills. The trees were enormous; their tops lost in the fog enveloping the peaks around us. It began to drizzle, adding to the horror.

A small sign reading Douane and Zoll, in French and German, marked our arrival at the border crossing. A tiny shack stood to the side of the road, and the Italian official waved us through. A similar structure, 50 meters ahead, housed two green-clad Austrians. Our driver stopped at the border sign, and both came out. *"Passports, bitte."*

We gathered all three, and the driver handed the bundle to the official. He flicked through the German's passport, stamped it, and held onto ours. The driver and customs officer exchanged a few brief sentences. The driver then told us that we were being asked to step out for a more detailed check.

He said he was sorry but couldn't wait. He had a long way to go and would get back on the road immediately. We sensed he was using this as an opportunity to get rid of us. What could we say? We barely had a common language, and the officials stood there impatiently. You could tell they were too eager and ready to make our trip miserable.

We were virtually ordered to abandon the ride at the top of the Prato Drava Pass in the high Alps, with very little chance of leaving in a hurry in either direction. We were shown into the cottage as the driver pulled off and sped away into the drizzle and thickening fog, without ever turning his head. It was one of the saddest moments on the road I had ever experienced.

Inside, we were ordered to place our luggage on a large table, empty our pockets, and unpack our bags. All our possessions were displayed across the table. Every item seemed to fascinate them. With an

Sarajevo's Elusive Spring

archaeological curiosity, each object was picked up, examined, and questioned: *"Was ist das?"* We tried to explain but couldn't say anything they understood.

They kept asking until they reached the two brand-new switchblades we'd bought in Istanbul. I knew it was a bad idea, but we couldn't resist buying such fine weapons at such a ridiculous price. This type of knife wasn't legal in Yugoslavia either. It was considered a weapon, carried by small-time crims, pickpockets, and wannabe street gang members. They certainly didn't want us entering Austria with two switchblades in our pockets.

When young anarchists of our age assassinated Archduke Ferdinand in Sarajevo in 1914, they had pistols and grenades. They might've carried folding knives too, ones they knew how to use for more than peeling apples. Also, the death of Sultan Murat I in 1389 at the Battle of Kosovo still loomed in the history books as a bad omen and a warning. Murat was assassinated by a small version of a switchblade, brought in by Miloš Obilić, a Serbian knight mistakenly taken for an unarmed messenger. Some of Murat's remains, his entrails, they say, are still interred in a mausoleum there.

Of course, we were harmless. But every Austrian would've learnt about Sarajevo. The Battle of Kosovo, the three-month siege of Vienna by the Ottoman army in 1529, and again in 1683, would've been taught in school and remembered at home. They still lived behind the Great Alpine Wall and viewed us Slavic nations the way the Chinese once saw the Mongols, wild and dangerous.

Personally, my greatest regret for Bosnia and Herzegovina is that we were torn away from the Austro-Hungarian Empire. It was the most prosperous period in our history. A highly developed foreign power had a serious intention of integrating our small land into the Western sphere. In just 43 years of their presence, they transformed a Turkish backwater province *(vilayet)* into a modern state, with Western-style infrastructure, education, communication, governance, and institutions.

Sami Tischler

Serbia, the land of our brave Slavic brothers, had a very different future planned for us. Looking back, when we counted our coins, we realized we'd simply fallen into the hands of a small neo-colonial power, hungry for territory and influence, with no genuine interest in our wellbeing. Bosnia became a playground for Serbian nationalistic and expansionist fantasies, a space to manipulate the ethnic and religious sentiments of its mixed population.

At the time, we couldn't have imagined that in 14 years, our country would be shattered into irreparable fragments, like a crystal bowl, and neither of us would be living there.

"My grandparents (all four of them) were born as citizens of the Austro-Hungarian Empire," crossed my mind.

One of them fought for the Empire in WWI and spent years in Russia as a prisoner of war. "Why would there be any obstacle for me entering the State of Austria today?" I was thinking as they separated items for confiscation. I couldn't express my thoughts about any of this, but I wished I could. I knew a few phrases and a whole bunch of words that had penetrated the Bosnian language over the years under Austrian rule, not enough to say what I was thinking. It was best to remain calm and obedient. Both of us understood that.

They were just doing their job. Unfortunately for us, they were very diligent, and painfully pedantic. Time was slipping by, and we weren't sure if this was the end of the road for us.

We were ordered to pack our bags, which we did with unusual reluctance, expecting a "return" stamp, refusal of entry, in our passports, sitting open on a side table. Neither of the two officers ever changed their facial expressions or body language. They maintained an official, cold, efficient, robot-like manner throughout.

"Where do they get turned off?" I kept asking myself, hoping to draw a smile, a wink, a loose hand movement, something, out of them. Cold blue eyes were all we got.

Sarajevo's Elusive Spring

One took a polished stamping tool and brought it down heavily on a page in each of our passports. He opened the front pages, looked at our photos, and handed them back.

"Willkommen, bitte betreten Sie unser Land" he said, with a tiny little smile and a gesture of the hand towards the Austrian lands beyond. I didn't understand the phrase, but the hand gesture, the small movement of his mouth, and the little shine in the blue depth of his eye said it all, we were free to enter The Empire.

"Danke schön." I certainly knew how to say that.

We hurried away across the ridge, further into the forest along an empty road that began to slope downward, fully aware of four blue eyes following us until we disappeared into the foggy wetness of the ridge. Once out of their sight, we jumped like madmen in the middle of the empty road, threw our hands in the air, and screamed our lungs out. We were still in the forest. There weren't any echo effects across the valley, which was beginning to appear through patches of cloud and fog below. It felt like a privilege to be there.

In 1976, Western economies struggled to maintain guest labour in jobs. Borders were tightly controlled to prevent desperately unemployed Eastern Europeans from entering the labour market illegally and placing additional pressure on the already struggling economies of the West.

Our aim was different. If we'd been looking for illegal work in the West, we would have arrived by train, with a decent amount of cash in hand, dressed well, presenting a conservative appearance. We knew the conventions and understood the lack of sympathy for the way we looked.

As pilgrims and travellers, we consciously rejected conservatism and despised conformity, whether Socialist or Capitalist. We were newage Gypsy travellers, the last Mohicans testing the boundaries of a world entering the age of regulation. Not that we were fully aware of our significance, nor did we understand that Woody Guthrie and the Beatniks had already practiced, tested, and promoted the same philosophy. Bob Dylan was the most recent prophet we knew. However, we barely understood any English, so his message remained virtually meaningless to us for much of our youth.

Still, we felt we held our own torch and constructed our own narrative. We were both determined to find our own way in and out of hippie clichés and the well-established culture, even within our "isolated" Eastern European sphere. We felt very safe in our ignorance of the underlying theories derived by authors, philosophers, and cultural icons of our time. We took small snippets from it all and idealized heroes of our own Socialist rebellion and revolution. We often interpreted their uncompromising radical message and enthusiasm as a set of guiding principles.

I admired their dress code from historic, grainy WWII images: a mix of working-class urban, military, and peasant hardware. They looked young, cool, determined, armed, and dressed ad hoc, people with vision and light in their eyes. I wanted to be working, fighting, screaming, and scratching a new world out of the ashes of the mess created in Palestine, Lebanon, Vietnam, South Africa, Congo, Bangladesh, Hungary, Czechoslovakia…

The world was burning, and it was hard to tell if that was just the beginning, the middle, or its permanent state. Our own leaders raved on about internal and external enemies, non-aligned international politics and about maintaining our own path of Socialism. I admired Tito for his bravery and charisma, but I couldn't stand his endless speeches, always downplaying or avoiding the elephant in the room: the failure to transfer power to a younger generation, and the absence of his own and his cronies', arse-lickers', really, retirement.

He was becoming indecisive and powerless against those who kept using his authority to protect their own scheming. Nationalism had always been there, and he was losing control over the forces preparing to exploit its monstrous possibilities.

It was interesting that Mao had already triggered a major, merciless clean-up among his comrades through his notorious Cultural

Revolution, where he empowered the youth to scrutinize the revolutionary morals of their leaders.

We had our own Cultural Revolution in 1948, but it was conducted too soon and in a typically corrupt Slavic Tribal style, resulting in a massive damage and little positive change or reform in the ranks of the Communist Party. I respected the gains and achievements of our Revolution but couldn't see its capacity to bring us out of muddy self-assured corrupt system they were running with no serious intentions for a radical revision or reform. I was expecting and hoping to see something very different on the other side of the Wall.

Sami Tischler

The Empire

The road descended through Western Austria and down towards Lienz. Grassy slopes, covered with large patches of forest, looked like the Promised Land. We were walking and scanning for potential shelter. The whole valley was wet, with little rivulets draining from the forest and gurgling under the road. We crossed some foaming creeks, with no villages in sight. A few cars drove by, completely ignoring our presence on the road.

If we were in Yugoslavia, looking the way we did and being so close to the border, we would have already been reported to the Milicija, ID'd or arrested. Around a bend, we spotted a wooden structure at the edge of the forest. You could tell it had massive double doors at the front. The building appeared windowless.

"There could be some access at the back we could sneak through for the night," I hoped.

We behaved like guerrillas in a war movie, slipping off the road, running amongst some bushes, avoiding the clearing, and sneaking behind the shed. It was even better than we'd hoped. We didn't have to break in or climb through high windows. It was a semi-open, covered lean-to, half filled with dry hay. Its open end overlooked the forest and the valley, half-visible through the fog below.

"We're set. Look at this residence. I think I spotted some wild pears and hazelnuts on the way. I'll go back and check it out before it gets dark."

I felt so grateful for his company. Hardi was always on the lookout for a free feed.

"I'll fetch water and get some firewood if I can find anything dry."

We both dumped our packs on the hay ledge and went our separate ways to find what we were desperate for before nightfall.

Later, we were sitting around the fire, smoking our YU cigarettes and chewing on small pieces of smoked beef we'd brought with us,

Sarajevo's Elusive Spring

listening to the sound of water rolling down the small stream just below the barn. Hardi found a chestnut tree on his forage and brought a pocketful back. Their heady aroma was spreading from the hot coals. He also brought a pocketful of hazelnuts and filled up the sleeve of his jacket with wild pears. We'd make a knot at the end of the sleeve and use it as a bag when desperate, it was one of those childhood tricks you'd learnt and loved using again.

We were, in fact, living out our childhood fantasies right there and then.

After Venice and the border experience, we didn't feel like rushing straight into the first town and getting arrested for begging or vagrancy. The next morning, we wandered around the forest and collected more wild food, rosehip fruit, a variety of berries, and more semi-fermented pears, which we ate all day. We saw a lot of mushrooms but didn't have the confidence to pick any. If they'd been edible, we could've lived on them for days. Some probably were, but the risk was too great.

We were resting in the open barn on our sleeping bags, thrown over the sun-drenched hay, feeling the mild effect of the fermented pears. The sun was still strong, and we'd had a good wash earlier in the stream, completely naked. We washed our underwear, socks, shirts, and T-shirts. They were scattered across low bushes and the barn structure to dry. Our Yugo stock fed our tobacco addiction well, and we had plenty left. The barn felt safe, out of the way, and we loved the fact we never had to break in to use it.

I was starting to fall asleep in the sun, half covering my nudity in an open sleeping bag. I had a cigarette in my hand, and that kept me in a state of semi-conscious sleep. Hardi was lying in another corner and appeared asleep and snoring when I heard a faint, unusual sound coming from the bushes.

"Something's there. That was the sound of a human making their way through the forest. Well, whatever it is, I'm not running away naked," I thought.

Sami Tischler

More noise, a grunt, and some rude-sounding words in German, then a figure of a woman appeared out of the bushes. I pretended not to notice and took another puff from my cigarette while watching her standing there, mouth open, unsure what to do, as she must've seen us lying there in the full sun. I was hoping she'd get scared, quietly disappear, and leave us alone.

Curiosity must have been stronger than fear, and she walked towards me.

"Guten Tag, junge Männer."

I played naïve, sat up and waved in response.

"Cigarette?"

I offered as she came closer. I looked at her, she was a woman in her forties, strong-bodied, wearing layers of clothes as country people and farmers do on a working day. She had no head cover, and her black hair, cut short, framed her round face beautifully.

"Ja, bitte," she accepted my cigarette and sat down on the end of my sleeping bag.

That was a bit awkward. As I went to light her cigarette, using both hands to keep the match burning, my sleeping bag slipped off and exposed my nakedness for a moment. I noticed her eyes scan the semi hard fixture between my folded legs. I saw her pupils widen happily as I tried to cover myself. As I said, the whole thing was awkward, and a bit strange.

She puffed her cigarette as I finally finished mine. The woman gave me an intense stare at the close distance we were sitting in. I felt like a little boy, embarrassed, but excited, and wanting something to come out of this, though I had no courage to make a first move.

She moved a bit closer and reached for the edge of the sleeping bag covering my crotch. Her hand stopped. A slight head movement upwards gestured a question: "Is my intention going to freak you out?" She must've read my confused naïvety as consent, and she went on. I sat there like a stunned mullet as her hand moved further, looking for the worm-hardening penis under the sleeping bag. She found it, just as stunned as I was. She kept looking straight into my eyes and started to stroke it. Her hand was cold, but I didn't mind. Her gentle movement, likely honed from many years of milking practice, took no time to get it rock hard.

Her gaze, so intense, the strangeness of the situation, and the masterfully sensual, gentle pressure of her hand brought me quickly to the edge. I didn't want to produce any milk yet. I wanted it to last forever.

She held my solid rod, came closer, took the sleeping bag off, and took it in her mouth as she went on her knees over it. I threw a glance across the barn and realised that Hardi was awake and watching. He had his hand over his crotch, still covered by his sleeping bag. I gave him a head C'mon movement, and he crawled out of the bag with his penis completely erect and looking gorgeous. She was too busy to notice what was about to happen. Hardi leapt forward and placed himself behind her on his knees. By then, she became aware of his movements and his presence behind her.

With one free hand, she reached for his erection and stroked it while Hardi dealt with her dress and panties, preparing for the penetration. I felt when he went in, she almost bit on my hot rod, but slipped my dick deeper into the depth of her throat instead and kept it stroking with each one of his stabbing movements deeper and harder. I didn't know what to do and wasn't going to ruin the good thing. I saw Hardi getting more in the mood, closing his eyes, groaning and giving her all he had.

I expected that neither one of us would have lasted long at this rate. "Let's swap Hardi," I said, not having any better ideas. After all, I never had my dick inside a woman and couldn't wait to get it there. "OK, OK, let's swap, but fast, I am nearly there, C'mon". We both gently came out.

Sami Tischler

She was there with her open mouth salivating heavily, and as we swapped positions, I entered smoothly. The feeling was great as she drove herself onto fresh meat behind and a hard one at the front. She pushed the tempo. We were such beginners, but we held on for a bit longer. Disrupted while changing our position and delayed; we tried hard to make it last.

I had to shoot my load and did so with a scream and a hard push against her resisting buttocks. Hardi moaned like a devil as he shot her a mouthful, and she kept stroking and playing with it until there weren't any left. I held my dying prick inside her juicy warmth, absorbing every squeeze and suction coming out of her lovely insides.

I felt so powerful holding her hips and soaking my penis inside her welcoming pussy. For fucks sake, we didn't even know her name. She sat on my bag, and the two of us sat beside her, all of us smoking and exchanging touches and kisses with her. For a moment, we looked like two puppies with their bitch mother, playful, sinful, craving to be breastfed since we didn't get any and didn't get to uncover that part of her warmth.

We didn't even undress her properly, but we were both naked. Her hair was sweaty around the edges, and her breathing was still short and excited. Considering what had happened a minute ago, she looked like a decent, mature peasant woman. The only thing that gave her away was the cigarette in her mouth and the way she sucked on it hungrily.

She held it in her worker's fingers, took more of it than necessary into her wide mouth, between full, big lips. There was no makeup on her round, childlike, innocent face. It was hard to imagine our cocks and our juices filling her throat. Despite that, as I watched her sucking on the cigarette, I was starting to get a hard-on. Hardi was laughing, and she did too as they noticed my erection shooting upwards amongst our closely entangled legs.

"Mein Haus heute Abend?" she was pointing out to my erection and laughing loudly. She was trying to explain where her house was, but

Sarajevo's Elusive Spring

we were completely confused. Hardi pulled out his notebook and a pen. She drew a little map for us.

We had to follow the stream and come out of the forest where it meets with a creek into a clearing where she lived *"solo, ohne Ehemann, mein Man ist kaput, keine Kinder und viele Tiere, moo Kuh, die Hennen, ein Pferd, keine Hund."* We could come and do some *"arbeit, essen, drink snaps"* with her and have a good time in a 3-some. She wanted to touch our cocks goodbye. "My name is Helga," she introduced herself as she touched each one.

We presented our names in a regal gesture, shaking hands with her. She behaved as if we were a little miracle she was praying for in her loneliness. Shortly, she disappeared in the bushes, and after a while, the silence returned.

You could hear the faint sound of water from the stream and birds celebrating the loss of our virginity. Hardi and I walked around naked for a while, like we owned the land we were sitting on. Strange, the sense of power that intimacy with a woman gives you. We were so shameless, too. All that struggle with young girls and suppressed desire for it appeared so far away. Here, we had this peasant woman, a farmer in conservative Austria, craving it, wanting it, as shameless as we, and wanting more.

I certainly felt that I hadn't finished with her and already fantasised about what we could do as a threesome. "We are going to give her more good time, Hardi, aren't we?" I sang it to him. "Fuck yeah, we will UFO, I cannot wait to learn more tricks from her. When are we going to do it, if not now, and with whom, if not her? She looks great, and I hope she can handle both of us."

I jumped in enthusiastically, "Of course she can. Did you see her buttocks and her hands? She would have sucked my underpants into my arse with her mouth through my cock if I wore any."

Hardi continued reviewing the event. "She took us bravely into her body on both ends, which wasn't a small task. My load was massive, and I hadn't emptied my balls for a long time. She got them properly drained and extracted the last drop. She has no idea what she is getting into, or perhaps she has done something like this before. We could be riding her all night. All she needs to do is feed us well," he sighed.

"I am looking forward to a good feed and a decent drink. I had had enough of eating pears and forest fruit. They are giving me shits!" he sounded so happy as he went into the bushes to find a good spot and empty his bowels.

"What a male chauvinist my friend is! Helga was so generous with us wankers. I feel so lucky and grateful for what I have just harvested from her body and her passion." I was a little disappointed with Hardi.

Threesome in the Forest

We found Helga's place easily. As we were getting nearer through the forest by following the stream, we could smell woodfire smoke drifting through the trees like a thin fog. The house sat in a cluster of farm buildings and sheds, neatly fenced. There was a horse and three big, fat cows in the paddock. Chooks roamed around the house, which was nestled within a small orchard on the hillside. The smoke came out of the chimney. The whole setup looked idyllic in the afternoon light. A high-pitched roof sat above two lines of small windows adorned with blood-red geranium garlands, facing the valley below. This was the sort of place you'd expect to be inhabited by an old couple, living their farming seasonal routine, unaware of the world ravaged by uncertainties and temptations.

Helga greeted us at the door. She had already changed into a single layered, flower-patterned blouse and a smart red skirt falling just above her knees. Her new dress exposed her stocky figure, strong but nicely shaped neck, and most of her muscly arms. All her visible skin was well tanned and healthy. She wore a red headband and gold earrings with garnets arranged like a bundle of grapes. The old-fashioned blouse covered her breasts completely, but their generous, shapely mass appeared hardly restrained by the thin fabric. She had a big smile, opened her worker's arms, and gave us both a big embrace as we walked toward the door.

At one point, our heads were squeezed together, kissing whatever was nearest. I kissed her small ear and felt the earring at the edge of my mouth. She kissed my neck, and as Hardi kissed her on the mouth, I had the nape of her neck in front of me, which I kissed and gave a passionate lick behind her ear. I felt her torso shiver.

"Willkommen in meinem Haus," she said, leading us inside and into her kitchen, packed with potent aromas. She had pots steaming; the oven was hot and baking in full swing. The table in the small room off the kitchen had been set, unopened bottles of wine amongst it. We sat

at the kitchen table and watched her pour us schnapps into three small glasses.

She stood there in front of the steaming stove with her legs wide apart, raising her glass as we jumped up and downed our drinks together. It was great stuff. We looked at each other for a minute, fully satisfied, while the alcohol high settled.

Suddenly, I was getting excited and hyped up by the anticipation of what was still to come. She refilled our glasses and went back to finish the dinner. Soon, she explained that the animals needed to be brought in and fed. I knew the routine. "It isn't any different than the way we do it in Bosnia," I thought, as we went to bring the cows and the horse inside. Then we brought in the chickens by feeding them near the coop. Once they were fed, they went in by themselves.

We had a good look around and realized that Helga had everything under control. Her place was clean, well-stocked with animal feed, firewood, farming tools and equipment. By the time we went back inside, Helga was ready to serve dinner. I was so eager to eat a homemade meal. So was Hardi. I could tell by the excitement on his round, big-eyed face. The bread was still warm, and the hot stew was sending steam over the table. Chunks of well-cooked beef in it looked so delicate.

Helga ate slowly and watched us stuff ourselves, like a mother making sure her children got their fill first. She was trying to work us out. We were only kilometres from the border, and she would've seen desperadoes before. We couldn't carry on a spontaneous or precise conversation, and she asked questions like: "Where are you going?",

"Where do you come from?", "What is the reason for your travel?",

"Why did you cross the border here?" *"Warum hier?"*

We showed her on the map where we'd been and where we were going, answering her questions using words, sign language, sketches on paper, mime, and role play between us. It had been our way of communicating for the previous three weeks anyway. We were becoming good at it.

We acted out some scenes from the riots in Istanbul, played out our trip through the corrupted state of Bulgaria as hosts of fellow Serbian truckies. She laughed a lot when we acted out the night we spent in Venice railway station. Hardi and I played beggars who came to bludge cigarettes from us. We mimed bartering cigarettes for wine. Wine bottles had been opened at our table by then. She was topping up our glasses and keeping up the pace. This helped communication and eased her anxiety about our unexplained arrival and existence.

Finally, we acted out the border incident and portrayed the customs officer as a fascist, using Charlie Chaplin-style mime from The Great Dictator. She recognized it and laughed long and loud, showing her immaculate, healthy teeth. With the three of us in tune, the night was coming along just fine.

We almost forgot about the main theme of our meeting, or at least what we thought it was. *"Wustenzeit liebe Männer,"* she announced. "Caffè?" Of course, there wasn't a thing we wouldn't take out of her hands. I wanted to help, and we cleaned up the table, washed dishes, and put leftover food away while she quietly disappeared. We were back at the table, sipping the wine and chatting, when Helga appeared with a tray of aromatic goodies, coffee, and a freshly baked and cut poppy seed strudel. "Oh, what a treat!" we both exclaimed. She was an amazing woman, we could tell, and on top of that, she had already changed into a nightshirt made of soft cotton with elaborately embroidered edges. The section partially covering her breast finally presented her secret weapon. Her breasts sat there with no support, like two small melons strapped to her chest. I could only guess their actual size and beauty, but her nightshirt suggested a miracle.

Helga poured out coffee, topped up our schnapps glasses, and took on the task of feeding us out of her hands. She made us eat the strudel without a spoon or fork and licked the smeared icing sugar and poppy seeds off our mouths. She took careless bites too, and we licked and sucked crumbs from her boobs and her lap. Finally, we kissed intermittently between the three of us. At one point, we had her tightly sandwiched between us, turned her around while pressing her front and back between our bodies and growing erections. She grabbed the freshly opened bottle of red and led us upstairs into her bedroom, into its semidarkness, between the sheets of crispy starched linen. She was such a proper Austrian Vienna school whore. She made us stand by the bed with our erections poking into her face. While sitting on its edge, Helga gave us a warmup with her skilful mouth and tongue. She was preparing for a more elaborate treatment, I could tell. She stopped and asked me to lay down on my back. I thought that she was going to give me a ride, but she had something else in mind. She mounted my chest and, while on her knees, brought herself over my face, lifted the nightie, and offered her pussy to me in the total darkness. I took it with pleasure. I wanted her to remember it.

During my last contact with her, I was pumping her madly from behind like an animal on heat, purely out of a raw need for it. This time, I enjoyed giving her pleasure out of my slowly developing repertoire. Luckily, she knew what she wanted, and her hands guided me to do it slow and easy. At times, I was so engaged that I almost forgot to breathe. I was gasping for air under her nightie and taking her juices hungrily. Things started to heat up when I felt Hardi's fingers slipping in from behind. Her pussy was getting hot and wet, and her hip movements got into their own spin and rhythm. I felt her hand on my completely hardened rod. I knew that she was ready for a ride. She slipped off my face and slid down onto it where I welcomed her. She took time to test its length, make herself comfortable, and find a home for it inside. Already settled into a rhythm, she asked Hardi, who had placed himself behind her and over my legs, to enter her from behind. It took a few minutes for him to get the painful penetration in. I was already deep inside as his monster finally settled next to mine. Small muscular division apart, virtually rubbing our dicks, and giving it to Helga two barrelled. She was moaning, laughing, squealing, crying and screaming at times while our three bodies worked ourselves into a drunken, breathless frenzy. By that time, she had slipped her shirt off. Her white melons were almost in my face, and I attached my lips, teeth, and tongue to the dark brown nipples, the size of a large cherry. It was almost a mouthful. She kissed my forehead and moaned; her eyes turned up, floating in the ecstasy of the moment. I felt Hardi's rod against mine, stroking, stroking, hard, solid, relentless, never giving up. I was getting there as I was feeling her body building up pleasure beyond the pain she must have endured. I was hanging onto her tits, Hardi had his hands on Helga's hips, locked inside. She was on her knees as we went together into the never experienced frenzy, like dogs, pump, pump, pump, stroke, pump, stroke…

We exploded like fireworks. I felt Hardi's prick ejaculating alongside of mine in tiny jerking movements as her muscles hugged, squeezed, and absorbed the cocktail of our love act. We collapsed on a pile sideways like a house of cards and panted for minutes in unison, breathing heavily into the flesh of our bodies the way we fell. She reached for the bottle, and we all had a sip to revive before we separated enough to light up a cigarette in the semidarkness of what we saw as a top-class boudoir. "Two Gypsies on the road, honoured guests in a boudoir of a Vienna class whore. That is something, isn't it, Hardi?" I said like I was an old Don Juan or a gigolo, as I was puffing on my Sarajevo-manufactured Blue Morava. Hardi laughed, and Helga asked, *"Was?"* We tried to explain without hurting her feelings. It was hard, but she got it. It was her time to act it out, and she responded in style. She used the word *Fuchs*, well known to us as a term for a cheap whore, jumped off the bed, stood up on a stool, took some time to get the balance on it. Finding it hard to remain on it, Helga opened her legs slightly and masturbated in a rhythm while singing some Austrian lascivious tune featuring the word Fuchs frequently.

We drank more wine and smoked Sarajevo-made Blue Morava like Hussars in the imperial Austrian Army, propped up on cushions filled with goose feathers. Helga started to do a slow spin on the small stool, maintaining a risky balance while stimulating herself between her unshaven honey pot lips. She was still there when I jumped off the bed to protect her from accidentally smashing herself into the bedroom furniture. The timing was perfect; she was almost climaxing when I caught her as she lost her sense of balance and swung her body in a single move onto the empty spot next to Hardi. She bounced and jerked her body in spasms of pleasure, completely unaware of what had happened exactly. I came to her and joined Hardi in attaching ourselves to her swollen nipples like two piglets on the belly of their mother, shameless, satisfied, and completely exhausted, as if we wanted to recharge our passion, make it last, and never stop. Completely naked, in bed, I had her melons against my face, my back, my chest. My dick found itself in the warm folds of her arse, belly, and her muscly back. At times it woke up, hardened, and kept me awake; sleep took over the night of passion.

I felt someone stroking my fully erected rod. It was time for the Morning Glory session. I felt her tits against my back and her pubic hairs on my buttocks as she stroked it gently in a magically erotic position, pushing her pelvis against my buttocks. She reached between my legs with the other hand and squeezed my balls gently as she massaged my cock. It didn't appear that she wanted penetration; she wanted to give me pleasure exclusively, and that was new to me. Everything was so new to me. I only had mini experiences and small segments of what good sex could provide. I was getting caught in an avalanche of sexual pleasure here in the Austrian Alps. It took no time to discharge my balls into her hands. She used it to massage my cock gently, absorbing small jerky movements into its own slippery lubricant and sending me back to momentary sleep. Hardi was asleep all the way through. We had drunk so much the previous night, and I was amazed that my energy lasted throughout the night and produced a massive erection in the morning. When I woke up, Hardi was lying there complaining about a headache. "What a night and what a headache! This woman is a sex machine," we both laughed. "More like a sex motor cultivator," I was referring to the mini tractor we saw in her shed the previous day. "If we want her to repeat some of her repertoire again, we will need to help her around the farm today. It will be hard with the hangover, but there must be work we could do and help her save energy for our erotic fantasies. I couldn't have imagined that a woman can do what she did yesterday and the last night. Besides, she gets up at dawn, jerks me off, and gets out of the house to start her farm work this morning." Hardi slept through the last part. "She owes me one; I'll try to get it tomorrow morning! That sounds exciting, but I was out, heard nothing. Well done, my friend!" I felt so good about it; just the intimate aspect of it was so different and intense. Both of us in the play drove her into a trance, and half of the time she looked and felt completely transformed, drugged out, tranced out. It felt like you could be doing anything to her, play any erotic fantasy or perform any stimulation, and she would take it on without fully realizing where it would lead, as long as it kept elevating the stimulus further and deeper. It was an almost scary thought: "We can try anything we wanted to and can imagine in our limited erotic vocabulary and play it out for our mutual pleasures." It sounds like total sexual liberation. "Oooh, another night of it, cannot wait! Let's get up and help our sex motor cultivator through the working day," I cried and jumped out of bed. "Yei, let's do it, UFO. This is the heavens! Isn't it?"

Sami Tischler

Day and Night on the Loony's Farm

Hardi was going to cook breakfast to start the day. I went out to find her and see if I could help with the immediate chores. She was in the stables milking the cows, just as they do in Bosnia. Helga was perched on a small three-legged stool. She held the side of her head against the cow's belly, both of her hands on its teats, doing exactly what she did so amazingly well that morning with me. I stood at the open door until she felt my presence and our eyes met. She just continued, locking her gaze on me and kept stroking and extracting effortlessly. She was daydreaming about the Morning Glory event; I could tell. It telegraphed through the devilish smile evolving around her mouth and the smoky shine in her eyes. She half closed her eyes and moaned gently, *"Mmmmein Gott, ich liebe mein schönes Bosnien."* I walked closer behind her and stood over, reached down under her blouse, found her own warm nipples, and gave them a gentle rub and a twist as she moaned and continued to milk the cow. The sound of milk spraying into the bucket gradually died, and she grabbed both of my hands, held them there for a bit, stood up, and unbuttoned her blouse. I looked at the glorious shapes in the dimmed morning light of the stable, fascinated. She reached down to the milk bucket with her hand and scooped warm milk with it, brought it to my lips to taste its earthy, raw richness, and smeared the rest of it over her nipples, pushing them out towards my face. I went for it, sucking and licking every drop of it as she closed her eyes and offered them right back to my hungry mouth. Then she grabbed my head with both of her hands and kissed my milk-smeared lips hard, sucking off any trace of milk from them. I was getting horny as much as she was, even thinking about where this erotic moment could take us. I could hear her broken breathing pattern getting louder and sexier when we heard the call from the distance: "UFOOO, Helgaaa, *Frühstück* is ready!" Hardi had prepared the breakfast for us. *"Mein verrücktes Kind, Wir müssen aufhören, mein hübscher Bosnier."* She mimed pointing with her hands," I'd love to do it with you alone in the hay." Helga bent over in front of me and pushed her buttocks into my hardening crotch, held it there hard against it, trying to get a physical memory of my erection to last her through the day. She swiftly grabbed the bucket, and we returned to the house as she rocked her hips for me, walking behind and in Hardi's full view from the front.

Hardi had breakfast and coffee ready. You could tell that our presence brought an accelerated level of excitement into her life. Helga really enjoyed the breakfast, amateurish as it was. Hardi tried his best with eggs, cheese, bread, and sausages, and she appreciated it. We ate well, and she told us that she had a plan for the day where we could do work, she had no strength to do. We jumped onto the tray of her motor cultivator, which had a bunch of tools in it already. We were driven across the large clearing and up the steep path into the forest to a small quarry. We were to dig large stones out of the ground, load them into the tray, and help her move them to a spot on the property where she planned to rebuild a retaining wall and protect the arable land from the flooding by the creek we followed into the property. I was happy to be doing some productive work. When she left to deal with her routines at the farm, I said to Hardi, "She may be trying to tire us out. She fears another night like the one she's just had with two studs. Have you thought about what we could be doing tonight? I thought we could…."

We both had some ideas and laughed a lot about them. We also wondered if this was a lucky break or a curse that we were living. We had a different plan and got sidetracked by this sex-crazed lady who really needed a young farm hand to bring some flavour into her life. Why is she alone here, and is this OK? How long can we last and maintain this dangerous game? Is she falling for me, and how are my feelings going to develop in this sensitive threesome? What about me and Hardi? Is this sexually charged experience going to pull us apart?

My dilemma played its crazy scenarios throughout the day as we laboured hard in the quarry, getting large rocks broken off or dug out of the ground. Hardi wasn't handling the physical work well. He complained about fresh blisters, bugs, mosquitoes, dirt, and sweat. He was an urban kid who hadn't done a hard day's labour in his life, unlike me, who had done heavy physical work throughout my childhood and youth. I had to help with our house build as well as assist with farmwork in the village during the school holidays.

"This is fucked, UFO. I cannot do this. It's too hard." He was sitting totally exhausted after we pulled out a massive boulder, smashed it down into smaller, manageable lumps, and loaded them into the tray of the small tractor. He broke a nail and tore up his jeans in the process. "All this for a bit of old pussy. I don't know about you, but I am not sure if I am even interested in this 'cocks and pussy' game anymore." He sounded serious. As I was developing a real liking for Helga and she appeared to be falling for me, Hardi must have sensed that he was being pushed aside, and this labouring today would have tipped the scale for him.

"Barren Island and breaking rocks are not my vision of free travel." He went on, referring to the jail for political prisoners in Yugoslavia. "After all, she is just an old *Fuksa*, don't you think?" I felt hurt by his comments. Helga gave me a sense of importance. I knew that she was desperate and lonely, but so was I. I understood that you don't get anything for nothing, and that is exactly why we weren't getting any from our young girlfriends. We had nothing to offer. We couldn't even take them back to our room because we didn't have one. We lived with our parents and shared rooms with our siblings. Our neighbours acted as guard dogs. None could enter without someone appearing behind their doors and window curtains. You hoped for little privacy and never got any. I was craving for free sex, and she was happy to give it, naturally expected something in return. I wanted to help her out, and I was starting to like her, as strange as it was. I had had enough of expecting intimacy from my young girlfriends who weren't ready, too paranoid about getting pregnant or being seen having intercourse virtually "in public." It had to happen in places like graveyards, corners of public parks, grassy suburban wastelands, mouldy cellars under the apartment blocks, and similar.

"I don't think she is a *Fuksa*. She isn't different from us. It takes courage and risk to do what she is doing with us. She is giving so much of herself, can't you see. I really admire her. I could see myself spending more time here, and to be honest, I don't mind a bit of hard work. I'd love to live on the land one day. This is a time to test yourself and possibly learn a few things. I was watching her milk her cows this morning. I have never learnt how to do it." He laughed with a zest. "It is the same as masturbation, that is why she is so good at it. Did she give you a hand job again, you bastards having it on without me. That is what I have thought, I am not included anymore." Hardi was getting angry about being rejected. "It's not like that, mate. She is just gentle with me. She said she likes big boys and adores my bold-headed tool." I knew that was a wrong thing to say, but I felt that sharing Helga with Hardi wasn't going to work anymore. "I don't care about her and her shrivelling tits; you can have her all you like. I am going to hang around here for a few more days and I will shoot through. You'll need to work out what you are going to do. I won't be joining you and your 'bride' for your engagement party or the wedding."

Helga came loaded with food and drinks around midday. She could sense that a rift had developed in her absence. I was glad to see her. I needed reassurance that what I was feeling for her was mutual. We ate together, had a few swigs of schnapps from the bottle, which changed Hardi's mood. However, he seemed to be avoiding eye contact with her. Before she left, she grabbed my hand and walked away with me. It was a rubber-stamped statement of our intimacy. She gave me a long kiss and talked about us being lovers "solo" from now on. She appeared a bit embarrassed about what had happened between the three of us and she asked me to apologize on her behalf to Hardi. I kept saying, "Hardi OK, *verstehen*, Hardi OK *verstehen*." I was glad that we had settled the issue for the moment. When I returned, Hardi was hugging the bottle she left behind a bit too much. Soon after, he disappeared into the forest with it. I called out a few times and couldn't hear any response. I kept on with a steady effort and filled in the tractor.

Hardi stumbled out of the bushes as I had sat down with a cigarette, waiting for Helga to come up. He was messed up, dirty, and drunk.

Sami Tischler

The bottle was nearly empty, and he was clutching onto it like a drowning man. I gave him a hard hug and sat him down. He couldn't sit up. He collapsed on his side like a bag of potatoes. Helga and I had to load his limp body up on a tarp she had on the tractor. The trip down to the farm turned out extremely hazardous. I had to hang onto Hardi's limp body and keep him on the pile of bouncing rocks we were transporting. Helga kept turning back, making sure she wouldn't lose us to holes, ditches, and rocks she was negotiating. We made it to the barn where she parked the small machine. Hardi was good for nothing. She suggested bringing him into the house to a small room in the basement where she had a simple single bed. We laid him on the small bed. I brought a bucket and a jar with water and placed them beside his bed. I expected that he may have to get rid of his lunch and the schnapps he had consumed in large quantity earlier.

She served dinner, a simple bake of vegetables with fresh bread and a freshly opened bottle of Riesling. "We are going to have a bath, after dinner, I'll set up the tub." I brought water, and we set up a big pot to boil. In the small room beside the kitchen, she had a massive copper tub and a tiled shower tray, designed as an old-style washroom. By the time we were ready, she had candles burning, towels, and clean clothes ready to wear afterwards. She showed me the gown I was going to wear. It was a male version of her nightie she wore the previous night. There weren't any knickers there for me or her. Riesling and glasses waited on a tray. I brought the big pot of hot water, poured it in, and mixed some cold with it. Helga mixed some soapy aromatic substances until the whole room smelled like the mountainside behind the house. We stripped off in the chill of the evening and slipped into the tub from two opposite sides like dolphins, washing off the salty sweat of the day. Soon, we were covered with the foam and soapy hot water. She turned her back towards me and let me wash her curves, tummy, boobs, nipples, her thighs, and slippery middle between her legs. Under my fingers, her skin felt like that of a mermaid. I loved every corner of her round body, every curve of her muscles and her soft flesh. She placed her head against my chest, and I gave her a wash, parting her wet hair around her small ears. She caught my fingers with her lips and licked the soapy foam from them gently, slowly with pleasure. It was my turn to be washed. I turned around and nestled gently between her legs and her cushion-like tits, dividing them with each on either side of my neck, as she washed my chest, stomach, legs, thighs, carefully avoiding my rod already swinging in the warm bath, hard and excited by this sensual erotic ritual. I was being treated like a little baby, except that Helga wasn't my mum, I had a well-developed hard dick between my legs, and my blood was getting pumped through my balls straight into my brain. What I was thinking no baby would ever be proud of and any mother would find highly inappropriate. She wasn't planning to finish me off there and then. Helga had better ideas on her mind. Hardi was out of the way now, and we had the whole night ahead of us.

Helga scooped warm water from the bucket beside the tub and rinsed me properly. I stepped out, dried off, and gave her body a rinse. I was fascinated with her motherly features. They got me truly excited. Seeing her in the candlelight intensified the erotic lines of her body shapes. Her glorious boobs just stood there, withstanding gravity's pull so gracefully. The black triangle between her legs and her short hair, now wet and shiny, was so mysteriously suggestive of sin and ecstasy. I felt grateful for her delaying the sexual intercourse further. I had a chance to enjoy being with her and the erotic gameplay she was so good at. We couldn't speak much, but that was perfect; our emotions and excitement were in tune and drove us ever so higher on our erotic voyage. She helped me put on the shirt, and I helped her pull hers down as I tucked in her boobs with my favourite dark brown, almost black, forward piercing nipples on them. Oooooooh! What a night and the memory of it. I forgot about Hardi, who must have been moaning in his drunken stupor below, like a Barren Island prisoner in the stonewalled cellar. Well, I deserved this treatment; I worked hard, praised Helga's beauty and intentions, like a proper traitor enjoying the fruits of Judas's betrayal. I followed her like a dog follows a bitch, sniffing and salivating as she climbed the stairs on all fours, exposing herself and her honey pot from behind so shamelessly in full view. Right at the top, I grabbed her feet, spread them apart, and buried myself between her legs and buttocks from behind like a dog would do, licking, sniffing, and stabbing with my tongue into the warmth of her vagina as she stopped and wiggled it back at me. She crawled forward, turned back swiftly, came behind me, sneaked her head under the tails of my shirt to lick my hanging member. She had it in her mouth for a while, and I was getting so excited that I thought I'd shoot it right in there. She felt that and pulled off, sat on the rug with her shirt rolled up to her stomach, and started to touch herself. "Prance around for me, *mein grosser Bosnicher Hund*." I stood on my hind legs, held the edge of my shirt up, and swung my erected penis in front of her for her enjoyment. She tried to catch it with her lips when I got close, but this time I teased her and got away until she jumped like a tigress and caught it in her mouth like a flying bird. I let her have it. We didn't make it to the bedroom before I emptied my first load. I did offload my rocks, not those on the tractor, and she collected it all except for a small dribble visible on her breast. Helga wanted more, and she knew that she was going to get it in a while. The night was still young, and we had nowhere to go. Besides, she was a patient woman who had waited for more than a few years for the gift she had in her mouth a few minutes ago.

I went down to get the bottle and wine glasses. I remembered my friend, decided to descend further down to the cellar and checked on him before returning upstairs. He was snoring and appeared to be completely out. There was no sign of vomit in the bucket. I brought glasses to bed where she lay with a cigarette in her mouth, looking like a real whore with some of my come still visible on her breast. It was so impressive, just seeing her there so openly shameless. All those little princesses I was trying to impress should have seen her. She certainly was a queen of whores, and droplets of my come on her chest were her medals. I poured us glasses, and she held my hand, brought me closer to the edge of the bed, lifted my shirt, and brought my soft rod into her half-full glass, giving the glass a wiggle which washed it well in the chilled wine. She lifted the glass in the air and called me to empty them together. We did it, and she drained hers without taking a single breath. I topped up our glasses again and slipped under the

Sarajevo's Elusive Spring

covers with her. It took some time and her sensational stimulation to get me hard again, but she was relentless, gentle, sensitive, and unstoppable. My penis migrated between her tongue, lips, tits, arse cheeks, fingers, and the lips of her vagina, finally sitting firmly inside her. Helga was on top for a while and got it rock hard with her strokes. She came off and guided me in from the back as she lay on her side. Shortly after, she changed her position, adjusting to doggy style. Finally, I was so hard that when I got on top of her, I thought that I might be causing her injury. She was yelling, "Nein, too hard, do it, stop, please, no, keep going!" I was trying to be gentle and rough at the same time, because that was what she wanted. I thought that I could last all night for the second round, felt so powerful, watching how much she was enjoying my strokes, her glazed over eyes radiating the state of trance and ecstasy she was reaching. When she got there, it was all spasms around my hot iron, her legs hooked over my hips holding me in as I had to join her in multiple strokes of pleasure and penetration. Her fingers dug deep into my muscles and stayed there until she relaxed into that post-coital state of semi-death. She was breathing hard under me as my hot rod splashed out its boiling pleasure. All my muscles, nerves, and blood flow exploded within. What a night! I didn't want to come out ever; she rolled me over and kept me in until there wasn't any of it left, squeezing him in small spasms, and draining its last drops out. We fell asleep virtually as soon as we separated and fused our sweaty flesh together right away in an impossible knot.

Sami Tischler

Reality of a Breakup

By the time Hardi emerged from the cellar, we were out at the edge of the paddock working on the stone wall. Covered in sweat, we were rolling large rocks over the bank's edge to be permanently seated at its base. It wasn't an easy job for us lovers, who had been fused together once more as the dawn broke. However, the sexual attraction between us was undeniable, and the energy it generated appeared to be inexhaustible. Dripping in sweat, we had already stripped off our surplus clothes. I loved watching her gorgeous tits popping up and out of her singlet as we bent, pushed, lifted, and climbed the bank to get another stone down.

When Hardi stumbled out of the field, looking like a ghost, we were sitting in the shade on a cigarette break. "*Guten Morgen*, I'd like to help you guys," he walked up, sat down, and lit up a fresh cigarette. "Are you OK?" we both asked, "Did you have a good night?" I tapped him on the shoulder playfully. He looked at me with sad, bloodshot eyes. "Not so well, I am planning to get back on the road. I'd love to help you guys for a while and get the booze out of the system this morning. I'll be aiming to leave in the afternoon, well before the night. Are you coming?" He certainly surprised me with such a rushed and unexpected decision.

"I don't know, Hardi. I am certainly wanting to track back on our trip, but not as soon as that." I was hoping to delay his departure, but he appeared determined to go and as soon as possible at any cost. "I'll leave today anyway. I'll be heading to Munich, and I plan to spend a week there. How about if we make a date and a place to meet? You can take your time and live it up with Helga for a bit longer. You may get tired of her by the time I get to Lienz, down the valley. What do you think?" He was looking at me with a genuine expectation that I was going to take the offer.

"Look, my friend, that sounds like a great idea. I certainly haven't lived out all my sexual fantasies in the last 3 days and have serious doubts that I will in the next week. I feel that there is an infinite space for exploration and fun here. Right now, I am loving it, but I don't intend to bury myself here forever. I really like Helga, and we are enjoying each other tremendously. Thanks for giving us space and sorry that the threesome didn't evolve further than it did. Let's work something out and we can meet in Munich in 10 days. We'll talk to Helga and figure out a city landmark where we can easily find each other."

We both stood up and hugged for a long time while Helga looked at us a bit puzzled, not understanding what exactly we were plotting in our strange Slavic tongue. We worked together till lunch and had completed most of the wall. We explained our intentions, and I could see a cloud of sadness descending on her as she understood that within a week she may be returning to her lonely existence on the farm. I felt sad as well. Although Hardi and I had decided to meet shortly at *Frauenplatz, Frauenkirche* (The Cathedral Church of Our Lady) and continue our adventure together, there was no guarantee that everything was going to work out.

At that moment, leaving Helga behind felt unthinkable and unreal. I wasn't ready to lose this passionate, lovable, experienced, real-life rich woman. As I looked at her working, I observed her even more intensely, realizing that we would soon be apart and possibly apart forever. It made all these moments more precious and unique. I decided that I wasn't going to cry about it or ruin the good time I was hoping to be reserved for our enjoyment.

Hardi went to the creek and washed after the morning shift on the wall. He was overhung and edgy, but the hard labour cleared his head soon. As the warmth of the late summer settled in, he went into the greenery around the creek for a body wash and came back a different man. He appeared reborn and his eyes somehow clearer. "I am ready to get back on the road, my friends. I feel refreshed and reenergized." Helga took his hand and gave him a man's hug, held him there against her breasts like you would hold a child. I saw tears in her eyes as she let him go and looked at his face for a while. He was touched when she suggested that he gets some *"Essen from speizekammer* and the kitchen" for his trip.

She placed something into his hand which I assumed was a bank note of some value.

I walked him up the hill and sat with him on the edge of the road for a while. There were seldom any cars on the road. We smoked cigarettes and discussed the scenario. "I'll be there, my friend; I wouldn't miss the opportunity to get back on the road with you for nothing. I'll see with Helga if she could help me out with the fare to Munich." I was trying to ensure Hardi that I was not abandoning our plan. "It is a pain to hitchhike on your own. I am about to do it now. Hope I'll get there without dramas. I've got to get out of these hills. I have someone in Munich, a lovely blonde I met in Dubrovnik this summer. I'll look her up and wait for you. Just one thing. I am not putting her up for a threesome. Let's be clear about that." I laughed it off. "That is OK, my friend, we shared Helga a few times and that was fun but wouldn't volunteer that again. It can be painful and destructive. She handled it well, but she's got so much of herself to give, neither of us came up shortchanged. Such boobs, hips and the backside, muscles of a labourer, it is lucky that we are both still alive."

We both rolled on the grass in laughter. "I am going back for more, isn't that crazy?" I looked at him and saw how sad he was, realized how close we were and how much we loved each other. I grabbed his shoulders and gave him a huge squeeze, felt his tears rolling on his cheek, held him for a bit longer and stood up to leave. "Good luck, my friend!" I walked down the paddock and when I turned back, I saw him entering a small orange VW Beetle. He waved as he entered the vehicle. I watched them rolling down the hill until they disappeared towards the valley below.

Sarajevo's Elusive Spring

Back in Helga's Hands & Between Her Legs

Helga looked so happy to see me. *"Zigarettenpause,"* we sat down on top of the finished wall. Helga had brought clean underwear and towels. We smoked, and she sang an Austrian folk song in a gentle, soft voice, in contrast with her strong, masculine features. She was rocking in a gentle rhythm side to side and touching my shoulders in time. I picked up the rhythm, and we gently bounced against our sweaty shoulders. We were like two kids, sitting on a wall in summer, smoking our cigarettes in secret, away from our parents. She taught me simple lyrics about the forest, flowers, river, village, and a happy girl making a wreath for her lover. I almost got the words when she invited me for a bath in the creek's natural pool just in front of us below the wall.

We both stripped off our dirty clothes and entered through the gravelled pathway through the bushes surrounding the shallow pool. We entered the pool holding hands. As we descended into the deepest section, we stood there like Adam and Eve in the Garden of Eden, completely naked and surrounded by untouched nature. The gentle sound of water rolling over the white pebbles was fully lit by the warm afternoon sun. She looked like a goddess with her regal, motherly body features, ivory coloured skin, and striking short black hair. Helga's pubic hair showed above the water only slightly, suspended just touching the restless surface. She was a mystical forest beauty, and I was under her spell as she scooped water in her hands and started washing my body as if I was a totem, slowly and with great respect and admiration, examining every detail, muscle, and crevice.

The water was chilly, invigorating, almost too cold. We stood in a sunny spot. It felt as if it was washing off the sadness left after Hardi's departure and heating up my bloodstream with this delicate, loving gesture. It was my turn to give her my response, and I took it in the most sensible way. I washed, massaged, caressed, kissed, and aroused every sensual spot on her body. We held hands as we walked out, wrapped ourselves in towels, and reached for cigarettes. Smoke gives you a fake sense of warmth and intimacy, and we were fuming from under our wrappings, drying out, laughing at our smoking gestures, puffing circles from our mouths. She picked some field flowers around us and started making a tiny wreath.

By now, Helga had her towel wrapped around her waist, and her boobs freely bounced between suspended, perched stance on her chest and swinging side to side motion. I was getting an erection when she brought the completed wreath. The towel was covering my crotch, and similarly to what happened on the first day, she reached below its end looking for my erected warm flesh. She uncovered it like she did at the creek, carefully as if she had seen it for the first time. It was the totem, her lingam erected on her altar. She was ready to leave the Garden of Eden and risk everything for it. She was in trans, repeating some sort of mantra, a combination of wards as she placed the ring of flowers over it. I was propped on my hands, bracing myself on the ground, looking at my phallus, the ring of flowers on it, and her face gently touching its smooth, warm skin.

She never touched it with her mouth or her hands but explored its hardness and warmth with every part of her neck, face, ears, and finally her glorious tits. She managed to embrace and hold my erected phallus between her tits as she rocked them gently side to side and up and down. Before I had a chance to return her any favours, she jumped on it and rode it hard with her closed eyes as I tried to hold onto her boobs and stop them from falling off, smashing the flower wreath at the base of my rod. Her frenzied body strokes released a potent scent of field flowers and herbs that reached both of our nostrils. She came careless of where she was, shivers going through her majestic body, wide open mouth repeating a word I didn't understand, extracting all I had for our pleasure.

I loved this woman and this place, which felt like Eden, or perhaps outside of it. I truly didn't care.

Sarajevo's Elusive Spring

Over the next week, I managed to help Helga prepare her small property for the oncoming Autumn and Winter. We brought firewood from the woodlands, repaired the roof, the fence, and stored the last harvest of hay. That was all hard work, but we were together, laughing, touching one another, flirting throughout the day, exchanging our emotions and built-up sexual energies at night. In the early morning, she would wake me up often with her hand, mouth, or her boobs on my erection. Other times, I'd bury my face between her legs or her glamorous tits and drink her erotic juices and aromas. She would pretend to be asleep but couldn't hold back the excitement of getting swept up by the floodwaters of an awakening ecstasy. The bathtub inspired us for more fun every time. I had found psychedelic music on the radio once and taught her how to dance to it, and how to get in the zone. Her stock of wine and schnapps helped a lot. I managed to get her to "bang her head" and "swing her hair" to the music. I taught her to move her arms as if she was in "space." The radio played "The Doors." I told her that I'd be going to pay respects to their dead singer, Jim Morrison, in Paris. She cried. It reminded her that I'd be leaving soon, she said. I held her in my arms as Jimmy sang: "I've never seen a woman so alone..." I cried on her breast when she held my head as if I was her child. We would calm down, go to bed, fuck in every possible position I could think of, climax in a sweaty pile of entangled flesh, and cry ourselves to sleep. "I'll be *zurück* before the Winter." I was lying, knowing that my plan was to spend the winter in Amsterdam. "Who knows if all that will work out? It may be a fantasy, communes in Amsterdam. They won't care about two penniless Bosnian freaks. This woman cannot get enough of me, and I am loving it. I am certainly obsessed with her, but this passive existence and its attraction isn't going to last forever. What about her friends or family? What are they going to say when they find me here, and how long could I be here before the police turn up?" It was hard to be realistic in bed with a gorgeous woman who worshipped every part of me, and even harder to imagine her feelings and sadness once she wakes up on her own again.

Sami Tischler

Helga surprised me with her strength when the date came closer. She called her lady friend in Lienz and arranged a train ticket for me to Munich as well as the lift to the railway station, carefully planned to make the meeting with Hardi in Munich. "Well, my boy, you will come and see me again; you have promised. I know I cannot expect to have you here for the rest of your life, and you cannot expect me, the old lady, to leave my cows and chickens on their own and wander around the World with you, the crazy Bosnian stud, can you? You need time and space to shag a few young blondies around Europe, now that I have taught you how." I think she must have thought as she watched the shock on my face following the news of my trip in her unexpected arrangement. Our last night together, we held each other completely devastated with the knowledge of the nearing separation. I sucked her tears, and she kissed my salty lips. We fell asleep in the early hours of the morning and woke up completely exhausted with just enough time for a quick coffee before her friend beeped the horn in the distance, high above the farmhouse. I didn't want Helga to see me off at the road and in front of her friend, whom I had never seen before. Helga slipped a small package into my bag and winked. *"Auf Wiedersehen meine Liebe,"* she said through fresh tears on her face. I held her trembling body and couldn't hold my tears back either. I hurried up into the forest and towards the road on the hillside above. Before meeting the stranger, Helga's girlfriend who generously offered to take me to the station, I stopped at the small creek and tidied up out of her sight. Perhaps, all she wanted was to discover who this mysterious young man was who had befriended and given Helga a new perspective on life, awakened her sexuality and zest for life. Of course, she tried to extract details from me. I was not necessarily the best person to give away such intimate details. I couldn't understand her questions well, and she didn't quite get my answers. I thought that Helga would best deal with that and satisfy her friend's curiosity anyway. I chose to smile a lot, look out through the window at the fascinating scenery as we descended into Lienz, and deal with the sadness of yet another separation from a woman I had attached my heart to.

Sarajevo's Elusive Spring

I jumped out at the Railway station and found my way to the platform and the train easily. As the train negotiated valleys, bridges, and tunnels, my mind recollected the time with Helga with an immense sense of fulfillment. It was so spontaneous, raw, wild, unexpected, sexually charged, and erotically adventurous. The memory of separation and the void I was left with the previous winter when I briefly met Lucy and lost her the following morning had a different colour. Helga and I gave each other so much over the previous two weeks, and there was a promise of meeting again which gave me a sense of safety and gentle anticipation. Anxious about the meeting in Munich, I had no idea if Hardi would be there or if the Austrian episode had affected the core of our relationship. At some point, just before the German border control, I opened Helga's parcel. There was pure love in it. Some dry food, her amazing bread, sweets, 5 packets of cigarettes, and a handsome bundle of Austrian schillings. I felt so grateful and impressed that Helga had an ability to be an amazing lover as well as maintain a clarity of a woman with a strong motherly instinct. There was a small cigarette box wrapped into a hand embroidered traditional handkerchief amongst the food items. I was touched, and tears came to my eyes. When I opened it, there was a lock of her black hair tied with a red embroidery thread inside. I couldn't hold my tears back anymore. I had to turn away from the world and towards the window where I watched the melting end of the summer colours with patches of changing autumn leaves. I was shattered and realized that she was a rare jewel and thought how foolish my decision to leave her was. I understood that she didn't expect me to hang on for too long. Helga had no illusions that this was my time to explore what is out there and enjoy the freedom one can only experience on the road. "The road brought us together and the road pulled us apart." I concluded as my tired eyes closed, and my mind shut off to sleep.

Sami Tischler

Munich

I made it to Munich. On the day of our meeting, I sat myself at the front of the enormous Cathedral and watched the crowd. I didn't have to wait long. I had cigarettes, Helga's food, and a handkerchief with embroidered roses on it, yet I felt so lonely. The weather was perfect. In the early evening, I could see the familiar figure coming across the vast Platz towards me. I jumped off the bench and ran towards him to meet him in an embrace. He was so happy to see me; I could tell. The decision to join him again felt right. "It is OK here; I found a great place to crash at night, and people are generous when I ask: *"Hast du ein paar Marken?"* Our precious 100 DM would have lasted one week max. A single loaf of bread costs 7 DM." I told him about the gift from Helga. "She has fallen for you for real. If you stayed another day, you guys would have married; I can tell." Helga's face came to my memory; in fact, it hadn't left my thoughts at all. It was sad to think that I would be sleeping alone shortly, and the comfort of clean linen, great food, a playful mature lover, and a roof above my head had all evaporated. "I think I have made the right decision, and I am sure I'll miss her. Who knows, if you don't make me happy, I may return to her." We laughed and laughed. I was glad to be on the road and sad at the same time. I was sad that she was left on her own. Overwhelmed by the Munich crowds, traffic, glamorous shops, and the mix of grand traditional and ultra-modern architecture, my mind wandered and marvelled at the vision. The German language, spoken and heard in snippets of conversations, appeared harsh and noncompromising. Austrian, Helga's version, never sounded so abrasive to my ears.

"You know, I did contact the girl I told you about, the one I met at the coast this summer." Hardi started to explain what happened over the previous week. "We met in the city, and she invited me over. I was so happy about that. We had a dinner at her place, and I thought that I was doing great with her. You won't believe this, but her girlfriend turned up, and they played out this jealousy sketch. Her girlfriend looks like a truck driver, twice my size, an evil-looking creature. Once she learned that we had met at the Adriatic Coast, she got so angry. It

Sarajevo's Elusive Spring

turned out that her father was a Yugoslav guest worker who had his real family in Bosnia and kept her mother as his second wife. She was yelling at me, calling us all swine herders and goat fuckers. She took my stuff and threw it out the window and onto the street. I had to get out fast. My sleeping bag ended up in the middle of the road. Cars were all around it; I had to get there before it got run over and destroyed. Once I was out, she wouldn't let me back in." I was listening and trying to imagine the drama he had to live through. "She used the most profane language in the original Bosnian dialect. Her father was from Zenica apparently. She was swinging a kitchen knife in the open window. There was no point arguing about the fact that I didn't do anything too serious with Anne, her girlfriend, the previous summer. We just sat on the beach around the fire, and I was trying to impress her with my flute playing." For a moment, I was serious and sympathetically compassionate but couldn't resist bursting into laughter while imagining Hardi with his meagre possessions in the street, trying to get back inside. It had elements of "The Flintstones," an American Hollywood cartoon: "Wilma, open the door!!!" The look of an abandoned dog left his face, and he cracked up into laughter. The rest of the evening, we spent around several locations where buskers played. We were both fascinated with the quality of what was on offer. These guys were more than casual entertainers. Compared to some bands we danced to in Sarajevo, they were fantastic. We didn't know if they studied music, travelled, and supported themselves with busking or just tested their creations while practicing performance in the street.

We joined the army of "beggars": alcoholics, drug users, Christian volunteers shaking their cans in people's faces, buskers of all levels of quality, homeless, and desperate. We asked passers-by for small change in German. Often, late at night in the red district, we would hear Serbo-Croatian, spoken by our compatriots working and partying in Munich. We never gave away our origin, asked them for money, or expected sympathy from them. Yugoslav official propaganda warned its citizens to avoid contact with nationalist antigovernment organizations and their activities at any cost. Some of them were causing trouble and managed to bring armed terrorists across wellguarded Yugoslav borders. They frequently planted bombs in overcrowded cinemas and eventually tried to rise an armed rebellion in Herzegovina (the southern part of our Republic). Their activities were senseless, crude, directed against innocent civilian populations, not very popular, and certainly lacking imagination and rebellious spirit, otherwise highly regarded by the population. The German government failed to suppress or control their activities, and we could have been a perfect target. Homeless, penniless, and clueless about their cause, reasons, and objectives, we just decided to avoid any contact with people who spoke our language, which generally became the policy on our trip. That may have been the reason why we left the city, 5 days after my arrival.

There was one thing I wanted to do while in Germany and in possession of the money gift from Helga. I went to the post office and made an international call to her. I was lucky to catch her around lunchtime. "It is you, my Bosnian lad; you have no idea how lonely it has been since you left." She was quiet and couldn't continue. "I love you, my baby, and I miss you," I said. I could hear her crying into the speaker. "I know, I know, love you too." I couldn't say much more in German and decided to sing her a Bosnian folk song into the speaker. That calmed her down. She was silent and listening. I sang the full version of a tragic ballad where two lovers separated as the young man went away to find remedy for his lover's deadly disease. On return, the young man just makes it to his lover's funeral, offering a large sum of money to the mourners to let him see her one more time. It is one of the most tragic Bosnian folk songs ever. I promised to return before winter, and she appeared happy about that. She wished me a safe journey, and I couldn't hold the line for long. It was costing me a fortune to call her. The next day, we left Munich.

Sarajevo's Elusive Spring

Some Welcome and Lack of It

We travelled by hitchhiking and slept in sheltered places away from busy commercial areas. It was perfectly mild early autumn, and our sleeping bags combined with layers of unfolded cardboard boxes provided comfort at night. It appeared logical to travel through Switzerland to France. It was the magic part of our trip. Zurich, Bern, Geneva, fascinated both of us with its tidy, immaculate urban order, architecture, and natural beauty. We got lucky in Zurich when two friendly girls offered shelter for a night. We asked two random girls for some loose change, and they started chatting with us. A combination of French and a few German words worked well enough. They were so relaxed and warm with us, kept asking questions about our trip, laughed at our humour and casual comments on the way we travelled. Travelling with no money, sleeping anywhere outside, appeared to impress them. Later in the evening, we got invited to their apartment in central Zurich. This sort of thing rarely happens in Sarajevo. Girls of our age had no space of their own, and their parents wouldn't dream of hosting two "bums" in their homes. When we got there, the girls offered the use of their bathroom and washing facilities. I had my first shower since the last one with Helga. We certainly smelled better after we washed ourselves, our socks, and underwear. The apartment was centrally heated, and I remember sitting around the table barefoot, eating a tasty, cooked meal, sipping red wine, and starting to think about sleeping arrangements for the night as we continued the frivolous conversation with two gorgeous girls.

Once they stripped their Autumn coats, shawls, boots, and vests, a darkhaired beauty with soft, oblong features and a full, womanly figure caught my eye. Hardi was trying to charm the fragile, skinny blonde with a big Afro hairstyle. I felt that we were doing well. There was that instant, fuzzy attraction between us, strangers, accidental passers-by. We both had a fantasy that girls in the West were sexually liberated to a point where intimacy wasn't a big deal. We also judged our girls back in Sarajevo harshly as conservative and sexually underdeveloped. Hardi suggested that I could ask our new companions about sleeping arrangements and lead them into sin. After all, I had some knowledge of a foreign language. I should know how. I reluctantly agreed to the plan. The conversation stalled after that and lost its momentum. The little bit of evolving erotic drama depleted while my brain raced into my thin knowledge of high school French. *"Volair vou cousher avec moi"* was the phrase that came up, and I couldn't think of any other subtle phrase to use. It was a song by Boney M. popular at the time and generally ridiculed by us freaks, together with Abba-produced pop. I hijacked the dead conversation and killed it with the suggested sleeping arrangements, which didn't appear to shock the girls. They laughed it off and told us that they needed to consider the proposal in the privacy of their room (rooms?). Not sure now if there was only one bedroom there and if we had placed the offer to the actual lesbian couple. Hardi and I sat at the table smoking and waiting for the verdict. "I fucked it up, my friend, with my bad French. It sounded like a peasant asking his goat to have sex with him." I was trying to be funny. "You were great, don't worry, it may all work out fine. Let's see, we may be shagging these beauties before long. You never fucking know with women." The verdict came back with a smile: "We like you; you are cute, but no, definite no! *Neine!*"

We couldn't return to the relaxed, intimate, erotic mood. My question and their response destroyed it in an instant. After a late cup of tea and disconnected snippets of conversation, the girls went to bed and left us to sleep on the floor rug in the lounge/dining/kitchen/hall. We were happy to be inside anyway. "We should have left it alone; this sleeping together offer. We might have squeezed another night of free accommodation out of them." I whispered to Hardi. "Doesn't matter, we are in this for a long shot. If we depended on the young girls' charity, we would have never left Sarajevo. There is more exciting stuff ahead. You know it yourself. Why would you leave Helga's bosom if you didn't." I thought about Helga and her boobs for a bit and managed to make myself comfortable on the hard floor while the two beauties giggled in the comfort of their beds next door, covered by clean linen, most likely dressed only in their soft skin. When they woke us up early, somehow it felt like we were intruders in their house.

Quick coffee and out we were in the chill of the morning. In the early evening, they walked by in the street, smiled politely, waved hi, and kept on walking like you do past an abandoned Bogomil necropolis. It was strange how a barrier grew between us so quickly. I felt that I deserved it. I was going to forget Helga so fast. We left Zurich the next morning.

In Bern, we hung around the old town and its red-light district. There were semi-naked, gorgeous-looking women in the windows. There wasn't anything erotic or kinky about it, sex for sale in a shop window looked so perverse. Besides, we couldn't afford their neon-lit skin. I felt a bit ashamed keeping my eyes on the wares on display. Sitting on a bench, watching passers-by, chatting with Hardi and smoking felt natural.

A drunk, long-haired freak collapsed hard on his face meters away from us and lay there, not moving. Passers-by ignored him. We jumped to his aid and managed to get him onto our bench. He was bleeding from cuts on his face and looked a total mess. He mumbled words in German, and we couldn't make out what he was saying. An elderly gentleman recognized him and asked us to assist in taking the longhaired loser home.

Once on the train, we realized we were leaving Bern and heading into the countryside. Our drunken friend had no idea where he was going. He was asleep in the seat while his grey-haired neighbour tried his best to convince us we were doing the right thing.

"You can stay overnight at his place; he lives in a large house by himself, and he won't mind your presence while he remains in this state. After that, you'll see. He should be grateful for what you've done for him. Although Hans, his name is Hans, has never shown much gratitude to anyone I know."

We made it to a small village and Hans' house late at night. The three of us carried him into his bed. The old man showed us around and left.

We were sitting in the kitchen of a well-furnished house with Hans completely wasted in his bed.

There was a sense of déjà vu, we'd had a similar scenario in Zurich with two young beauties. The difference this time was that neither we nor Hans had any interest in sharing beds with each other. Also, this time, we didn't care. We'd helped the man and decided to take advantage of the situation.

"Let's hang around here, whatever happens when he wakes up," declared Hardi as he inspected the fridge filled with food and cans of beer.

He took two cans out and we relaxed into armchairs to enjoy them. There were foam mattresses in the second bedroom, a missing ingredient in our outdoor accommodation. It was a great improvement to our comfort in the room we took over for now. We both had long, hot showers, just in case, and washed some underwear, which we hung over the furniture in the bedroom to dry.

When we got up, Hans was still completely wasted and out of action. We scrambled a breakfast, lit the fire, and sat in our armchairs flicking through illustrated books and magazines. In the daylight, we realized the village was very pretty, surrounded by paddocks filled with cows, a typical Swiss scene of hills, forest, green valleys, and fields.

Hans woke up completely shocked by our presence and sense of domesticity. Hungover and angry, he walked around like a nervous dog and talked about not wanting us there, at least, as much as we could figure out. We were determined not to go anywhere. We insisted he owed us hospitality for the generous help we had provided. He had no idea if that was true or not and eventually walked out.

We found spare keys to the house hanging on a hook by the door. With the key in my pocket, we left the house unlocked and took a hike into the hills above the village. We also carried a few of Hans' cold beers from the fridge.

Up in the hillside, we sat down and drank our beer, smoked cigarettes, and looked over the valley. It was pure serenity, distant mountain tops, green fields crowded with cows, a train line cutting through the valley, a red train shooting through, almost silently, muffled by the distance. "I could live here, Hardi. This is so perfect."

Hardi was silent for a while, then responded in his slow-paced, measured speech:

"If I lived here, I'd most likely become an alcoholic like Hans. This is all so manicured, sterile, and artificially perfect. Even these trees look like someone trimmed them this morning. They keep cows just because they wouldn't have any idea what to do with untidy natural grass otherwise. I can't see their cows ever being slaughtered. Imagine if they suddenly disappeared from the postcard-perfect landscape, what would they do with the mess?"

We rolled in laughter, victims of our own cynicism.

"I think I'd rather live in a cave somewhere. I hope to see how they live in an urban commune in Amsterdam or Copenhagen. Otherwise, I'll take to the hills. We have plenty of those in Bosnia. I'd love to have a go at it there."

We came back home as it was getting dark and found Hans cooking dinner. He was surprisingly in a better mood and offered us wine, which we were happy to accept. At dinner, Hans wanted to know about our plans. He seemed happy to let us stay with him for a couple of days. We were starting to enjoy the evening when his girlfriend turned up.

Sami Tischler

Hans' Sweetheart

She looked just like those window girls in Bern, displaying her wares for us to enjoy while hiding her eyes behind heavy make-up and massive fake eyelashes. She wore an ultra-mini leather skirt and layers of jewellery. Not all of it looked cheap. She didn't seem to fit the profile of this neighbourhood, made up of people wearing their working clothes at any time of the day. She pulled out her kit and rolled us a big hash joint. Soon we felt like mates and laughed a lot with them.

Hans played music on his stereo – screaming hard rock we had never heard before – completely wrong for the occasion. We were going through another bottle of wine, having a matching conversation on top of our voices, trying to out-yell the stereo. She looked at her watch, stood up on her gorgeous legs, paraded between the kitchen, the loo, and the bathroom mirror where she checked herself out, gave us an impressive salute as she sprung out her hardly covered small tits, and they left. Apparently, they were going out to Bern, and we weren't invited – naturally.

"This is perfect!" I screamed, found the only Rolling Stones record in Hans' collection, and set it on the record player. We had some wine left; she had left crumbs of hash, tobacco, and a few *Rizzlas* on a magazine. Party time – yeeeei!

That's how it was for a week. Hans turned up late, slept half a day, woke up overhung, had a few beers, disappeared, came back late, and woke up late. Some days we hardly saw him. We got into the habit of exploring the hills by walking on narrow roads leading to a single farmhouse or jumping fences and walking through the fields. We assumed the right to do so – it was generally legal in Socialist Yugoslavia. Pathways to springs, river corridors, beaches, ancient access roads and footpaths retained free public access as they had in ancient Balkan communities. In Bosnia specifically, formal feudalism existed during the Ottoman era. Bogumil communities didn't seem to have much sympathy for any institutional structure and preferred communal living, sharing both burdens and benefits.

Occasionally we spoke to farmers, shared smokes, and chatted with them as we did in Bosnia. My French started improving in short leaps – school knowledge buried somewhere deep in my brain surfaced and started making sense through repetition and listening. I started thinking in French and even had dreams speaking it.

Hans' ugly scab on the left side of his face was starting to peel off as we systematically prepared to leave. We couldn't stay there any longer. The fridge was virtually empty. The little money we had couldn't be wasted on groceries; it was preserved in case authorities requested proof that we weren't vagrants. The village was too small to start asking random people in the street for small change.

Hans' sexy girlfriend turned up one morning. Hans was still in his comalike state and not getting up. We made coffee, and she rolled a fat joint. She was in a great mood and wanted to dance. She found some slow tunes in German and wanted us to dance with her. Hardi wasn't getting into it, so she dragged me up on my feet.

I loved dancing and thought of myself as a great dancer – certainly the case when I danced on my own. Apart from my original feet, hands, head and torso movements, I was able to spin like a dervish while doing those simultaneously without ever losing my balance. Dancing to slow music with girls wasn't something I had practiced, and I always felt a bit awkward. I could get into a close embrace and rock to the rhythm without stepping on a girl's feet any time. I knew how – and had the courage – to sneak my hands into spaces where they weren't welcome. Low back and top of a girl's bum, as well as over the girl's breast, were my favourites.

Recently, with Helga, we went as far as I could have imagined going with a girl. I also taught Helga how to loosen up and let go to psychedelic music, and we had our own mad parties in the Austrian hills. This was something different. This girl looked so foreign to me. She smelled like a rose garden – and the earth the roses grew in – at the same time. I could almost taste the hash that came with her hot breath as she brought my body close to her made-up face and against her prickly little tits.

I felt a little scared facing her piercing blue eyes behind the massive fake eyelashes, almost a death mask. Her eyes were glazed over after the fat joint we smoked, and I was feeling a bit doughy on my feet. The song in German sounded strange. The whole idea of her boyfriend being completely wasted in the bedroom next door felt so weird.

"Ich bin Irma," she introduced herself for the first time, as a sign of giving some recognition to my existence.

"Ich bin UFO," I responded.

"Schön name, sehr schön," she whispered into my ear and bit it playfully as she placed my hand onto her spiky tit. I had no option but to leave it there. We moved slowly, close together. My hand on her tit found the nipple easily and gave it a gentle massage through her thin blouse. That made her press even tighter against me, my hard cock forming against her belly. She held her belly there and circled it around my muscle.

My left hand decided to help on its own. It went down to her small round buttock encased in the leather mini skirt and held it tight, making her grind very effectively. Her butt moved in circles as we moved around, and my hand found its way between the cheeks. I saw Hardi in the lounge chair watching intently and shaking his head.

The stereo played another German song, as slow as the previous, hardly any rhythm in it. We almost stopped moving without letting go of the territory gained, just standing there, grinding pelvises, progressing into kissing everything but each other's mouths.

There was a sound of movement in the bedroom next door, followed by a dry, deep-chested cough. Irma froze for a moment but never detached herself from my enraged cock. We both listened, there was no further movement from the bedroom. We looked down the corridor, but no door opened. She continued for a minute, but my cock

Sarajevo's Elusive Spring

wasn't in it anymore. I felt guilty. We were guests in the house. Despite all his grumpy gestures, we had drunk Hans' wine and beer, emptied his fridge, enjoyed total freedom in his home, and now I was about to be caught with his girlfriend, and not just flirting. She was just about ready to ride me.

It would have been a great experience, but it was going too far. She stood there, confused for a moment, then stumbled away to the bathroom, a great way for a woman to escape reality. When she came back into the room, she looked immaculately gorgeous. Makeup perfect. Hair spotless. Even her nipples stood to attention through her blouse in a perfect salute. She gave us a little wave, wiggled her arse atop her perfect thin legs on the way out, and made screaming sounds with her sports BMW as she left the scene.

Hans came to in the late afternoon, completely unaware of what had happened while he was in a coma-like state. His scab was peeling off, and his eyes looked watery and fogged over. He sat in the armchair, smoked, drank beer for breakfast, and moaned in pain. Before his regular nightly disappearance, we told him we were leaving. He looked a bit sad, probably relieved too. Hans went out and must have celebrated hard. We couldn't wake him when we took off in the morning. He was completely wasted, having made it home in the first light of day. We decided to leave him to his troubles.

In Geneva, we befriended a group of hash-smoking youths and had a hash party at the beautifully calm lake, late into the evening. They played music, switched between German and French, and behaved as if they owned the world. Although in clear sight of passing dog walkers, none paid much attention to the joint ritual taking place just meters away. Hardy claimed to be a target of homosexual harassment repeatedly. None bothered me. I wasn't sure if he was making it up or if he had qualities popular with those looking for a same-sex partner.

We used immaculate public lavatories where we kept ourselves clean, washed our clothes, and often sat around in sunny park areas, having clothes spread over bushes and benches to dry. No one bothered us, no police checks, no harassment. Homosexuals had been a nuisance on the road. A young man once stopped and drove us a long distance. At first, I wasn't sure if he was serious. The conversation led into an argument: "How do you know you don't like men if you've never had sex with one?" He pressed for an answer but clearly hoped to get in our pants, thinking we were desperate enough to do it for some reward at least. He was so aggressive that I felt relieved when we got out of his car with our arseholes still intact.

Later, we realized certain areas must have been hunting grounds for homosexuals and tried to avoid them, public toilets at any time of day, large city parks at night, and "friendly drivers" who prowled the roads. We never thought about the possibility of male hitchhikers doing their trade on the highway, servicing the gay community in their cars or in secluded carparks. It was a new experience for both of us. We were aware of gay communities and their existence in Yugoslavia at the time, but they must have run their business in extreme secrecy since it was punishable by law.

The weather held well; dry, warm days rolled on for a long time. Autumn was in full swing when we decided to get out of this magnificent place and leave Alpine Europe before it got too cold.

France, here we Come!

We entered France through the Lower Alps and Provence, all the way to Lyon. Motorways with trespassing restrictions and travelling away from places and people didn't make sense to us, so we tried to use old country roads between Lyon and Paris. We travelled in short rides between picturesque southern towns, inhabited mostly by old people, each with a Post Office, small grocery shop, and a church.

It was hard to hassle people for money. Living on a diet of bread and yoghurt became a drag. I had studied French for eight years at school, since the age of 11, but my conversational French was rather poor. When first asked "Where do you come from?" in French, I had no idea what the question was and had to ask the guy to repeat it a few times. It was only when he started listing countries that I recognized it. However, after a week in the French-speaking part of Switzerland, I was getting the hang of it.

We travelled with a small A5-size map of France and got lost in the labyrinth of country roads in Provence. At times, we stood at intersections with road signs pointing in nine directions, none of the names existed on our tiny map. Rides were often too short, hardly worth the effort, taking us from one bad spot to another. We would walk out of a half-deserted village, then another few kilometres before finding a good spot to hail rides. By then, we were virtually in the next village, or we caught rides there anyway.

"This isn't the way to get to Paris," I said to Hardi, as we slept in a hay barn, virtually in someone's farmyard, where we'd sneaked in late one evening after a long walk. Another night, we slept in a gazebo built in the middle of a large cemetery. Morning dew and fog were becoming a real pain, we couldn't sleep in the open anymore and had to seek shelter. There wasn't much choice. Our presence in small villages couldn't be made less obvious, and I was starting to worry about attracting police attention.

We sneaked onto a brand-new motorway illegally one foggy morning and entered Paris the following day. At the time, Paris offered a wealth of opportunities for a carefree, penniless existence. We slept in parks until we discovered that every Parisian gay used them as hangouts and places to mate. Eventually, we found a quiet park next to a crèche. It was fenced and safe, although the fence wasn't high enough to stop us entering.

Our main reason for coming to Paris was not its cultural, historic, or artistic charm. We came to pay our respects to Jim Morrison, the legendary singer of the American band The Doors. We had read that he was buried in *Père Lachaise* Cemetery with the rest of France's greats. Of course, we knew of Victor Hugo too. Our local library was well stocked with works from legendary French authors – Rimbaud, Sartre, Camus, Hugo – and I had read all of them.

The pilgrimage was a disappointment. By 1976, Morrison's remains had been moved back to the US. (Interesting! No one had told us about that.) We realized that Yu media and the editor of Jukebox magazine were at least six months behind and badly out of touch. The grave site and the way to it were well desecrated by graffiti, Morrison's poems, and hippy symbols. All in all, it was one grand act of vandalism – far too radical, even for us native Eastern European primitives.

Paris was easy. Tourists gave money casually, any time we asked. We smoked *Gauloise*, bought decent food, and stole some too. Hardi and I, natural small-time thieves, developed a technique where we would say hi to a grocer while stealing a piece of fruit from the street display at the same time. We couldn't see anything wrong with that – it was like taking a piece of fruit from a branch hanging over the fence back in Bosnia.

Buskers of great quality played everywhere. We followed those we liked to different locations around the city. We walked around the old town, checked out buildings, parks, and watched artists at work and at their stalls along the Seine. Everyone looked less bohemian than us. Most of it seemed like an act for tourists – fake beret, fake pipe, over manicured moustache, trendy shoes with a trendy hole in them. We wore the ones with genuine holes and slept rough.

Sarajevo's Elusive Spring

We were both artists in the making, becoming artists without even realizing it. That same winter, back in Bosnia, I started carving wood – a natural progression from always making something with the pocketknives I had owned since I was five years old. A few years later, in exile in Australia, I studied furniture design and making at ANU under world-famous furniture designer and maker George Ingham, which I still practice. In time, Hardi began colouring silk scarves using Indonesian batik techniques with wax and knots. He made a living working with silk and silver wire for years and died as the owner of a jewellery shop in Vitoria, Spain.

At the time, in 1976, we were genuine *clochards* – homeless Parisians, temporarily nevertheless, through our own choice and circumstances. The Seine was magic, with its stone banks and bridges. We came back repeatedly to Notre Dame. I tried to imagine scenes from Hugo's writing and a hunchback on its roof. It didn't look possible, but what the heck – such a small detail wasn't worth ruining such a great book.

Neither was the fact that Jim Morrison wasn't in his grave anymore, nor that the beautiful Gioconda wasn't a match for my Helga, the "woman wolf" in the Austrian Alps. Although there was some resemblance, I had to admit Helga's breasts were a creation of heavenly genius, and the fact that I was able to touch, fondle, and bury myself in them had immeasurable advantages. I wasn't going to destroy my own illusion and refused to spend time scrounging money for a ticket from tourists in front of the Louvre to see a dead painting. The living memory of Helga was too valuable to me. Mona Lisa had to remain a mystery.

We killed some time in the beautiful gardens around the Eiffel Tower, where West African illegals sold souvenirs to tourists. In Trocadéro Gardens, across the Seine and along the large ramp-like sets of steps to the Palais de Chaillot, we observed a new trend. Kids rode what became known as skateboards alongside these endless ramps. They seemed to have an original fashion style and were evolving a new street subculture we had never seen before.

Metro stations and tunnels leading to the platforms were great performance spaces for buskers, mime artists, singers, and actors. When we found someone, we liked, we hung around and came back to see them again the next chance we had. Eventually, we followed our favourites to different locations in the city centre, and they started treating us as friends, offering us cigarettes, wine, and on a few occasions, sharing joints with us.

I felt honoured to be accepted into this weird society of freaks, evolving their existence on the verge of civilization – same as we did. I was starting to believe that the commune we were dreaming of finding in Amsterdam was a logical reality and a real possibility for the approaching winter.

Ten days in Paris had taken its toll. We started feeling bored, running out of places where we could hang around and feel inspired, calm, and genuinely interested.

Sarajevo's Elusive Spring

Mao's Death in Paris

One rainy day (9 Sept. 1976) I found a discarded daily paper and read the shocking news; Mao had died in China. I didn't know what to think. There was an image on the front page: an endless, orderly mass of people standing in Tiananmen Square, paying their last respects to their legendary leader. Black-and-white photo, no colour, bits of grey, the rest grainy black.

Paris didn't seem to care much. Life went on. "Who the fuck is Mao?" someone would have asked. I was puzzled by the lack of interest. I wished I had been there when President Kennedy or Martin Luther King were assassinated, just to have seen people's reactions. When they decapitated their King Louis XVI, I knew they celebrated. Perhaps that was what the Chinese should have done.

Mao's death marked the end of the Cultural Revolution, one of the darkest periods in Chinese modern history. There was something sinister in this event. "What do you think is going to happen when Tito dies?" I remember asking Hardi that unthinkable question.

"That is a scary thought, my friend, indeed." Hardi went silent for a moment, rocking his head side to side. "That may be the only way to get rid of those old farts, useless fake revolutionaries. See what Mao did? He got his youth to get rid of them before he left for the Eternal Hunting Grounds. Perfect solution. China is liberated now. There will be some good things coming out of there. They'll certainly get rid of their blue pyjamas, don't you think, UFO?"

He had my mind in a lock. I just couldn't imagine the future without Tito for us in Yugoslavia. I liked China and their shining path, but I couldn't see myself in a blue loony jacket. I'd only just rid myself of my compulsory blue school overcoat a few months earlier.

"What did Jim Morrison think about China?" I would have liked to know at the time. And what would a Chinese audience have done if they saw Jimmy stimulating himself on stage?

Sami Tischler

The world without Mao would never be the same. Yugoslavia without Tito might not survive, but China would. This city had had its Revolution in 1789–1794 and had shown the world what people's power could do when masses moved together. Now, they didn't seem to care about revolutionaries anymore. They sold old stories to new tourists instead, showing off kings' palaces and art, they'd purchased from starving artists or stolen from colonies. Fake artists must have painted every façade, alleyway, café, bridge and balcony, selling their cheap canvases to hordes of gullible visitors.

The whole thing was starting to look like a theatre of fakes. Tourism wasn't our thing; we detested it in all its forms. The time was right to move on.

Paris →Nancy → Antwerp → Brussels → Rotterdam

Hardi was famous for his address book. He collected hundreds of addresses of people he'd met at parties all around the Dalmatian Coast, Belgrade, Zagreb, Ljubljana and Sarajevo. He met Michael in Belgrade that summer. Michael had been born in Yugoslavia, but his divorced mother married a French doctor, and they lived in Nancy.

It took us two days to get there. We found Michel, who spoke perfect Belgrade lingo. Welcomed and entertained in his parents' house, we felt like royalty. They hosted a series of formal dinners where I managed to hold a decent conversation in my broken French, encouraged by a generous quantity of great wine.

Michel knew everyone at the university, where he was a student at the age of 30, something virtually impossible in Yugoslavia. After a certain age you could study for a degree by correspondence as a feepaying student; otherwise, education was free.

We were invited to house parties and cinema screenings of "Midnight Cowboy". Many of Michel's friends lived in converted attics, some of which may have been squats. We slept in clean beds at his parents', had regular showers and clean clothes for a week.

Michel was planning to visit London, and we were invited to join him. It was a unique opportunity to get closer to Holland and Amsterdam. But the offer to travel to London held no attraction for either of us, we knew that being penniless on an island couldn't be much fun. When I thought about it, I realized this was the perfect excuse for Michel to get rid of us. I wasn't going to tell Hardi. Michel was his friend after all. We'd had a memorable week as his guests, and there was no reason to hang around Nancy any longer without him.

He drove across northern France, which looked gloomier and gloomier the further north we went. We were dropped somewhere on the highway at a massive intersection with numerous overpasses, ramps and huge road signs listing cities in Belgium and Holland.

Sami Tischler

The weather turned nasty, and we got stuck at an intersection in the middle of nowhere. In the semi-darkness of the highway junction, we discovered a control room under an overpass. It was amazing luck. The space was dry, clean and warm. It even had a working light. It was a vagabonds' castle.

Bad weather had caught up with us and began following us around. In Antwerp, we sneaked into a locked block of apartments late at night, hoping to leave before anyone came out in the morning. Our calculations didn't work out, a young couple came home late and found us sleeping on the landing, virtually at their front door. They weren't put off by the sight and invited us in.

These wonderful people brought out food and drinks and sat around with us until the early hours, talking and eating. They put us up for the night and left for work in the morning, leaving us in their apartment. We felt that one night with them was more than generous, so after breakfast we left a "thank you" note and went back on the road.

Belgium appeared a bit grey and lifeless. We were missing Paris and hoping to find something new in Amsterdam. Within a few days, we were in Rotterdam. Autumn was turning depressingly wet and dark.

The road into the city centre went under the New Meuse River through a brand-new tunnel. How fascinating! We walked through a well-lit, wide passage full of good-looking, well-dressed people on their way home, to work, or simply out to town. They didn't care about the weather, nor were they looking for a dry place to sleep. It was hard to imagine they lived in flats and houses like the rest of humanity. The whole set-up seemed futuristic, like a cocoon in a space colony.

In the evening drizzle, we walked the streets looking for shelter and wandered into suburbia. Funnily enough, people did live in flats and houses. Human residences looked unreal with their curtains drawn open. We could observe domestic scenes, dinners, and families gathering after a day at work or school.

Sarajevo's Elusive Spring

After wandering through the city centre, void of a friendly face, infested with good-looking, well-dressed aliens, we searched for an apartment block and sneaked in after a careless resident. It had a typical basement where tenants kept their bikes. Once inside, we set up for the night. Someone must have come down to get their bike, spotted the two sleeping vagabonds, and reported it to the police.

The arrest took place while we were still in our sleeping bags. The authorities denied us an opportunity to be properly heard, investigated, or formally sentenced. They took all our possessions, belts, shoelaces, and passports. Each windowless cell accommodated only a single person and not one ray of natural light.

On the sixth day in jail, I turned 19. Hardi was yelling out of his cell across the corridor: "Happy birthday, UFOOOOO!" I was trying to read a couple of books left in the cell for my entertainment. They may have been religious books, with a Bible amongst them, who knows. I couldn't tell. They were written in Dutch, which I had never heard or seen in printed form. I spent hours trying to decipher enigmatic, illogical text just for something to do and keep my mind occupied.

You could only tell the time by the pattern of meals they shoved in. We walked once a day, circling the roofless top of the jail building in total silence for 15 minutes. You could only see the grey sky above. The autumn sky in Rotterdam never offered any consolation, always grey, murky, and depressing.

On the 12th day, the police confiscated our 100 DM bills to pay for the "exclusive" accommodation and transport in the company of two plainclothes cops. They issued a receipt and dumped us at the French border. After 11 days in a high-security prison, we were expelled from all three countries of Benelux (Belgium, Holland, and Luxembourg). The French police at the border didn't seem to have anything to add. We were free to go.

"Let's go to Germany. We could swing across to Austria and spend some time with Helga. Farming season is coming to an end. She will love to see me, and I'm sure she won't mind you, if you behave yourself." Hardi was smoking his *Gauloise* again and thinking for a while. I was anxious to know what he thought about this idea.

"You know what? That's a great idea. Fuck Amsterdam, we should drop that dumb idea for now. A commune in Amsterdam could have been a great way to spend winter. Smoking hash and flirting with goodlooking blondies will have to wait. Things have changed, and there's no going back. Losing those two 100 DM notes to Dutch Nazis feels more demoralizing than being pickpocketed in an empty Sarajevo tram. As for Helga, she may decide that change is not such a bad thing and dump you as her lover. I understand she prefers your skinless sausage, but you never know. If you're not freaking out about me being around, I'd love to try it."

I took it all light-heartedly. We had no other alternatives. I craved Helga's intimacy, and my head held fresh memories of our adventures in bed. I wasn't afraid of Hardi's presence there. Helga's place was less than a day by train to Graz, the Austrian city on the border with Yugoslavia. If it didn't work out, Hardi could easily get back home from there. I was starting to feel warm around my heart at the thought of seeing her soon.

It took us a couple of days to get to the Strasbourg border crossing. German customs officers bluntly refused to let us into the country. It was a result of an impressive one-page "Refusal of Entry to Countries of Benelux" stamped in our passports, and the serious absence of funds in our pockets. We were devastated to learn we couldn't get home through Germany either.

We decided to try Switzerland as an entry point and a way to Austria. At this point, our passports had one more "Refusal of Entry" stamped by German customs. At the Swiss border, we were met with an uncompromising refusal after the police confiscated a pair of *Opinel* folding pocketknives we had acquired in France. They officially stamped our passports with another "Refusal of Entry" in case we tried another crossing into Switzerland.

Sarajevo's Elusive Spring

We felt like the guy who was caught at an international airport without a visa. We had no restrictions in France, but both countries we could have transited on the way home wouldn't let us in anymore. We were completely penniless. Italy appeared as our only hope, but we had to get there first.

The weather in the Alpine ranges had already turned to a fog-and-rain pattern. Hitchhiking was no longer an option. Sleeping outside was out of the question. I scored a pair of leather gloves lined with fur, left behind by a scooter rider at the set of lights in Strasbourg. The gloves were a gift from heaven. They had a separate space for the index finger and thumb, making them amazingly practical. I could smoke without taking them off. Black leather matched my heavy black winter coat. They must have cost someone a fortune.

As their new rightful owner, I felt great comfort and warmth around my heart. I had a sense of being looked after by someone, somehow. With the misery surrounding us, rejections at the border, the possibility of not seeing Helga again, I needed something, and this was it. As small as it was, it was a sign I wasn't abandoned; some force, my mum's prayers, or Helga's love surrounded me and took care of my needs.

We boarded a train without tickets and got caught by a plain-clothes inspector. He issued a fine we couldn't pay. We were taken off the train at the next stop and escorted back into the street. We managed to scrounge some funds for two train tickets to Chambéry, a large city in Provence. Completely wet, depressed, and miserable, but on the move again. Hope and enthusiasm crept back in.

"It must be a bit warmer there. We can relax for a few days and see if we can work something out. You know, Hardi, my friend Boya crosses the border to Italy without a passport. Did you know that?"

"Of course, I do, half my neighbourhood does it. We could slip through the border, I'm sure. If they can do it, so can we."

I was glad I had a travel companion with some guts. For a moment, I thought about the Spanish International Brigades fighting Franco in the 1930s. They would have sneaked across borders into war-torn Spain to die for the cause they believed was right. The survivors would have been in a similar pickle making it back home, where they faced united German and Italian fascism shortly after.

At the time, we were doing this for the love of adventure, but it felt like our cause grew bigger as we advanced through southern France, negotiating merciless regulation, increased government control, and suppression. We were so exposed, unprotected, and easy prey to a growing monster of regulation, intolerance, and discrimination.

Hustling in Chambery

I had a brilliant idea. If we had train tickets all the way through Italian territory, the Italian authorities couldn't deny us our right to return home. My memories of Trieste and Italian customs were of relaxed lenience and indifference. They never displayed the authoritarian attitude of the German, Austrian, or Dutch authorities. It was a gamble, but we had run out of cards, and this was the only one left short of crossing two borders illegally.

At the Chambéry train station, we asked the ticket clerk to quote a fare to Sežana, the first major station in Slovenia, on Yugoslav territory. We were surprised that the sum wasn't astronomic and that we should be able to raise it using our well-established practice of asking passersby for spare change. This time, the sum was well above what we normally collected or needed. We gave ourselves a week to make it happen.

Winter hadn't reached the south yet, and we were confident our plan had a chance of working. After an intensive begging spree in Chambéry over a couple of days, we were getting close to our quoted sum. Working in the street all day was exhausting. Although French citizens in the south were surprisingly generous, there were those who asked uncomfortable questions:

"Why don't you find work and earn your own money?"

"Aren't you ashamed to be begging in the street?"

"You are so young and already useless."

It was hard to answer any of those questions, and I was glad only a few asked. My French had improved by now, and I was able to reply politely. At some stage, generosity dried up. By that time, we must have already asked half the city's population for small change. Citizens had seen us in the street for three consecutive days, and we started spotting those who crossed the road to avoid us. We were so close, yet still short.

Sami Tischler

Life wasn't cheap in France. We bought food and cigarettes out of funds reserved for our tickets. Longer we stayed further away we were.

We worked constantly in sight of each other, covering both sides of the busy city centre streets. It wasn't going well, and we were starting to lose hope and motivation.

A man approached and pulled out a 20-franc note. He knew what we were about, you could tell by the way he passed the note with discretion. I didn't get a chance to ask anything. I was so impressed and thankful.

"You can have more if you like, but you have to come with me to my place," he said.

I instantly saw it as an invitation to paid sex from a gay man. Reluctant to respond immediately, and since he had already given me 20, I was momentarily speechless.

"I live a short walk from here, and I don't have much money on me, but if you come along, I'll give you 100."

The number flashed in front of my eyes. *"Bien sûr, allez,"* I said, grabbed my bags and walked past Hardi, giving him a thumbs-up and a wink to let him know everything was okay and I'd be back shortly.

As we walked through the centre, I had a chance to observe the gentleman taking me to his place. He was in his thirties, shorter than me, but tall and handsome, nevertheless. He wore fashionable clothes, safari trousers, a creamy vest, and fashionably long hair. He spoke educated French and kept a relaxed, cool façade as we conversed.

I was nervous and ran endless scenarios through my head: "What is going on, why am I following this man? What is he hoping to get out of this deal?" I wasn't afraid of him or his intentions. I didn't think I could be raped by someone like him, I'd defended myself from far more dangerous characters in my own neighbourhood and in Sarajevo's dark alleys. This guy looked harmless in comparison, and even likeable.

Sarajevo's Elusive Spring

"Would he be capable of getting me into something I wasn't ready for? What am I ready to do for 100 francs? How desperate am I? Why am I still following this man?" I churned these questions over in my mind, keeping myself on edge as we walked.

It took a while to get to his apartment. I was about to give up when he said, "We have arrived." There was no point going back, I would have lost too much time for nothing, and yes, I was desperate. "What can go wrong? I can always refuse to let him be on top. After all, what the hell, he's so nice and handsome."

He showed me in and sat me down, then brought out a bottle of red. "That's grand!" I thought. His place was beautifully furnished and stylish, modern artwork and objects from North Africa filled a spacious apartment. Loaded bookshelves and LP records collection looked impressive and chic. He played French Gypsy jazz on his stereo and set about rolling a hash joint for us. He pulled out a lump of hash and the rest of the kit from a delicately carved Moroccan box.

I was starting to relax, and the wine was amazing. The joint brought a feeling of lightness between us and a lively conversation about travel, exotic places, Morocco, art, and music. I realized I was talking to a freak. I had nothing to fear. We were so much alike. All my suspicions about being dragged into becoming a boy for sale evaporated like the hash vapour I exhaled. This guy, Pierre, was just trying to help.

What a relief. I completely forgot that Hardi was left in the street, puzzled as I'd lost track of time in Pierre's company. "I've got to get going, Pierre!" I remembered suddenly and got up.

"*C'est bien, mon ami*, it was nice to meet you!"

I wasn't going to remind him of his promise. It didn't feel right somehow. I was at the door when he called out, *"L'argent, mon ami, l'argent, ici, vrai copain."* He gave me 100 francs and a bear hug at the door.

Sami Tischler

"Bonne chance, bon voyage!" I heard as I went downstairs and back into the street.

I felt my wings growing, my feet hardly touching the ground all the way back to where Hardi patiently waited.

"Where have you been? I was so worried. I thought I'd lost you for good to some poofter."

He looked at my excited, happy face as I pulled out the 100.

"Don't tell me you slept with him for that. You're crazy if you did. What happened? Tell me, what's going on?" I couldn't take the smile off my face.

"Are you jealous, you prick? Adventures with Helga, now this gay, I know it's too much for you. But I love you, and I only love you, my greatest friend."

I had him in my arms, and the tears were coming. He was crying too.

"We have money for tickets now, what a day, how fantastic!" I screamed, and we started dancing in the street like two madmen.

We went to the shop and bought food, wine, and cigarettes. We also bought supplies for the trip: bread, salami, cheese, a bottle of orange juice, tins of sardines, biscuits, chocolate, and extra cigarettes. In the nearby park, we celebrated. I told him everything about Pierre. We toasted to his name and emptied the full bottle in no time. We even sang some Bosnian *Sevdah* folk classics at the end.

Then we remembered we needed to purchase our tickets. It took the clerk some time to count our small change and bundle of small notes. The 100 francs stood out, and I was sad to see it disappear into the money drawer.

We had just purchased two train tickets from Chambéry to Sežana via Trieste and Villa Opicina. The corner of the park and thick layers of cardboard were our home, as they had been for the previous three nights. Neither of us wore a wristwatch, and we both kept an ear open all night for the city's bell tower, counting its hammer's blows. We couldn't afford to miss our early 5:10 am train.

The night was mild, and the morning chill woke us before our due time. We sat on a cold bench, all packed up, eating our dinner leftovers. Everything was closed except the train station down the road. We boarded with a few early travellers, hardly speaking to each other, anxious about the upcoming border control.

It took only a couple of hours to get through some deep canyons before we faced an Italian customs officer.

"Passaporte."

We pulled ours out. He looked at one, then the other, stamped them both, and handed them back. He hardly glanced at us. If he had paid any attention, he might have suspected we were smuggling the most dangerous contraband. Completely numb with fear and anxiety, we were such easy prey, but he couldn't be bothered. Our Italian angel.

I felt my mum and Helga were there, screening us from his police trained stare, letting us come home.

Sami Tischler

Back in Italy on an Iron Horse

As we made it over the Italian border, the train route, and my eyes, followed the Alpine foothills. Helga's face came to me in the night and followed the train through the frozen landscape. I felt her hot skin and warm breath on my cheek. There was no way of returning to her for the time being. I planned to phone Helga from Sarajevo.

It was a long trip to Sežana, the Slovenian town on the border with Italy, where our tickets expired. From there, we travelled on trains without tickets. Somewhere between Doboj and Zenica, we got caught in an overcrowded train by the ticket controller. Completely penniless, unable to pay a hefty fine we were handed over to the armed train escort. Our homes were only 70 km away.

He offered us cigarettes and wanted to hear details. We certainly had a story to tell, five months on the road from Istanbul to Rotterdam via

Belgrade, Zagreb, Venice, Munich, Zurich, Bern, Geneva, Lyon, Paris, Nancy, Antwerp, Brussels and back, along the German, Swiss, and Italian borders, penniless. All the way to Sarajevo along the autumn fog engulfed railway lines. There was something almost heroic in our story. The big policeman decided we were worthy of respect for what we had done.

We left the train with the big man together. "You'll be welcome to travel on my train any time," he promised as we parted.

Our reputation among freaks in Sarajevo grew to legendary status. The three of us, Hardi, UFO, and Chuck wore the new label with pride. Chuck couldn't travel outside the country. After spending time in juvenile detention for a minor offence of vandalism, authorities wouldn't approve his passport application.

With our new followers in tow, we hung around the city during the day and the club Cactus at night. Random people invited us to parties. We never missed a concert in Skenderija, went to the movies a lot, and just wandered the city. Its mosques, small parks, and the cultural

Sarajevo's Elusive Spring

hub in the subterranean Skenderija, heated in winter and out of the wind, became a perfect shelter and refuge.

I tried to call Helga from Sarajevo's Grand Post Office, built by the Austro-Hungarian Empire. I remember walking into the international phone booth, taking off my legendary gloves, and listening to the signal. There was no answer. I was waiting for her voice, but it never broke the line. Nobody was home.

I went back to the counter to make a payment and walked out into the freezing winter day. A couple of hundred meters down the road, my hands felt cold, and I remembered the gloves I'd left behind in the booth. I sprinted back, but there were no gloves in the empty booth.

I realized the torn-out page with Helga's number and address was gone too. I rushed to the counter.

"Excuse me, has anyone found my gloves and a piece of paper in the booth?" I was devastated.

"Sorry, young man, we have better things to do than look after your gloves and bits of paper."

I was puzzled for a moment and wondered if everything around me was a case of a liquid psychedelic reality. I reached into my pockets. My hand landed on the box with the strand of her hair tied with a red thread. My hands were shaking as I realized she did exist. She was real, but that fine thread connecting us had gone, evaporated into the cold, grey fog.

The life turned monotonous, predictable, and comfortable too soon. Boredom was setting in too quickly. Playing a game of cat and mouse with shop security guards all day in Skenderija Centre just to stay warm had annoyed us enough. We started taking lengthy visits to Belgrade, where we linked with the local young freaks who were doing the same routine there. Generally penniless, I found that citizens of our capital gave freely. They were well-groomed by jobless and penniless Belgrade freaks, who practiced the same craft daily.

Sami Tischler

We were often invited by teenage girls on school holidays to small day parties while their parents went to work. We sat in these grand apartments owned by the new socialist aristocracy, entertained their young daughters, and checked out their musical taste. That wasn't the only thing we checked. Their collections of exotic foreign spirits and wines became our favourite objects for exploration.

Unfortunately, we couldn't sleep anywhere decent. Our looks, clothing, and Bosnian dialects attracted young girls but certainly inappropriate to be paraded before their parents or neighbours. At the end of the day, generally very late, we'd retreat to our atomic shelter two levels underground. No one else used these spaces. In the absence of nuclear war, they made fantastic, trouble-free accommodation. The temperature down there appeared mild and constant. Flattened cardboard boxes made a clean surface and a thermal barrier from the concrete below. We kept stacks of candles there and enjoyed the same cavernous shelters during many of our wintertime visits to the capital.

Sarajevo's Elusive Spring

Karlo

I met Karlo at Chuck's house in Malešići (Ilijaš). Chuck was adopted by his elderly aunt from a large family when he was a small boy. When he moved to live with his new parents, he was separated from his twin sister Jadranka for the first time. I met his old aunt and helped her while Chuck served his time in jail and the army consecutively. I'd go and visit, chop up firewood, and help her understand bills and legal documents.

By this time, she had died a while ago. Chuck had no job, nor a passport. He owned his house and a decent-sized block around it at the age of 20. Karlo had lived in Germany since the late '60s. He went there with his father intending to work as a *gast arbeiter*. Karlo's father died after a few years, but Karlo stayed behind.

In the early days, he got attracted to numerous communes sprouting up all over Germany and eventually settled in one fashioned around new interpretation of the Bible and the teachings of Jesus. Its members indulged in communal living, open-sex marriage, hash smoking, music playing, and generally having a good time while criticising the harshness of the German government and its omnipresent eye over its population.

They had no idea what the control of population was. In Yugoslavia, we were frequently ID-ed, checked, and raided. We had no unemployment benefits, had to forego 15 months of national service without pay. There were no drugs to take, and all our girlfriends went home by 8.00 pm.

Chuck was lucky to have his own place, but the local police were onto him, and raids were frequent and aggressive. This time Karlo came back to Yugoslavia to arrange his long-delayed national service. He postponed it for a long time by residing in a foreign country. Finally, he had run out of excuses.

We met, exchanged our ideas about government control, life, drugs, religion, and jammed some improvised Eastern sounds for hours at

Sami Tischler

Chuck's place, as was customary. We had no drugs to consume, but we drank cheap wine instead.

Soon, Karlo went to the army to serve his compulsory unpaid national service. He left his personal copy of the Bible with me for safekeeping and a read. We exchanged a few letters, I read the Bible from cover to cover, and six months later he came on his leave.

His long hair and beard were gone. He looked like an escaped convict in his second-hand winter coat and JNA (Yugoslav National Army) boots. Sarajevo can be depressing in winter, engulfed in smog and its sky hardly seen through thick layers of fog. The snow gets dirty after a few days, you walk around in wet boots, cafés are your only escape, and waiting for Cactus to open in the evening becomes a drag. Getting back home late at night on a bus with bad draught seals around the doors was a serious health risk. We generally dodged the fare on government-run cheap buses and had no right to complain.

I suggested that we take a couple of days, hike through my home country on Treskavica slopes, and escape dreariness, boredom, and claustrophobic depression. Sarajevo could make you feel claustrophobic in winter, small cafés, buses, trams, cinemas, and discos, packed with overdressed people, filled with cigarette smoke and stale gossip. A vision of white snow-covered mountainside and the idea of breathing crisp, cold air haunted me for days. Smogcovered Sarajevo felt like a trap, a gas chamber of sorts.

Time Travel to Ledići on Foot

Upon our return to Bosnia from our adventure in the West, Hardi and I made a bundle selling Christmas cards door to door. We travelled around Bosnian towns and pretended to be students on a mission to make some cash and support ourselves through door-to-door sales. It turned out to be a very profitable venture, and we both felt that we had broken a secret money-making code.

At the start, I needed some starting capital. I was naïve enough to think that my uncle Ibrahim was the right man to ask for a loan. So proud that I was starting to think like a businessman I had to let someone important know. He looked interested while I was laying out my business plan but refused to support it in the end. I was asking for something like $50. It was my long hair and appearance, as well as my parents' disapproval of my travel, that would have made his decision for him.

Hardi and I worked it out between us. We used his funds as our starting capital. Within days, I had made enough to pay him back, and if my uncle asked to borrow some cash, I had enough stashed aside to impress him.

I started looking through classifieds and house-and-land sales, hoping to find a small property in an abandoned village somewhere and start up a commune. It was a mad idea. The elusive commune we fantasised about while travelling in the West wouldn't leave my mind. When I thought more about it, I realized that we could start one ourselves.

Now that we'd discovered a way to make money fast, land ownership was becoming achievable. It was a matter of time before we'd stumble onto an abandoned house and land somewhere in the southern parts of Bosnia and Herzegovina. We all agreed that Herzegovina would be a perfect choice, due to its mild climate and proximity to the sea. We were hoping to find a property out of the way, out of sight, away from people's curiosity and the militia's attention.

Sami Tischler

Hardi, Chuck, and I spent many an evening talking to friends and freaks about it, while searching for clues on locations and lesser known corners of Bosnia and Herzegovina. The village Ledići came under my radar. It is the only village on the plateau between Treskavica and Bjelašnica inhabited exclusively by Bosnian Orthodox people. The rest, including the village of my birth, Trebečaj, were settled by a mix of Muslims and Orthodox Christians. Someone told me that the village Ledići was virtually abandoned and might have properties for sale.

I suggested to Karlo that we could take a bus trip to Pendičići, on the way to Dubrovnik via Foča, Gacko and Trebinje. A four-kilometre walk would take us to Trebečaj, where we could drop in on one of my many relatives there. We would walk to Dujmovići, my mother's village, and stay with one of her first cousins overnight. The following day, a hike of an additional 3 to 4 kilometres would take us to Ledići.

He was very excited, and when I told him about a string of Bogomil tombstones covering the landscape, he could not wait to get on the bus. "It sounds like we'll be going back in time. The past is my favourite tense. Present is *shaise!*" he swore in German. "Let's get on the road and out of this shithole!"

I tried to match his euphoria by performing my famous "Dervish Spin" in the middle of the street while negotiating the crowd of passers-by.

The next day, mid-morning, two creatures, two urban freaks, could be seen trudging a muddy path up towards Trebečaj. Sure enough, the village of my birth is an ancient Illyrian/Slavic Bogomil settlement, surrounded by a large stone necropolis *(stećci)* on three out of the four roads crossing the village. On opposite ends, there are Muslim tombstones. The only Christian Orthodox graveyard shares one of the sites, separated by the road. Bogomil tombstones are everywhere else, including the area around the road dividing the two cemeteries. In some cases, they have been integrated into our yards, orchards and wheat fields.

Sarajevo's Elusive Spring

Karlo had only ever seen these gravestones in books and museums. He didn't know how common they were in many parts of Bosnia and how natural they appeared in this ancient landscape.

The Treskavica Mountain rises close by, all the way to 2,000 metres in altitude. As we entered the village, I was spotted and recognised by my cousins Ramiz and Nurko, Mehmed and Sabaha's children. They hoarded us into their house, greeting us with a loud and hearty welcome. Sabaha brought out a simple lunch of cheese, sour cream and bread, and asked us hundreds of questions about family, city life, our plans, and reasons for the trip. They gave us free tips for the next leg of our journey, collectively, and all at the same time. My country folk had never learnt to speak one at a time or listen, unless you were representing an official authority.

There was a long walk ahead of us, so we decided to continue before the afternoon light turned grey. Large areas of the hills were still under deep snow. While the roads looked clear they had turned muddy during the short period of midday warmth. I decided to take the forestry gravel road, visible as a cutting across the lower Treskavica ranges. I knew that was a safer option and that the snow would be cleared for the forestry trucks carrying timber from logging sites on Bjelašnica.

We descended into Dujmovići in the late afternoon. I found the old Vilići household. Sevda, Besim's mother, welcomed us. I mumbled some fake name when introducing Karlo, and no one asked again. I can vaguely remember, but I believe we spent the evening with Devla and Sevda, who served us a great dinner and voiced their concerns and warnings about the risk of going to Ledići, where we did not know anyone. They were puzzled about our motives for wanting to go there.

Their old, spacious house felt so welcoming, and a bit strange, in the absence of my male relatives, who worked and studied in the city. The following morning, we were awoken by the smell of coffee and a cooked breakfast. It was a real feast of their own produce and a farewell. The women had their chores in the stables and around the house to attend to.

We put on our boots and took off, following the line of forest across the ridge between the two villages. The mountain above looked enormous, and it made rumbling sounds while we walked across the white expanse, as if it was sending us a warning. Within an hour, we walked over the ridge crowned by a long line of *stećci*, some monumentally large. A distant memory of a time in the past flashed before me, when my mother, village women and I took part in a procession praying for rain. My mother always denied that she ever participated in such a pagan ritual. My memories of it were so vivid, but I seem to have many of those.

There are certainly elements in this story that happened, but there are those I must have dreamt about, and certainly lots of details and events I cannot vouch for to be true.

From there, we gradually descended into the village of Ledići across frozen patches of snow. It reminded me of Trebečaj, houses on the hillside, water running through the village, old shingle-roofed houses covered with rusted sheets of metal salvaged from recycled tar barrels. The only difference was that most of the houses had a small cross planted at the ridge of their roof. Muslim houses had a spear-shaped point as a rule. Smoke was coming through the *badža* (roof opening) on a few of them.

There were no people in the streets, and many houses appeared in disrepair, neglected and half-abandoned. We took a cautious walk along the ghostly streets, admiring the rustic architecture and the strange beauty that invades dilapidating structures as soon as humans desert them. It was daring to imagine our life in these houses, repairing crumbling render, patchy limewash, rotting shingles, empty stables and chook houses. Small village plots wrapped in broken fences woven from hazelnut sticks appeared so romantic, craving a new enthusiastic owner.

Sarajevo's Elusive Spring

An old man appeared and called out, "God be with you, lads." We greeted him warmly with, "Good day, Uncle."

He asked who we were and what business brought us there.

"We heard that there were houses and properties for sale, and we came to have a look. I have family in both Trebečaj and Dujmovići, and my father owned the only bakery in Trnovo in the 1950s," I introduced myself using conventionally expected references.

He appeared a little suspicious. I was extremely irritated by the fact that he did not know who my father or my mother were. My grandfather owned the land a few kilometres down the stream of the river Bijela, at the site of the famous Husremovac Springs. My father owned the bakery in the regional centre, Trnovo, the only bakery within a 25-kilometre radius, 10 kilometres away, in the late '50s and early '60s. My parents' families made up more than 80% of the population in Trebečaj and Dujmovići, and this slow-talking and even slower-thinking character behaved as if he had never seen the rest of the world or interacted with my numerous relatives, virtually his next-door neighbours.

Although this was my first visit to Ledići, the village was often mentioned in my household. My mother told us that a band of partisans (Tito-led communist rebels) came to Ledići one winter, possibly in early 1942. She was 10 years old, and their scouts came to Dujmovići demanding food for the troops stationed in Ledići.

My extensive research had proven that Tito wasn't there at the time.

Villagers refused and brandished their weapons supplied by the Independent Croat State (a Nazi-style puppet state created by Ante Pavelić and supported by Mussolini). They were no match for the partisans.

At the time, communist partisans held a loose alliance with the *Četniks* (Serbian nationalist irregulars), and the Bosnian Muslim population did not trust them. The *Četniks* were held responsible for the massive slaughter of Bosnian Muslims in Foča and Goražde, only 100 km to the east.

It was a freezing winter night, and the snow was over a metre deep when the partisans attacked the village. They came covered in white bedding sheets and started setting fire to houses and stables on the edge of a narrow strip of dwellings leading up to the thick, forested side of Treskavica.

The village men were on guard and started the fight in the darkness of a moonless winter night. From my memory of cold, silver, moonless nights in my own village of Trebečaj, it would have been a battle of shadows, visible only in black and white. Villagers were armed with one machine gun and an assortment of small weapons. The gunner kept changing position, creating the impression of multiple machine gun nests. The flames from its barrel would have been the only flashes of colour in the ghostly grey and white of the village and the towering mountain above.

Villagers used their knowledge of the terrain to their advantage, moving around swiftly, confronting the partisans, and returning fire fiercely. The partisans failed in their surprise attack.

My grandfather got up on the roof of a house and kept yelling at the top of his voice: "Hit them hard, brothers! *Allahu Akbar!* Do not be afraid, help is coming!" He had a hoarse, deep voice, the voice of authority.

Several houses, stables with animals in them, and farm buildings burnt down. There were dead partisans who had their pockets loaded with nails. Villagers were puzzled by this and speculated that their intention was to crucify or burn people alive in their homes.

Afraid for the safety of their families, the following day they evacuated the village, moving women and children to Trnovo on sleighs, horses, and on foot. From there, they were transported on Croatian Army trucks to Sarajevo as *muhadžeri* (refugees), where they spent the next two years with distant relatives.

As a result, no Muslim from these villages joined the partisans during WWII. They fought as Croatian "home guard" regulars, joined the *Ustaše* (elite Croatian fascists), or enlisted in the German Army. However, those who remained at home were armed by the NDH (Independent State of Croatia) and capable of defending their homes and lives in desperation from a variety of irregular armed groups and military formations. Times were bad, and life was cheap in these mountains.

Thirty-five years later in Ledići, we were talking to an old man in the street when a few more joined our gathering. Our conversation was not getting any friendlier. The questions directed at us were the sort you'd expect from the city militia when they decided to harass you. They wanted to see our IDs. We refused to show our documents out of principle.

Eventually, a young man about our age materialised from somewhere and addressed us in what we identified as an urban slang. It turned out he was a student in Joša at the Railway College, close to where I lived. Several people I knew had studied there. We cross-referenced a few names, and the stalemate eased a little.

Sami Tischler

House Arrest

Someone suggested that we go inside a house, sit down with a cup of coffee and a drink. We were keen to get this sorted out in a civilised manner. So, we did. As we sat there being treated as guests for a while, more people emerged until the small house got packed. By then we were fully encircled by Ledići's male population. At some stage one of them declared: "Sorry lads, but you will not be going anywhere until we get a few things checked out and some information clarified." We both protested and insisted that we lived in a free country. "We are entitled to free movement, without restrictions. This is house arrest, and you aren't authorised to enact one."

They insisted that they were going to wait for the response from an official who happened to be in the village of Dejčići, only 4 km away. They had already sent someone there and it should not be too long before they had an answer. They maintained that we should not have anything to fear and once cleared by the official, they would be more than happy to let us go. Arguments continued and, in the process, we naively disclosed more suspicious information to them.

Karlo declared that he was on his Army leave, that he was religious and believed in Christ, same as they did. If he hoped to get their sympathy, he failed. It only had the opposite effect. They recognized his Catholic references, and this made them even more suspicious. They rolled out stories of madhouse escapees, jailbirds on the run, Croatian terrorists trying to escape from encirclement in Herzegovina to the Bosnian side of Bjelašnica, the mountain behind and above the village.

It all looked hopeless. Tense hours went by in the smoke-filled room. Everyone smoked, except Karlo. It was late afternoon. Shadows were getting long while the temperature plummeted. A Land Rover jeep with the Council of Trnovo insignia and red rego plates rolled up with a bald-headed, short official in it. The chubby fellow emerged through its mud painted door. We answered more questions and repeated our "story" one more time for the full audience.

Sarajevo's Elusive Spring

The official, a Bosnian Muslim and distant relative of mine, whom I had never seen or met before, knew all my family from both my father's and my mother's side. He advised everyone that he was going to drive us down to the main road on his way back to Trnovo where we could catch the bus back to the city. He appeared to be satisfied that we had no ill intentions and that we were just naïve city boys with romantic feelings for the village life. The sooner we went back to our dirty city the better off everyone was going to be.

They all laughed a big, loud collective laugh, exposing their dental disasters. A variety of yellow, rotten, gappy mouths with decaying teeth displayed their wares all at once. Mouths of Hell, a scene from a Fellini socio-psychedelic film noir fantasy. We sat in the Land Rover relieved that we were getting out of there, following the canyon of White River down to Kijevo, one-third of the way to Sarajevo.

Sami Tischler

Freed But Handcuffed

It was nearly 7.00 pm when we left the village as it was about to disappear into total darkness. The mountain behind the village appeared to be sitting on its rotting roofs and squeezing the last fragments of life in the form of smoky haze swallowing everything living in it. Our conversation in the darkness of the rattling Rover, as it crawled between potholes and the frozen surface of the rugged road, grew more sinister with each kilometre.

The official appeared apprehensive and worried about his promise. Getting dropped off on the main road wasn't on his agenda anymore. He started building a case for taking us back to Trnovo, 30 km out of our direction. "Those rednecks back there will walk all the way through the snow just to make sure that I had done the right thing," he whined. "It could backfire badly," he continued, "I cannot afford to put my reputation on the line for you guys. I hope you understand how sensitive this situation is."

He kept on appealing for our sympathy. "You don't have to worry about anything. Militia will check your IDs, and you can catch the bus from there to Sarajevo easy," the brown-nose champion elaborated. Trnovo had always kept a fragile balance between the Bosnian Orthodox and Muslim population, result of those events in Dujmovići and Foča as well as similar horrors committed against the population during WWII. Everyone felt on edge all the time in these parts, suspicious of the new multiethnic Socialism based on principles of "Brotherhood and Unity".

We could see that he was looking for a way of getting us back to Trnovo whether we liked it or not. After all, they all had our details, all the way from Ledići to Trnovo now. There were no phone lines in any of those villages and no chances to cross-reference or doublecheck information. The whole business was 100 kilometres out of our way, getting out of hand, helpless and more complex by the minute.

Sarajevo's Elusive Spring

Sure enough, he drove straight to the "Milicija" building in the middle of the town. We went in of our own will, and he ushered us to a room while he had a short conversation with the policeman on duty behind closed doors. We never saw "my cousin" again. Two policemen entered the room shortly after. We were handcuffed to the hydronic heating pipes. They questioned us just to kill some time while they waited for the response from Sarajevo. They also searched our pockets and confiscated our documents.

In the big inside pocket of Karlo's coat they found a pocket Bible and his Army ID. Those two items did not belong together. In combination with his name, Karlo Miler, the whole thing appeared a puzzle, too hard to resolve in their thick skulls. My Bosnian Muslim background and the location of my origins looked just as bad. The pieces simply did not fit. The militia were instructed to bring the puzzle down to Sarajevo immediately and hand us over to someone who knew how to read and connect all the fragments.

It was after midnight when we were brought, handcuffed, into an office 300 metres from Skenderija and our favourite Club Cactus to face a plain-clothes drug squad policeman. We had no drugs on us, and they did not know what exactly we were accused of or why and how we were brought to them. Sure enough, they did a fair share of questioning, provocation, and harassment before we were released, well after 1.00 am.

At that time of night in those days, Sarajevo was a dead place with no public transport in operation. The only warm place where you could spend the night was the railway station. We went there and sat in a large waiting room next to a boiling radiator, trying to process what had happened in the previous two days. We felt lucky to have made it out of those mountains so dear to me and so foreign to Karlo, who grew up in Sarajevo only 30 kilometres away.

Tito would have felt the same as he left Ledići in the summer of 1943 with the knowledge that the village of Dujmovići was completely abandoned except for some 30-armed men shooting at the back of his column from the forest nearby and refusing to let go of any livestock as they had the previous winter. Some of Tito's bands certainly knew how to discredit and sabotage his heroic efforts to unite the population against the aggressors. By 1943 Tito had clearly broken a shaky alliance with the *Četniks*, but some of their crimes stuck to his name.

Višegrad, Narrow Gauge Narrow Minds

It was winter, may have been my last year of college in former Yugoslavia. Hardi met a guy in Split at the Adriatic Coast the previous summer. Joško turned up in Sarajevo. He was a coastal freak, spoke Dalmatian dialect typical for Split. We took him around to Cactus, Nightingale Bar, daytime cafés and hangouts in the city. It was starting to look like we had nothing else to impress him with.

When we travelled on the coast, local Dalmatian freaks generally ignored us Bosnians. We owed nothing to Joško either. However, it was a matter of pride, and we were trying to show off to our rare visitors that Sarajevo had evolved into the modern world where things were happening. Hardi suggested that we could go to Višegrad, a famous city featured in the book by Bosnian Nobel Prize winner Ivo Andrić. Hardi's mother came from a village on the opposite side of the Drina River just a few kilometres downstream from Višegrad.

We had heard that the narrow-gauge railway line built by the Austro-Hungarian Empire would be closing soon. It would mark the end of the steam train era. Steam trains had run for 100 years and earned the nickname *"Ćiro"*. We thought this was a one-off opportunity to get this ride under our belt and explore the famous destination of Višegrad. Although penniless, we knew that we could gather funds fast by asking passers-by for small change. We called it *"žicanje"* in Sarajevo.

It didn't take long, and we had money for train tickets, cigarettes, and a meal of *"ćevapčići"*. The train was leaving soon, and we decided to do more "business" when we got there. We boarded the train at the old station in Pofalići. Within 20 minutes the train climbed to Hrid, high above the Old City, and disappeared into the canyons and hills of Romanija.

Once we reached Pale, a small town in the highlands, the train was virtually empty. Buses had already taken over the transport of those travelling further and across the mountain. The ticket controller and three of us sat on hard wooden benches. The official employee of the doomed railway line produced a bottle of homemade plum brandy and an endless lament about good old times.

The moonshine on the sly often appeared in unexpected places while travelling on trains and within factories and workplaces, I discovered later. Working-class Yugoslavs consumed alcohol at home, at work, on trains, on buses, at roadside buffets while travelling, driving, and socialising. It was a massive social problem but largely ignored by the government. It was perfectly legal to distil alcohol out of your own fruit and if that wasn't enough, government distilleries and wineries topped up the deficit and sold cheap alcohol throughout the government-owned shops, cellars, hotels, workers' canteens, bars, and restaurants. It wasn't uncommon to see policemen on duty standing at the bar in the middle of the day having a few "quick ones" on the house with the manager of the establishment, both employed by the government.

We went through amazing countryside, including 23 tunnels on a 20 km stretch of the line (4.2 km of tunnels). We came out of the empty train a bit tipsy and landed in the small provincial town of Višegrad like a gang of bandits in an Italian spaghetti western. Longhaired, dressed in daggy clothes, wearing earrings, rings and bracelets. It wasn't hard to get spotted and be declared "a danger to society" in this sleepy town with a grand reputation, featuring an ancient and beautiful bridge over the Drina River and housing the peasantry of eastern Bosnia and western Serbia.

We were as naïve as Karlo and I had been a short time before in Ledići. To make things worse, we went to the busiest location in town, the bus station, and started with our business of *"žicanje"*. Surprisingly enough, we were doing great. Hardi met one of his cousins whom he recognized in the street, and they hung around while Joško and I kept collecting funds from passers-by.

It didn't take long before two uniformed policemen swooped on us and asked for our IDs. We were ordered to the police station, only metres away. We had to accept "the invitation" and followed them in.

Sarajevo's Elusive Spring

They ushered us into the building, one ahead, the second behind us. It was as bad as the Milicija in Trnovo. Luckily for us, Hardi and his cousin weren't arrested.

It turned out that Hardi's cousin worked in the local government office and, while we were sitting in an empty room with our pockets full of change, he negotiated our release. He told us later that he knew both policemen and blamed it all on our desperation to get money for the bus to the village downstream. When one of the two came to let us know how lucky we were to get away with our "crime" this time, we could see how disappointed he was. They would have had a great time locking us up properly and giving us a decent beating just as a warning.

"I want you to disappear and I don't want to see your faces again in my town, and don't forget to thank the young man who bailed you out."

I felt like a Mexican bandido who had to leave the town without a gun, horse, or saddle. Once reunited with Hardi and his cousin, we walked four kilometres to his mum's village. On the way there, we made up a story for the family in case the whole episode leaked to the village.

In fact, we had a great couple of days in the village, being a major attraction for young girls who had not seen young urban youth like us before. They giggled and laughed and giggled again as they walked within our proximity with obviously nothing else to do. It would have been a bad idea to respond to their flirtations and get ourselves in trouble with Hardi's family.

After two nights there, we decided to sneak back on the train one evening, hoping that the policeman so keen to try his truncheon on us wouldn't be on duty. We had a lucky break and returned safely across the mountain back to Sarajevo. As *"Ćiro"* descended into the night lights of our little metropolis, it felt as if we were escaping a siege, returning to the Garden of Eden. Like the survivors in the movie Deliverance floating along the river into the safety of the concrete jungle.

Sami Tischler

Within a relatively short span of time, this little metropolis would be held in the claws of the famous Siege of Sarajevo for a total of 1,425 days. The types of characters we kept encountering amongst government officials, teachers, militia men would be amongst snipers and those blasting heavy artillery guns into this beautiful valley, its inhabitants, their homes, hospitals, schools, libraries, places of worship, cemeteries, indiscriminately.

Exiled from the White City

Shortly after our trip to Ledići, Karlo went back to serve the remaining portion of his national service, and I was already called up to do mine. Many of my close friends did theirs around that time since we were all similar age, unemployed and not studying at the university. It was a boring period of waiting for the inevitable 15 months of compulsory national service, and friends kept disappearing at random times to serve their time.

Earlier in autumn I travelled to the capital again to see off my friends Hardi and Boldy on their trip to India. They were going to slip out of the country before they got called up. Army duty was to be delayed through a "disappearing act" and served afterwards.

It was late autumn and nights were getting cold. We made it to Belgrade on the night express from Sarajevo. The three of us masterfully moved ahead or behind the ticket controller, silently walking past him as he did his rounds and systematically checked tickets within carriage compartments. A few times we left the train at a station, walked on the tracks and skipped around the controller, then back into the section he had already checked.

Secretly, I was hoping to get caught and handed to the "big militia man" who promised to host us on "his train" and test his hospitality. I hated this style of travel and the risks we had to take. I preferred lifting my thumb on the side of the road and getting rides from sympathetic drivers. Although doing it in cold and damp autumn wouldn't have been the best choice either.

Finally in Belgrade, we stored our sleeping bags in our atomic shelter two levels underground, within a multi-storey building close to the city centre. This had become our legendary pad. We used it, bragged about it to everyone, we even gave out its location and address to friendly freaks travelling to Belgrade. Walking around the city with a sleeping bag over your shoulder was considered risky business amongst us "freaks".

Belgrade had a plain-clothes police force like no other city in Yugoslavia. Friends told us about their raids, especially when foreign dignitaries came on official visits. They arrested anyone suspicious, homeless, or penniless to ensure a clean image of our White City, Belgrade, and our squeaky-clean regime. We stood out with or without sleeping bags. Besides, we came to Belgrade for a begging spree.

Hardi and Boldy had managed to save some money. They had no idea how long their funds were going to last or how exactly they were going to manage a long journey by land and a whole winter in India. We usually did well in Belgrade, and people were generous when asked for small change. Once we had enough for a meal, cigarettes, a bottle of wine, cover charge for a concert and similar, we moved on and had no problems with police in the past. This time we were planning to push our luck further, much further. The memory of the Chambéry miracle lingered fresh in our minds, and we were secretly hoping to see a repeat of it in Belgrade.

We figured out that we should try it away from the busy shopping zone and ended up in a smart street, not far from the National Parliament. "Business" was going extremely well. We worked the passing crowd selectively and in sight of each other, carefully avoiding hassling the same people.

I was completely unaware that we were operating in the most patrolled part of the city. We got arrested in a swift move by a pair of undercover detectives who we thought were just ordinary citizens. They knew exactly what we were doing, and we were caught red-handed. One of us must have asked a plain-clothes policeman for money or, even worse, asked his or her boss.

They walked us over to a police station just around the corner. It was well known to every Belgrade citizen, certainly not for its gourmet food, kind staff or comfortable cells. We were dumped into a cell, barely the size of a large bedroom, with a bucket in the corner for the toilet and no other furniture apart from a low, well-worn wooden platform.

Sarajevo's Elusive Spring

There were only a few cellmates there when they brought us in. The numbers grew throughout the night, reaching 28 by the morning. They were vomit-covered drunks, troublemakers with broken teeth and swollen lips, quiet, well-dressed innocent-looking crooks, talkative Gypsy swindlers, beggars, and dimwits. Only half of us secured a spot on the wooden part of the floor; the rest stood leaning against the long wall or squatted between us on the floor and those standing.

Every now and then, uniformed policemen would open the heavy metal cell door and chuck another unfortunate soul amongst us, already struggling for air and space inside. A few times they ordered someone by the door to pick up the overflowing bucket and empty it somewhere outside of the hellish cell. On return, the cellmate selected for the task moved away from the door and made sure that he wasn't going to live the exceptional experience again.

Our money, a large quantity of coins, and our smokes were confiscated at the time of the initial arrest, and we craved a cigarette, same as every other smoker in the cell. We survived one sleepless night in "Hell" and had no idea what was going to follow. In my naivety, I thought that we would get released back onto the streets. One night like this felt like a crude and merciless punishment, more than enough to put us off begging small change for a day.

There was no breakfast in the morning. I guess there weren't any beds to serve it in. More experienced crims told us that we'd be taken to the Small Court and have a judge decide what to do with us. Streets were full of Gypsies begging, and we felt that we hadn't done anything worse or worthy of additional punishment. We didn't realize that begging was tolerated and reserved for Gypsies only, unofficially considered a form of exclusive welfare support.

It took forever before uniformed cops started taking individual detainees out. Everyone appeared to be anxious. Hardi and Boldy kept talking about their trip to India and how they were going to get on the road and hitchhike that very afternoon. I couldn't wait to get out of this place and head home to Sarajevo. I was just helping friends get cashed up for the trip anyway. I had no other reason for visiting the capital at that time.

Hours passed and we were taken out through long corridors and stairs to the section with small offices, where we faced a judge seated behind an office desk in a small room with a middle-aged woman typist behind a second desk. We never sat down. He never asked any questions, and we had no chance to say anything in our defence. He read out our crime and sentenced us to 14 days in the low-security jail of Padinska Skela *("Padinjak")*, 50 kilometres north of Belgrade.

Uniformed policemen shoved us into a half-full paddy van and drove off. In one hour, after driving through a flat, fog-covered countryside, we arrived at a barbed-wire fenced compound made up of low barracks and warehouses in the middle of an endless open landscape covered with dried corn stalks, last harvest leftovers. There weren't any signs of a village, river, or hill. It ominously looked like a German concentration camp.

Police made lists of our possessions, counted piles of our coins, made us strip our clothes off, pumped up DDT powder over our hair and naked bodies, and gave us government-issue rags. In another room they shaved our heads. Within an hour we were transferred from street-smart looking "freaks" to bald-headed, disoriented losers dressed in misfitted, prison issued worn-out gear. Worst of all, we had no cigarettes.

It turned out that we could have ordered cigarettes but had just missed the only day when those orders were taken. Cigarettes were the currency in the jail. All three of us, full-time smokers, had none. Days went by very slowly. We begged cigarettes from those who had them, but they wanted favours for it. Some of those favours were humiliating, and others could have been more degrading. But I befriended a Gypsy they all called Count, and he was well connected and loaded.

I told him about our travels and some of the stories I picked out of books I had read and he hadn't. He loved my company and made a place for me on a long bench as soon as we went into the dayroom, where many played endless chess games or just harassed those without cigarettes to kill the time.

There was a long synthetic runner rug from the entrance into the room to the opposite end, running between tables and bench seats on either side of the large space. The unwritten rule was that nobody was allowed to walk on it. If anyone did, someone would sneak behind their back and pull the end of the runner rug under the loser walking on "the red carpet". They virtually pulled your feet from under you and often you heard the thud of the skull hitting the floor. This would cause the room full of people to explode with laughter. Some would yell abuses at the unfortunate person concussed on the floor. Nobody showed any sympathy for them.

We just waited it out. Having my mates and cigarettes made it easier. Most of the prisoners were on short sentences for minor offences like ours. Typical ones were vagrancy, being involved in a drunken brawl, getting caught at the railway station without ID or cash, caught with a prostitute or a man in a public toilet, theft of a goat for personal gratification and similar.

All in all, a pathetic bunch of small-time criminals, and metropolitan underclass rubble.

One foggy morning we were released out of the barbed wire fence. We were never given back the proceeds of our crime. As I stepped onto the open road, I didn't know if I felt released into freedom or back into the oppressive reality that had led me into this situation. Unfortunately, over the following 18 months, my sense of limitless freedom withered, and I had to take radical steps to survive and come out the other end intact.

This was the second time I was formally arrested, and it wasn't the last. That is exactly what Count told me in *Padinjak*.

"You'll come back," he said, smiling and showing off his golden teeth. "You enjoy your freedom too much. You don't fit this uniformity and their moulds. That is the biggest crime in this country.

Sami Tischler

You know that, I am sure. You know your crime. You believe in your innocence and the right to exist unharnessed. You just don't realize how easy it is to upset the system and get a label. It will be hard to get rid of it. You will leave this country sooner or later. I saw you on a boat crossing a big sea in a dream last night," he said prophetically.

Sarajevo's Elusive Spring

Bold in Sarajevo

I made it back to Sarajevo with a shaven prisoner look. It didn't have much of an impact, punk looks and shaven heads were starting to appear on the street. My parents suspected that I had finally got unstuck.

"Why are you fussing about this? Everyone in the capital has shaven their hair. It is a new look. You better get used to it," I explained as they shook their heads in disbelief.

I decided to try and have a great time before going to serve my 15 months of compulsory Army duty next spring. Sarajevo can be great in autumn and winter if you accept its claustrophobic qualities. Everyone goes to disco clubs, cinemas, live music on Friday and

Saturday nights. White Button rock band had just started out and played a series of concerts at Skenderija. If there ever was a Bosnian style of rock 'n' roll, this was it.

My cousin Gev and I had a great time dancing to their tunes, dancing to visiting bands like Smak, Josipa Lisac with Clan, Formula 4, as well as great DJ sets at Club Cactus next door. My circle of friends expanded. Some of my new friends enjoyed reading and had great collections of music. I was starting to attract the attention of city girls too. For a long time, I had felt invisible, and with my shy nature wasn't getting ahead in this sphere.

My suburban neighbourhood didn't interest me anymore, and the only place there I frequented was the cinema. I remember seeing "Gimme Shelter", the famous Rolling Stones live concert documentary, as a Sunday morning matinee. The cinema was full of school children. I preferred this session time to the evening ones, when the hall filled with local violent gangs of youths looking for another fight and another weirdo to smash.

Chuck got himself in trouble for a reckless episode of vandalism and ended up in jail for 18 months. We were so close, and I felt I had finally made a deep friendship. Before I knew it, he was gone.

Sami Tischler

It was a wild winter in snow-covered Bosnia and fog engulfed Sarajevo. It felt like Kafka's story where a small town gets cut off from the rest of the world by deep snow and develops its own magic reality and characters not existent anywhere else. New friends popped out of the woodwork. I had places to go and friends to meet. Some lived in the old town or close to the centre of the city. One of my school friends played concert piano, which sat in the middle of a huge hallway. The rest of his family's massive Austrian-built apartment appeared as if it were missing walls. The ceiling hung high above your head, making space for enormous chandeliers. His three elder sisters, with their conservative dress style and manner, came right out of Kafka's creative fantasies.

I met a short-haired, trendy-dressed girl who hung around the places I went to. She seemed very interested in what I had to say, what I had done, and how I danced to "Sympathy for the Devil" by the Rolling Stones, often played by DJs at Cactus. We had a great time on the dancefloor and snuggled up against each other in darker corners of the club between sets they played for us freaks.

One time, with a group of friends, we went up the Miljacka river and out of town where the river comes out of a deep gorge. Spring was just entering the town and the sun broke through all the barriers of fog and smog. We drank cheap wine and played a bit of music amongst big boulders in the riverbed. The river was flowing at full strength, discharging rainfall from the hills above the city down into the valley through Sarajevo.

I was nearing my Army National Service. They were my last free days before the regimented period of 15 months coming up. I walked into the water in my clothes and got completely drenched. The freezing stream wasn't cold enough to stop me from enjoying it, and I expected that someone else would be drunk and crazy enough to join me. They all stood there on the riverbank in disbelief. Eventually, I came out a bit disappointed, and we walked back to town. Cold wind swept from the hills, and I was lucky that my heavy winter coat had remained dry. We used it as warm protection from the dampness of the riverbed.

Sarajevo's Elusive Spring

When I decided to jump into the icy water, my girlfriend's lovely round backside kept my coat dry and warm. This same lovely, shapely round backside wiggled beside me on top of her glorious legs all the way to the warmth of a tram and the Club "Cactus" further downstream.

Sami Tischler

Senta

There wasn't much time left. Hardy and Boldy wrote a letter from Goa describing beach havens, tropical fruit diets, *ganja* parties and a carefree THC-infused life. My immediate prospects weren't looking good. I got the dispatch paper to the small town of Senta, near the Hungarian border on the river Tisa.

Following a wild party for 20 in my room of 16 square metres, I was asleep on an overnight train to Subotica, a charming Hungarian jewel of a city north of Belgrade. I slipped past Army police picking up the recruits at the railway station destined for Senta. That was easy, they weren't authorised to ID civilians or approach them unless they looked completely lost. There were loads of them, young guys from villages who had never travelled more than 50 km from their homes.

I certainly didn't fit into this category and wouldn't miss the opportunity to explore yet another new place, especially one in close proximity to my destination, which didn't promise to be of any great significance.

It turned out to be an excellent idea. Subotica was laid out as a grand city during the Austro-Hungarian era and was fully intact. I walked on grand boulevards lined with old trees and public buildings, as well as town villas built many years before the former peasants took over and ruled all aspects of life in the post-WWII socialism.

This was a zone where the original *"Volksdeutscher"* population were labelled as collaborators and ethnically cleansed at the end of the war. After the Last One, their property was confiscated and taken over by the government to be distributed to the poverty-stricken, war-ravaged Bosnian population sympathetic to the Revolution. Careful analysis would have uncovered that they were changing the demographic map by expanding the Serbian population and getting rid of Germans and Hungarians in the process of consolidating the newly acquired territories.

Sarajevo's Elusive Spring

At the time, Subotica was an eye-opener. It was my homeland, as was the rest of the SFRJ. I felt richer for this jewel being part of it. After all, I was joining the glorious Yugoslav National Army, which grew out of a heroic struggle against Serbian collaborating nationalists, and the cataclysmic coalition of Italian, Croatian, Hungarian and German fascists. At the same time, it bravely and cleverly fought off Stalin's neo-colonial plans and calculations. This grand Yu creation, the JNA, had to wait until I had a good look at this beautiful place, so different from Sarajevo.

My city sat at the other end of the cultural spectrum as a regional centre of another collapsed empire. There weren't any hills in sight and all the towers in the city wore a cross in a variety of interpretations. What always fascinated me was the fact that all Oriental cities had a diverse mix of cultures and religions, manifested so clearly through their presence in architecture. Cities in the West always appeared monocultural and ethnically clean. Yugoslav capital Belgrade had 217 mosques at the time when *Evli Çelebi* visited Serbia in the 17th century. There is only one left now.

Less than six months before, I had wandered between Sarajevo, Belgrade, Istanbul, Trieste, Venice, Munich, Zurich, Geneva, Paris, Rotterdam... Sarajevo and Istanbul were the only cities where the visible evidence of mixed communities of Christians, Muslims, Gypsies and Jews still existed. It turned out that evidence of Ottoman presence in the flats towards Hungary barely existed, except for the resilient Roma communities who stayed behind. They adapted to this flat, foggy, waterlogged, muddy and fertile land and followed the predominant Christianity.

I must have arrived in Senta on the last bus from Subotica. I recognized a few stragglers who were on the same voyage and trudged my way towards the Army barracks at the edge of the town. Senta appeared almost deserted, its long streets lined with walls, nontransparent gates, limewashed low houses with small curtain-covered windows. It hardly gave away anything about its Hungarian population, hiding from another influx of fresh meat and reinforcements to the occupational forces.

After entering the guarded gates and barbed wire fence surrounding the Army barracks, the stragglers and I got "processed" with the same efficient routine as Hardy, Boldy and I had been "processed" a couple of hundred kilometres east at *Padinjak*. This time, it wasn't against our will, and we were issued sets of clean army uniforms, including underwear, socks, and a good dose of DDT all over our naked bodies after a collective shower. It had the taste and smell of yet another concentration camp.

The next morning, we were standing in line, part of a group of 30, two soldier-ranked officers and one professional sergeant. Things evolved very fast. It took them two weeks to get us all to jump when they said "jump", move together in unison, stop when commanded, turn around when directed, make up our beds exactly as designed by the regulation book, and line up our little cabinets with our folded uniforms and caps with a red star on them in such precision that when they stretched a string line across the room, which they did every night before bed, the red enamelled stars lined up perfectly.

They taught us how to dismantle our weapons and keep them clean, how to clean showers and latrines, how to "guard" us soldiers from ourselves in shifts during the night, how to salute and march. There was no escape. From 6.00 am till 10.00 pm, your every minute was accounted for and enjoyed collectively as eating, learning, exercising, manoeuvring. The challenge was finding a minute for a smoke or a chat with your new mates. Almost "Mission Impossible".

I came out on top again. My jail experience proved to be invaluable. Being denied cigarettes and freedom, fighting withdrawals had left a bad taste in my mouth. I wasn't going to live the same misery this time. Most of my village relatives smoked contraband tobacco. It originated from Herzegovina, the southern, coastal part of BiH. It was of exceptional quality, but not fashionable in urban communities. Everyone smoked tailor-mades and couldn't be bothered with rolling smokes and cigarettes without filters. Bosnian factories produced Marlboro and Kent under licence and most of Yugoslav youth smoked those as a status symbol.

Well, in my bag I had one kilogram of raw contraband tobacco neatly packed in a flat cardboard box they sold business shirts in. It even had a cellophane window in it where you could see the colour and the quality of its cut. This tobacco was surprisingly cheap, but you had to know where to get it. It wasn't much different to buying drugs these days. You had to be personally introduced to a dealer by someone the dealer knew and already serviced. My dealer turned out to be a waiter in a busy Old Town café in Sarajevo, just behind a mosque and a tram station.

The main advantage of possessing a box of tobacco was that you virtually never ran out of it, not daily anyway. My parents, who knew I was a full-time smoker, had already promised to replenish my stock for the length of my service. Their pledge gave me a sense of safety and a currency for being the most wanted man when everyone else ran out of cigarettes or compassion for those always short of funds. Very few knew how to roll tobacco, and my spare time often went into rolling smokes for desperados. While rolling, smoking and chatting afterwards, I managed to build a large fan club, a great asset under the circumstances and a precious resource for the following 15 months in the Army.

Let's make one thing clear: I never charged anyone for a smoke, and I have bludged many from friends, passers-by and even smoked cigarettes left at grave sites after a funeral by the bereaved family over my short smoker's career. I was a soldier now, and the whole world had changed.

As I said before, there was nothing much to discover for me in the army. The initiation cruelty of a gang of soldiers and the terror a group of young macho males can inflict on others wasn't anything new. Fear and oppression delivered by uniformed men was an old knowledge, and I had already been a victim of it in two short stints in jail and in free life outside as a freak. I was too cool to be bothered by either. I wasn't afraid of thugs, whether dressed as army officers or as soldiers with a stripe on their shoulder, but I respected what they had to do. I never caused any trouble or harmed any of my fellow soldiers physically or mentally.

What I couldn't handle was being stuck behind those barbed wire fences, behind armed gates, banned from free movement, and even from the local disco, all while not being paid to serve my country. However, I had made a voluntary pledge to the People, Tito, and the Country. Having to do it with a bunch of immatures, aggressive, inconsiderate youth added another layer of frustration.

I had brought a tiny radio transistor with me from home. It was small enough to fit into the breast pocket of my blouse. Beside a wristwatch, wedding or engagement ring, or musical instrument, a small radio receiver was one of the rare items from civilian life we were permitted to keep. Progressive rock music had already become my obsession, and I picked up a radio station from Novi Sad where they played a good selection, some to my taste (still limited), and lots of it very new: good jazz, traditional blues, reggae, and punk, which was just starting to take root in major urban centres of Yugoslavia.

Rock-folk band Bijelo Dugme (White Button) ruled the scene, and I remembered with great sadness the previous winter when they played for 2,000 people in Skenderija three Saturdays back-to-back. Punk sounded exciting. I'd always loved the Rolling Stones, and this stuff was just a rougher version of what they were about. I can't say I liked their looks, but the kids on our streets, though none in Senta, appeared cool and brave. The system fought against rock'n'roll, hippies and freaks. Finally, punks turned up as radical as they come, much more radical than their predecessors, and they weren't arrested *en masse* or forced to cut their hair. Their hair wasn't long enough to bother the Milicija anyway. Sleepy YU Milicija would take a couple more years before realizing that there was a new subculture on the scene.

Sarajevo's Elusive Spring

Aggression was their norm. New drugs and chemicals, as well as alcohol, petrol and glue fumes, were driving their minds. I was glad that time had come when uneducated cops, conservative politicians, and sleepy old revolutionaries, with Old Tito at the top, would have to understand that the world was powering ahead, with the punk subculture as its bulldozer. In fact, there was already a band in Slovenia with that name, and they had cleared and levelled the terrain for these young cultural revolutionaries.

Ethnic and religious sentiments weren't obvious or popping up at the time. Slovenians, Albanians and Macedonians often stuck together, but so did the boys from Bosnia. The only difference was that Bosnian boys came from the full variety of religious and ethnic backgrounds. Still, separatist behaviour or attitudes weren't obvious. As for me, they all loved my free tobacco and generally hated my choice of music.

I felt untouchable with the transistor in my breast pocket and endless supply of tobacco. My fans loved my tobacco, free of charge and rolled by the master, but they hated my radio station. That was one thing I wasn't going to change for anyone. I've always believed I had to defend my freedom to play my music or my radio station, and I still do to this day. I also had a gift and a need to educate my peers, and I practised it from an early age with different levels of success. I didn't see anything wrong with teaching people new music and telling them straight to their face how bad the common pop was. I certainly knew how bad it was. I'd taken the time, listened to it, and learnt it on my own skin.

They had never heard what I liked and promoted, and they never bothered to try. So, I took the liberty of introducing it to them on my radio and educating them at the same time. Most lasted only a couple of cigarettes, the time it took to roll and smoke them. The less patient ones left as soon as they lit one and joined a group listening to the "new folk" in the form of commercialised and bastardised Serbian traditional music. Others preferred Yugoslav pop. It was a government-subsidised collection of crooners keeping the neutral, politically correct middleclass educated elite happy.

Sami Tischler

Music competitions like Belgrade's Spring, the Festivals in Split and Opatija paraded through the YU music scene, all hoping to succeed in the Eurovision contest. Government-owned and censored record shops, radio stations, recording studios and TV promoted and pumped their "soft pop" products while their pictures and gossip filled popular magazines.

Sarajevo's Elusive Spring

Getting Out of There

With all due respect to Tito and his brave revolutionary elite, this whole circus was getting on my nerves. It was all a bit too much. I lasted four months but never stopped thinking about my friends and my life in Sarajevo. Over that time, I wrote numerous letters and received a few in response. Eventually, I wasn't getting any.

My younger sister wrote frequently. She told me how she'd got herself in trouble by failing the first grade of the technical college she was enrolled in. Our parents were giving her a hard time, she was banned from leaving the house, had to quit smoking, couldn't use the phone, and our father gave her a beating. Punk might have made some impact in the UK, US and the large urban centres of Yugoslavia, but things were a bit medieval and heavily agricultural in my household. I felt my sister needed help.

I requested to see the captain, who gave me 10 minutes of his time. He promised to investigate, but a week later, nothing had come back from him. One warm Friday afternoon I sneaked out through the barbed wire fence and walked out of the Senta training garrison onto the main road. I raised my hand, and the first truck stopped. Before it got dark, I had crossed the River Sava into Bosnia.

I was getting rides one after the other, even late into the night, deep into the mountain ranges towards Sarajevo. A soldier in uniform couldn't be ignored in Serbia and Bosnia. The sense of camaraderie between former soldiers, my drivers, and current ones like myself was to be admired. People took my reasons for travel without questioning.

I changed my story a few times during the trip. I told some drivers I had urgent business to attend to and couldn't wait for the slow rail connections from Senta to Sarajevo, which was partially true. Other times I told them about my travels before the army and how I'd been missing the open road and hitchhiking so much that I had to go on leave using it as my mode of travel.

Sami Tischler

They stopped and fed me at the truck stops, offered good cigarettes, gave me a packet before we parted, and even offered money to help with the rest of the trip. I didn't volunteer the fact that I was travelling without a permit. None ever asked, anyway.

I was at home before midnight. My parents were shocked. That very morning, I didn't know myself if I was going home. I told them openly that I came without a permit. My father wasn't happy about that.

"In my days, you would have been court-martialled for it."

I told him: "Don't worry. Times have changed," hoping that was true.

My mother, in shock, set about organising a feed and withdrew into the safety of her kitchen. My sisters were happy and didn't look too worried. They both sort of expected that I wasn't going to obey strict

Army discipline and weren't surprised to see me turn up unannounced.

I sat down to eat, and the phone went off. It was around 1.00 am. I knew it was the Army.

"Don't tell them that I've made it home yet!" I said to my father before he grabbed the set.

I was listening to my father's part in their conversation. I heard him repeating a lie to my commanding officer, replying frequently: "I will, yes I will."

When he came back from the hallway where the phone was, he looked guilty, as if he was a runaway himself, and disappointed for acting a liar.

"I'm not going to lie for you again, and the next time the phone rings, you'll be answering it and explaining yourself!"

I felt so sorry for him. He served over two years in the Army around 1949. They held his generation on extended service due to political tensions with Russia at the time. Before that he was recruited into a "voluntary" working brigade, building a new railway line between Sarajevo and the Croatian border in North Bosnia. He was a true and honest working-class man, a shift worker, breadwinner and baker – a cog in the engine of our new society.

He didn't sympathise with my irresponsible attitude. I didn't feel guilty whatsoever. My generation had lost patience with the old worn-out socialist rhetoric. Besides, there were some weird things about the Army. If you had a job before the Army, which was considered super lucky but possible, your Army service was counted into your pension benefits, and your job was "waiting for you" on discharge. However, if you were unemployed your time in service counted for nothing. The small symbolic allowance couldn't even pay for your smokes, and at the end of service you'd return to your parents, 15 months older and still jobless.

Unemployment benefit didn't exist. The cost of your existence was the responsibility of your family. All that discipline had the same flavour as police terror and control on the streets – not much different to the way you were treated in jail. We were force-fed obedience. The system had obedience as its key objective and used any platform to impose it, civilian or military.

I had certainly experienced all of it already and wasn't afraid of the system or its servants. During those mock-up raids when we were woken in the early hours of the morning by the sounds of sirens as part of training, I watched all our overweight, pompous officers running around wearing old-fashioned tight uniforms hardly fitting their pot bellies, puffing around us young, fit recruits, expecting us to take it all very seriously. They had to. They were getting paid – and paid very well.

Active officers were educated at the expense of the government – in other words, society. They were given permanent postings, apartments and other privileges like reduced retirement age, exclusive Army health care, access to military-owned holiday resorts, and who knows what else.

I was there just because I had no choice. My parents funded my smoking habit, and the Army dentist refused to repair my teeth.

Hence, I decided to get them pulled out, which he was happy to do. I wasn't going to let my teeth rot away over the following 15 months just because the Army couldn't afford to keep us recruits in good health.

I guess I was meant to feel sympathy for the government and the fact that the permanent staff cost so much. There was one person who never lost my sympathy, and I paid my respects to Marshall Tito exclusively.

I was too tired and went to bed. My parents and sisters did too. I slept well. My parents wouldn't have slept a wink.

The phone rang as soon as daylight sneaked through the curtains. I grabbed it.

"Hallo, Mido speaking," I said. Officers addressed us by our surnames.

"I order you to get to the rail station right away and return to the barracks in Senta!"

"I'm sorry, comrade Captain, but I'm not able to do that. There are things I must do, as I've already discussed with you."

The Captain cut in with my surname again: "You must come back right away, or I'll be sending Military Police!" he threatened.

"I'm sorry, comrade Captain, but I'm not able to come back right away. I need three days to sort things out. There's no point sending the Police over. They won't find me. I give you my word I'll be back in three days. Now, with all due respect, comrade Captain, I'll have to hang up." Which I did.

Shortly after, I left the house wearing my civilian clothes and with my civilian ID card in my pocket. I returned to spend time with my family and slept another night at home.

The rest of the time I did a range of different things. First night, I went to Club Cactus and met a bunch of old friends. The club was full of young punks too. They just looked like punks, but still danced to all

Sarajevo's Elusive Spring

the groovy psychedelic, progressive and rock'n'roll music. They had no choice. Everyone saw it as a new fashion only. There was nothing revolutionary about them.

I really liked girls who suddenly looked dangerous and cool. I fitted right in with my crew cut hairstyle.

My long-legged girlfriend was nowhere to be seen. I saw her later at a newly opened trendy bar, a new feature of Sarajevo nightlife, hanging onto a trendy young man, neither a freak nor a punk. She hadn't written back to any of my letters, nor had she ever promised that she would.

I had a heavy heart for a bit afterwards. She gave me a faint smile over the noisy crowd drowning in the heavy smoke and pumping sounds of the latest Yugo rock originals.

I was with my cousin Gev, who was working full time and loaded. We did a pub crawl and ended up crashing at his place, in the basement of his parents'.

Sami Tischler

Time to Go Back

When I woke up, Gev was already at work. My time was up. I walked down into the Old Town and bought a fresh 1 kg box of tobacco from my dealer at the coffee shop behind the mosque, took a tram to the railway station and purchased a ticket for a night train. Back at my parents' we had a great day. They all relaxed when I told them about the ticket. We certainly enjoyed that day, and I kept them amused with funny Army stories and stupidities. Mum prepared a feast and kept offering delicacies all day. By night-time I was riding a train north.

I was back in Senta before lunch the next day. The captain saw me briefly and told me to change into "working clothes". I wasn't scared. "I've done what I've done, and I am up for whatever they throw at me. They cannot beat or torture me; they can only lock me up," I thought. When I reported back to the captain dressed in my working clothes, I was handed over to a low-ranking officer and escorted to a building renovation site within the base.

In a large room with a deteriorated concrete floor, I met another soldier who apparently hadn't done anything wrong. We were given a sledgehammer, crowbar, pick and a pair of shovels. The officer told us our task was to find a sewer line in the room.

"Do you have plans or any idea where the pipe may be located?" I gathered a little courage to ask. "Unfortunately, the sewer plans haven't arrived from Vienna archives yet. We'll let you know as soon as they do. Ha, haa, haaa, you bloody greenhorn fuckwits!" he rocked his head in disbelief and laughed as he left the room.

I rolled two cigarettes, and we smoked them. Then I walked around the room and picked a spot randomly. I spat into the palms of my hands, grabbed the sledgehammer and went for it. I had to break through a slab 200 mm thick. My comrade poked out the broken bits with the crowbar. Soon enough, we were both covered in sweat and concrete dust.

Sarajevo's Elusive Spring

I rolled and we smoked another two cigarettes. I spat into the palms of my hands, as was customary on YU building sites. My head was exploding with fury as I kept going with the sledgehammer to widen the hole. I was swinging it like a madman, working up more sweat and sending broken shards of concrete everywhere. My co-worker stood behind me the whole way through, hidden and afraid of getting them in his eyes. He cleaned up the broken segments of concrete, exposing a large patch of soil below.

We laughed like madmen when he said, "We've dug a hole to the bottom of the (former) Pannonian Sea." Next, I took the pick and started digging into the soil. He shovelled the black earth out. We had more rolled cigarettes, spat into the hole as we smoked, and discussed the absurdity of our situation and the "hole-searching project".

I remember he said: "When the hole is deep enough, we'll fuck it." We both thought this hilarious but had to keep our laughter down. After all, this was meant to be the start of my "punishment".

I was standing on the edge of the hole, hitting the bottom of it with the crowbar. We had dug a hole about 600 mm deep and 900 mm in diameter. He jumped in to remove the soil I had loosened. The last bits he took out with his hands, exposing the side of a ceramic sewer pipe buried there since the good old Austro-Hungarian Empire. We couldn't believe our eyes.

It felt like finding gold. There was no point celebrating. We kept it lowkey, fearful someone would come and move us to another job or tell us we'd uncovered the wrong pipe. Our shovels placed across the hole made a great seat. I rolled and we smoked more cigarettes. I told him about my escape and adventure. He was afraid for me and couldn't understand why he was here with me, or why I was there with him.

We jumped up as Comrade Captain walked into the room, swearing at us for sitting down and doing nothing. We stood there "at attention" while he inspected the job. He couldn't hide his awe at what we'd done and how lucky we were. He turned to me and said (using my surname again): "Get the fuck out of here and out of my sight."

I walked away feeling lucky. Somewhere deep inside, I knew that this small red-faced official and "comrade" wasn't going to forget the insult and would find a way to pay me back for it.

The end of our training was getting near. Things started to slip into a survivable pattern. I worked out the best strategy to escape additional duties. We would spend a little free time hanging around the canteen where you could buy sweets, snacks and cigarettes. This turned out to be a zone to avoid. Low-ranking officers looking for victims hunted in that area, and those lurking around tended to disappear on shortterm jobs around the barracks. There was always another renovation job to put a fresh labourer on, "cigarette butt foraging" duty, or an extra kitchen hand required to clean up the mess.

Straight after lunch I would grab a couple of my smoking friends and disappear into the tall grass out of view. Summer was just around the corner and cool, shady spots were plentiful. Short breaks between lunch and compulsory activities in the afternoon were too precious to waste slaving in the kitchen or at a building site.

At this stage we were given permission to go into town every second Saturday after lunch for about seven hours. There were limits to what you could do. We weren't allowed into the local disco club, we couldn't stay overnight, and we couldn't cross the river to visit Čoka, a Serbian village 7 km away. There were pubs we were advised not to enter. Gypsy whores operated in them, and Gypsy bands played in the late afternoons and weekend nights. They were always full of drunken soldiers whenever I passed by.

I wasn't much into drinking and didn't have the funds to get drunk at a pub anyway. Most of those guys who went there on the weekend and spent their money getting wasted would come and bludge smokes off me all through the week. As for the Gypsy girls, I just couldn't see myself competing with hordes of soldiers for a couple of desperate girls from poverty-ridden communities in the area.

Sarajevo's Elusive Spring

Although banned from the local disco, I walked in, and to my surprise nobody stopped me. I was pleased about that, but I didn't like it anyway.

They played shit music, and eventually I had to sneak out the back when the military police walked in on patrol.

I opted to spend my free time on park benches along the walkways on top of a high levee built as a flood barrier between the river Tisa and the town of Senta. The river was wide and deep enough, navigable and used as an industrial waterway. The opposite bank appeared level with the river, covered with ancient willow and oak forests and a narrow belt of marshland. Beyond the tree line stretched endless flat land, the bottom of the former Pannonian Sea and the most fertile soil you could imagine.

Irrigation canals created a grid of waterways between the river Tisa and the Danube further south, an engineering masterpiece of the socialist government. They managed to drain swamps and marshlands, providing temporary storage for floodwaters, irrigating crops in summer, as well as being a permanent barrier between Belgrade and Russian troops firmly stationed in Hungary.

Yugoslavia kept a cautious political distance from Russia, and there was a time in 1948 when Tito had to make a stand and keep Stalin's imperialist ambitions in check. The Hungarian uprising in 1957 and the events in Czechoslovakia in 1968 proved his wisdom as a statesman and foreign policy strategist, clearly displaying his courageous, uncompromising vision for the independent socialist Yugoslav state. He knew the Russians well.

Tito had fought them as an officer of the Austro-Hungarian Empire. He was a prisoner of war there during the October Revolution. As a communist leader from Yugoslavia, he was educated and financed by the Russian-led Comintern. During WWII Tito became the leader of a significant military force and fought Germans, Italians, as well as Yugoslavia's own nationalist factions, very successfully. Stalin benefited greatly from the resistance led by Tito but failed to support him. Tito realized that Stalin had a different plan for Yugoslavia.

Unfortunately, he underestimated the confidence of the new Yugoslav state, which successfully built and maintained strong relationships with the West. These irrigation canals, I'm sure, made Tito sleep better.

He also colonised the new fertile farming land with his supporters, subsistence farmers and refugees from war-ravaged Bosnia and Herzegovina, making sure the remaining Hungarian population there became a minority.

Senta felt uneasy. You could tell the population lived a compromised existence, faced with the constant influx of new recruits rotated every five months. We were constantly briefed on scenarios, procedures and strategies during regular classes on military theory. "Report any suspicious activities, report anyone taking photos around the perimeter fences, report cars with foreign registration plates …"

Limited freedom of movement ensured an action-ready force, designed to face any potential aggression from Hungarian territories. As far as I could tell, it was Cold War paranoia in full swing. People in town spoke Hungarian among themselves and addressed us soldiers in Serbian. In a way it felt like I was serving my duty in another country. Any exchange I had with the local population was formal and businesslike. We were clearly seen as an occupying force, not much different from the Russians in what had remained of the original Hungary.

Field Manoeuvres

Shortly after my return from Sarajevo, we were woken up at the break of dawn and given emergency orders. We took our war kits, consisting of a backpack and our personal weapons. I carried a 1200 mm long aluminium pipe equipped with a telescopic device and a trigger handle. I had already used it in target practice several times. It was a propelled grenade launcher. It threw flames through its back and launched a small self-propelled anti-tank missile at the front.

It was the middle of a rainy spell leading into summer. At around 3 am, 1500 of us recruits lined up, battle-ready helmets on our heads, waiting for an order. Broken into formations, we marched out of our fenced base and out of town. I don't know what the Hungarian population thought or felt as we walked and rattled our gear past their windows at that ungodly hour.

As soon as we came out in the open, we were ordered to get off the road and walk through the farmland. Apparently, the road was being investigated for land mines, and we did see a special squad scanning random spots on it. We walked on dirt roads designed for tractors, trucks, and farming machinery for a while. It didn't bother anyone, though it did get muddy at times.

All around us were endless fields engulfed in wet darkness. We couldn't see much of it in the dark, windy cold, with drizzle coming down. We all wore woollen winter coats, jackets, and trousers underneath. Immaculately polished leather-strapped boots fell softly on the wet, slippery ground.

We expected to spend part of our training in the field, on strategic manoeuvres. None of us knew exactly when, where, how long, or what we were going to do there. We certainly knew this wasn't real war, and I thought it couldn't be much worse than travelling penniless, sleeping rough outside without a tent, getting up in the middle of the night half frozen or drenched by rain, and having to find shelter in the dark. I'd already done all that, and in foreign lands too.

Sami Tischler

Well, we kept going along the muddy agricultural track. The light started changing, and we could see black freshly turned soil on either side of it. No surprise there. There wasn't anything else for hundreds of kilometres other than upturned soil or the fresh greenery of young crops.

Order came down the line: "Take a right turn along the edge of the wheat field", through the freshly upturned soil with burrows created by deep ploughing up to our knees. I couldn't believe the absurdity of it. Before we knew it, we were trudging through the soft sticky mud on uneven terrain, slipping and falling. My leather boots instantly filled with liquid soil. It was dripping from my coat and trousers, already soaked and covered in filth.

To make things worse, the sun never came out. Both wind and rain intensified, and now that we could see properly, the dark threatening sky appeared almost fused to the land, with hardly any visible space in between. All you could hear was the rattle of the war kits we dragged with us, including a fold-up shovel strapped to our belts, and the groans of young desperate recruits.

We were all facing a challenge we couldn't have imagined when we smoked our last cigarette before bed the previous night, or while some of us performed a lonely indecent act a bit later as we lay under rough army blankets dreaming of warm, silky, desirable female skin.

Officers were yelling: "Move, faster, move, for fuck's sake, you are holding everyone back, comrade!" as I was trying to pull my foot out of the deep mud and bury it back in again.

By the time we came into a grass-overgrown paddock and out of land reserved for crops, we looked like the defeated German Army on their retreat from Russia in autumn 1944. We were ordered to stop and rest in a dry irrigation canal, the size of a small riverbed. I looked around at a pitiful sight. Soldiers were handing cigarettes to each other, behaving like survivors of a tragic event, lucky to be alive.

We gulped down breakfast from the food parcels in our backpacks, smoked another round of cigarettes, and started feeling a bit better. A few made jokes about our struggle, appearance, and weaknesses displayed by some during the march.

Our commanding low-ranking officer stood up, his round chubby face under a battle helmet that hardly fit his head and gave us orders. We were going to sneak up on our enemies somewhere ahead in the marshes by crawling through the wet, rain-soaked grass, forge a deep irrigation ditch full of water, then run ahead in a full-frontal attack through the open field and destroy "the fuckers".

We did our crawling bit and got soaked in the mud. That was the end of anything dry I had on that day. I felt cold water penetrating through layers of my mud-soaked woollen uniform while the rain took care of my well-exposed back.

We made it to the irrigation ditch, about 200 m away from a concrete bridge which was apparently under fire. We were clinging to the grass on the steep, slippery slope of its bank. The water in the ditch measured about 2.5 m across. We didn't know how deep it was. The opposite bank was identical, designed and constructed with engineering precision.

The order came: "Forge the irrigation ditch!"

We all sat there reluctantly. One soldier made a one-step run down the slope closer to the water's edge and jumped across. He landed on the steep slope on the other side, but the weight of his backpack pulled him back and, in slow motion, as he fought gravity, he splashed back into the canal, completely submerged for a moment, then emerged looking like a frightened rat. He crawled out onto the grass, completely soaked.

Another soldier threw his backpack across to the "wet rat" and managed to stay on shore by grabbing a lump of grass on the slope. I couldn't care less and simply walked through the canal, water to my waist, and came out on the other side. "I have dry clothes in the backpack," I hoped.

We grouped on the slope, mostly soaking wet, and jumped out together when the command came: "Troops, attack!"

"Hurraaaaay, Hurraaay, Hurrayyy!" we screamed and yelled as we ran across the open field under the threatening sky, dripping wet, covered in mud, holding our weapons with no ammunition. I could feel my useless aluminium pipe bouncing across my back on its strap as I ran into my heroic mock-up battle, screaming my head off in anger, full of aggression, completely forgetting the absurdity of the whole thing.

We were commended on our successful manoeuvre by a short, fat, grey-haired general who turned up in a covered jeep, polished boots showing no trace of mud. Even the rain stopped as he came to inspect his forces, lining up in this foreign landscape we had apparently won. We were led to a site at the start of a thick oak forest where we were ordered to set up camp. Logistics teams brought big tents on trucks, which we had to assemble ourselves. We were issued field beds and dry blankets. It took us a long time to get smoky fires going.

In semi-darkness around the campfire, we were served a hot meal. The rain had stopped, and we were all trying to dry out wet, muddy clothes. Before bed I took off everything damp and pulled out dry underwear, a singlet, shirt, fresh socks, and slept like a baby in a cot. I had my wet clothes spread across an improvised rack made from salvaged firewood we'd gathered earlier. Most of the next day we spent cleaning ourselves up. The weather had improved, and the sun broke through the clouds enough to allow wet woollen fabric to lose some of its moisture. I washed some dirt off my clothes and cleaned my boots and feet in the nearby irrigation canal. Officers ignored us moving about the camp semi-naked. It seemed all the boring nonsense rules had been abandoned for the day. I suppose, according to them, we were winners after all.

By evening everyone's spirits had lifted, and with tidier appearances and dry clothes our good mood returned. We sang some patriotic songs around the fires and had another night in tents, deafened by frogs' mating calls all around us through the night.

The next day we packed up the tents and marched along the road back to Senta, feeling like liberators. The people of Senta barely acknowledged our column and went about their daily business as if we'd never fought and won our ridiculous war. No doubt they laughed at home as they described our muddied uniforms and battle gear in total disorder. The older ones would have compared us to the old Austro-Hungarian Army or German legions and wondered how much worse things could get, and how long this Godless Empire was going to last.

Sami Tischler

Far Away from Home in Raška

At the end of the fifth month, the entire generation of recruits was transferred to different locations around the country to serve the remaining 10 months in roles we'd been trained for. I was trained in the communications unit as a telephone exchange mechanic. On the transfer list, beside my name, was the town of Raška. It turned out I was being sent south to the opposite end of the Republic of Serbia.

Raška was the last proper Orthodox Serbian town, and beyond it, all the way to the Albanian coast, lay lands inhabited predominantly by Muslims: Sanjak, Metohija, Kosovo (all parts of Serbia at the time) and finally Albania, over the high mountain range known as the "Cursed Mountains". Albania was as ethnically mixed as southeastern Yugoslavia: Catholics, Orthodox and Muslims made up the majority. I had never been there, but once I found Raška's exact location on the map, the proximity to Kosovo made it an interesting prospect.

We were all being sent in different directions, and the friendships we had invested in were coming to an end. It felt a little sad, but the fact that we weren't going to be treated as greenhorns any longer was promising. Food packs, travel orders and train tickets for the journey, with exact times of departure, transfers and arrivals, were issued efficiently and with great urgency. I took my personal travel pack and walked to the station with a group of soldiers leaving at the same time.

I had seen these scenarios in movies. The main character sets off from one army camp to another. In the movies, it usually means trouble, the hero carries a past, an accusation, a traumatic experience. He is being moved to a new environment for a fresh start or as punishment. I feared this move to the very south of the Republic of Serbia was a form of punishment for my escape during training. It certainly looked far from Sarajevo on the map and was not connected by rail. I had no plans for escape at the time, but I promised myself I would be wiser next time: "You aren't going to ask for permission, and you will not get caught." Raška garrison sat on a small plateau above the old Serbian town across the river Ibar. It stationed a massive force of infantry recruits in training. A beautifully organised set of buildings housed its own bakery, large library, troop carriers, trucks, artillery and ammunition depots in the middle of a large, forested base. I had scheduled work and guard duty in our workshops and troop carrier yard, where we maintained mobile battlefield-ready radio units. We kept batteries charged and sat inside the workshop at night when our turn came around.

During my last escape to Sarajevo, I had bought "English in 100 Lessons". It came with mini records you could play to practise pronunciation. I left the records at home, knowing I wasn't going to use them. The weather was great, and as a soldier who had completed training, my free time was generally mine to organise. I had two things I was interested in: the library and studying English. English was my priority.

I was planning to travel to India as soon as my national service was over. I felt that a journey to the source of the Ganges, in the footsteps of my mates Hardi and Boldy, was the best way to wash off the Army experience. I had no idea if, or how, I was going to find work or fit into the predictable life patterns of the Yugoslav working population. The idea of travelling to India seemed extraordinarily exotic, promising an opening to another world full of unimaginable adventure. In the late 80s we knew little about that part of the world. Yugoslav president Tito had been one of the leaders behind the Non-Aligned Movement with Nehru, Nasser, Nkrumah and Sukarno. Yugoslav national TV filled the news with his visits to these exotic places, showing welcoming crowds and progressive post-colonial communities, promising democratic freedom from oppression and poverty.

After my trip through Western Europe the previous year, I knew that my real interest lay in the Developing World: Eastern mysticism, African music, the communal and unsophisticated lifestyle of people who worked hard but still took time to enjoy and share the simple pleasures of life, food, music, drugs, and being together. What a fantasy for a young socialist mind, thinking that anywhere in the tropics, people could live from the fruits of nature and smoke weed growing in abundance everywhere. I thought poverty and homelessness in big cities must have been leftovers of the colonial era, and that the solution would simply be to go back to the land. I had money saved and planned to find abandoned land for myself. But first, I was going to see India, and not just India. I wanted to travel by land and revisit Istanbul, see more of eastern Turkey, Persia, Afghanistan, Pakistan and finally India.

We called India "The Promised Land." I read as much as I could find on Hinduism and Buddhism. I was completely ignorant about the tensions and details of the partition of India with East and West Pakistan. Although I was marginally aware of the civil war in East Pakistan and its separation from the West, I had no idea what the reasons were. Nor did I know that Afghanistan was about to go through a bloody Communist takeover, instigated by Russia, just before the time of my planned trip the following year. Not that I knew it had even happened when I eventually travelled through. These "minor" political events in these "marginal" places, most of which people didn't know existed, were certainly going to make a huge impact on my own life, and on the lives of many across the globe, over the next half-century.

It didn't take long before my presence, my tobacco box and its contents, the sounds coming from my pocket radio, reading and writing in English, and borrowing books from the library, attracted the attention of soldiers with similarly unusual interests, music being one of them. I befriended two Bosnian boys, Iliya and Mirso, who were into music. Mirso had brought his guitar and a small cassette player. I had a small collection of music tapes compiled by Chief, full of songs we listened to at the time. With a cassette player and a keen guitarist wanting to learn some of the songs, I'd transcribe English into phonetic form and translate whenever possible. A great exercise in listening, comprehension, and developing friendship.

Sarajevo's Elusive Spring

Iliya lived in Zagreb and spent summers in Modriča, north Bosnia. Mirso came from there too, near the city of Tuzla, where he lived with his parents, who were farmers. He wanted to be a rock guitarist. Iliya worked as an operator in the internal petrol station, filling up Army trucks, vehicles and drums that were transported across the region's network of Army installations.

As I said before, I wasn't aware of major global issues, but I knew a little about tensions within my own country. Iliya, who had been initially trained in Raška and spent most of his first year there, told us about the paranoia that encased the garrison. Albanian separatists had been very active in the region for years.

"Soldiers were shot at and killed!" he said. "We aren't allowed to visit the town of Novi Pazar, 14 km away. The place is full of Albanian Muslim separatists and very dangerous."

"I'll take a trip to Novi Pazar next time I get a 10-hour permit," I declared.

"You're crazy. The military police patrol the road, and they'll arrest you," Iliya warned.

I wasn't going to argue.

Sami Tischler

Forbidden City Novi Pazar

The fact that we were banned from visiting the place sounded like an open invitation to me. It was easy enough to leave the garrison at any time, but there was nowhere to go. There was a cinema, and soldiers were banned from attending the Army Social Club, which was exclusively reserved for officers and their families. The band, formed for the officers' entertainment, was made up of great musicians, recruits like myself. The musicians were treated like stars and given a range of privileges. For us ordinary soldiers, their music was out of bounds.

On my next outing, I left the barracks alone and walked past the cinema, which was showing an old Western I had already seen. My itchy feet carried me out of town towards Novi Pazar (New Marketplace). I stood casually at a bus stop, scanning cars as they passed. As soon as I lifted my finger, a car stopped, and I was on my way to the forbidden place.

It seemed a bit randomly developed, missing the order of a Serbian military town. The River Ibar left the gorge and the town of Raška within it, and was now flowing across fertile flat ground, spreading itself through the town. It moved downstream completely liberated. People sold goods in the open, wore clothes like those seen in Istanbul, and a few minarets poked into the sky, just as they did in Sarajevo. The smell of grilled meat and smouldering charcoal fires drifted along the narrow streets. Pastry shops and cafés were full of young and old smoking tobacco; many used long cigarette holders, as in Bosnia.

I sat down in one of the eateries, and the owner struck up a casual conversation. He was disappointed that not many soldiers visited the place. He was impressed when I told him about my origins and how I had travelled with a friend to Istanbul a year earlier. I spoke of meeting his compatriots who had migrated to Turkey, where they lived and traded in leather, gold, and fabric. He reminded me that Istanbul was to them what Trieste was to us in the western Yugoslav states. Half his family, he said, lived in Istanbul and owned shops and manufacturing businesses there. They didn't visit; afraid the government would expect them to serve National Service.

"I have been to Istanbul more often than to Sarajevo or Belgrade," he announced.

At the end, he wouldn't let me settle my bill, it was "on the house", and he ordered Turkish-style tea from next door. I offered the golden contents of my tobacco box, which he accepted, saying he hadn't rolled one in a long time. There we were, puffing on illegal tobacco from Herzegovina, discussing the latest smuggling trends and the price of gold in Istanbul. I wasn't much of a smuggler myself, but I had certainly travelled with smugglers on trains and coaches.

My first trip with my brand-new passport at 17 took me to Trieste, where my parents had sent me to purchase and smuggle Western clothes and consumer goods for our household. Idris, the shop owner, arranged for one of his boys to take me back to Raška, as they were travelling in that direction. The young driver dropped me off in an alley in town, conscious of the risks. He returned to Novi Pazar straight away, I was the only reason he had come to Raška.

Back at the barracks, I told Mirso and Iliya about my trip and meeting Idris in his shop as we lay on blankets in the sun. I felt they were jealous, but I knew that the lone-wolf strategy was the one to play. The last thing I needed was a greenhorn companion, a common occurrence in the Army where many men felt vulnerable and insecure, needing someone to hold their hands, watch their backs, and even keep them company on trips to the loo.

I hadn't witnessed any homosexuality, but the sounds of collective masturbation when the lights went out were a frequent and fascinating phenomenon. I was more than happy to join in this rare collective fun. Otherwise, I kept a safe distance from the crowd. From then on, I planned and executed my outings alone whenever I bent the rules. Most of my outings did, one way or another.

Sami Tischler

Smak Concert

A popular new Serbian band in the late '70s, and the greatest competition to Bijelo Dugme (White Button), was Smak, based in Kraljevo, a small city in south-eastern Serbia. They played a concert in their hometown. Serbian radio stations played their tunes daily and promoted the event.

I had seen Smak when they visited Sarajevo the previous winter and really liked their guitarist, known as "The Wheel", a Roma by origin. They had a strong following among progressive hard rock fans in Sarajevo. There was an ongoing argument about his abilities compared to those of "Bijelo Dugme" leader Goran Bregović, "Brega". "The Wheel" had great technique: he was a furiously fast player. But "Brega" was something else. He was a sensual player who created a formula for authentic Bosnian rock 'n' roll, revolutionising the stagnant Yugoslav music scene and fashion trends. He managed to integrate Bosnian folk, Gypsy music, urban culture and poetry with punk, progressive rock, ska, reggae, new wave, and classic rock influences.

"Brega" became a legend, the only contemporary musician and composer from the former Yugoslavia known abroad. He worked with Ofra Haza, Cesária Évora, Rachid Taha, Iggy Pop, George Dalaras, Zdravko Čolić, and wrote soundtracks for numerous films. Even at nearly 70, he still travelled the world, performing reinvented versions of music he had written in his twenties.

I really wanted to see "The Wheel" on his own turf. I knew this was a once-in-a-lifetime opportunity. To travel 200 km to Kraljevo and return the same night, I would have to hitchhike in the dark and come back to the barracks after midnight.

My head officer was a cranky Bosnian who must have received the file with full details of my adventures in Senta. I knew he kept a keen eye on me, so I managed to keep my head down for the time being. The junior officer was a young graduate from officers' school, younger than me, inexperienced, and unwilling to accept anything creative beyond respect for schedules and routines. I heard he would be away that weekend.

My direct supervisor, the soldier-officer, was an older Bosnian I didn't trust much. He was always "brown-nosing" anyone above him. Nothing unusual in the Army, but important to keep in mind when planning something against the rules. I wasn't on duty that night, so it all depended on whether he would notice my absence in the evening and, if so, whether he would report me.

"If I get caught coming back late from town, that's a small breach and not a very serious offence," I thought. "I might get extra duty as punishment and a verbal warning from my commanding officer. That sounds manageable, something I could take on. I must travel and come back unnoticed. I've done it before; I should be able to do it again."

I was left with the dilemma of how to get back into the barracks, past the gate and the guards, in a garrison enveloped in paranoia about Albanian separatists' activities. We had an Albanian in my squad, and I had already made friends with him. I was genuinely interested in his life as a rural Albanian youth. It turned out he was involved in a blood feud, a typical archaic pre-Christian custom still practised among Albanians and Montenegrins. He was from a family that owed blood (one of his relatives had killed a member of their rival family), and he felt very safe in the Army.

"None dares to kill a soldier," Selimi said. "When I go home on leave, I can walk around freely while the rest of my family stays indoors, afraid to leave the house and the protection of thick boundary walls and windowless rooms. When my service is over, I will have to go back inside those walls. I am a free man now, but who knows what awaits me when I'm released."

I really sympathised with him and shared my tobacco with him many times as we exchanged stories about our lives. I told him about my freedom, travels, and the girls I had kissed. Poor boy was denied all that, and it seemed his life would only become more miserable once he left the Army. I felt so sorry for him. He appreciated our friendship.

Sami Tischler

Not many soldiers had time for Albanians. They struggled with our official Serbo-Croatian language, and everyone thought they weren't interested in Pan-Yugoslavism. That was a big sin in Yugoslavia at the time. We were all so proud to be Yugoslavs, I thought.

Albanians stuck together and didn't easily bond with others. However, in this garrison, they were influential and strong. Albanians worked predominantly in the kitchens and bakeries, producing great bread and popular pastries. The previous garrison in Senta didn't have its own bakery. This was a great privilege, and if you were good to them, you could get their produce outside of your scheduled portions. In the Army, where your next meal is the most important event of the day, these favours meant a lot.

I told Selimi about my plan. He hardly knew who the band Smak were. It wasn't the style of music he appreciated, but he could tell how important it was to me. He wanted to help. We found out which soldiers were going on guard duty that night, and Selimi arranged a parcel of pastries for them. We went to see them together, and they met me personally. The arrangement was made to let me come straight through the gate. The guard officer would be in his office, most likely watching TV or sleeping, while the guard would pretend to check my pass and let me through. The rest was up to me.

I kissed Selimi on the cheek multiple times when we stepped out into the open. He was so embarrassed, his cheeks went red, and he didn't know what to do with his hands.

My trip was a complete success. I even got out of town with the permit. Instead of coming back by 8:00 pm, I returned six hours late, around 2:00 am the next day, and snuck back into my bed. The concert was great. "The Wheel" was virtually worshipped in this small, charming city. The entire Gypsy population of Kraljevo was there in their colourful dresses, very different from Bosnian Gypsies, trendier and more prosperous.

I felt lonely, though. No one noticed the Bosnian soldier in the small but enthusiastic crowd of young fans shaking their long hair to the

Sarajevo's Elusive Spring

hard rock pumping from the stage. No girl paid any attention, nor did anyone offer me a cigarette. Concerts in Sarajevo tended to be real celebrations, and virtually everyone hung around the dance floor. Most rock concerts didn't provide seating, and numbers weren't strictly controlled. We travelled in overcrowded buses, trains, and trams. Being squashed in the massive crowd was a great feeling. The energy of the crowd inspired the musicians on stage, and the concerts were full of a wild party vibe. Hardly anyone sat in the stands. Revellers spent hours on their feet in semi-darkness, going wild. Alcohol had a lot to do with it, of course. Hard drugs weren't available, but the youthful energy of students and school-aged youth was inexhaustible, and it drove everyone into a frenzy.

I remember leaving concerts at night, in winter, completely soaked in sweat, and not caring if I had to walk outside in temperatures below zero. I'd catch a bus and eventually get home; all fired up inside from the fresh experience of music and dance on the overcrowded dance floor.

Kraljevo felt well behind that level of excitement. I sat on my seat for most of the concert, as did most of the fans. On the way back to the barracks, late at night, hitchhiking went well, and I told my drivers where I had been. I didn't think anything was wrong with what I was doing.

My soldier-officer noticed my absence and threatened to report me, but he didn't. I'm not sure why he didn't. Maybe he didn't have a snitch in him. He was just a loyal, honest, old-fashioned good man, and I was lucky again.

Sami Tischler

Aliens in Raška

One day, in early autumn, my friend Hardi, who had already returned from India, wrote to tell me he had found out where I was posted and promised to come by for a visit. He had spent most of the summer combing the Dalmatian Adriatic Coast with a bunch of hippies from Sarajevo, Belgrade, and Zagreb. It sounded great, and it was obvious that my Sarajevo friends were building a reputation within the well-established network of YU "Freaks". This network was "ruled" by an older generation, and we knew all the legendary unofficial heroes across the country. Our time had come, and we were becoming well-known and accepted as part of the avant-garde movement of the new generation.

I couldn't wait to see him and hear about his experiences of travelling in India and Nepal. He had spent the previous winter far away from the debacle and imprisonment we had lived through outside Belgrade before his departure. It didn't take long, and one afternoon, I was called to the gate to meet visitors. Hardi was there, as dark as an Indian, wearing a faded, daggy outfit, adorned with Indian jewellery and fabrics. He had just spent about nine months of summer between India and the Adriatic Coast, and you could tell by the way he looked. He resembled an old truck on the move, covered in road dust, with faded paintwork, neglected and battered at the edges, but full of energy and life, radiating a new self-confident image and manner.

After we kissed, hugged, and patted each other's backs forever, I was reintroduced to his travel companion, Bernarda. Yes, we had met before. She was the girl who arranged the lift to Istanbul for us, and I had met her in Belgrade a year ago. Bernarda was as skinny as a rake. Her tiny, firm breasts were visible through her thin Indian tunic. Her beautifully shaped mouth, full of big teeth, sat handsomely on her tanned face, surrounded by faded, sun-bleached, short-cropped punkstyle hair.

Last time we met, I hardly got to talk to her. She'd changed a lot since then. I liked her straight away. She looked at me as though she had just seen a giant, which I was. I had eaten well for the previous seven months, and my Albanian connections in the kitchen had provided a steady supply of pastries and additional kilograms.

Army rules stated that you could get a permit to spend a night outside the barracks if you were visited by your parents or fiancé. They suggested registering Bernarda as my fiancé to get me an overnight permit. So, we did. I went back to my commanding officer, who granted me the permit. We didn't waste any time. They produced some cash, and we bought a few bottles of wine, food, cigarettes, and a small tin of contact glue, then headed to a small, wooded area on the outskirts of town, by the riverbank, across the plateau from where the Army barracks stood, across the river. It was a heavily overgrown area. We felt safe, protected, and thought it was the best place where we could enjoy our special moment and have some private time.

Their appearance could have upset the local militia if we stayed in the open town park area. The authorities' concern for public safety could have ruined our reunion. We gathered some dry wood, set up a fire, sat around it, smoked cigarettes, drank wine, and sniffed glue. Sniffing glue was the latest craze brought on by punks. I didn't really like it much. The high was violent, and the smell of glue was awful. Bernarda, a real punk, loved it and kept sniffing the glue from a plastic bag. Hardi appeared to enjoy it. He filled the quiet moments with stories of his adventures over the previous nine months of travel. I joined in now and then, sniffed a bit, felt sick, and eventually stopped using it. They both laughed and fooled around a lot. I enjoyed this fresh air of freedom piercing through the grey cloud I'd been living under for too long.

I missed being on the road with my sleeping bag over my shoulder, with little money, no plans, and no schedules to meet. It was great to see Hardi and the change he had gone through. He kept doing Indian bows with his palms clasped together. He called me Baba UFO and showed me his chillum he brought from India, with a cobra snake spiralled around it. They had no hash, unfortunately. They'd smoked often during the summer, much more often than we had before Hardi went to India. It appeared the doors were opening to us, and all those fantasies we'd had about smoking dope freely were becoming a reality. The sad truth was that I wasn't part of it yet.

We sat up late that night, and Hardi played tunes he had learnt in India on his flute. Bernarda came and snuggled against my big frame, and I held her slim body in my big hands. Her small frame just fitted there so neatly. I needed this so much, and she appeared so vulnerable. She told me she lived with her grandfather in Zagreb, and that her mother, who lived somewhere in Germany, had abandoned her when she was three. She moved effortlessly between exhilarated happiness and the saddest tears you'd ever seen, without warning. I was very touched by her fragility and openness.

I never realised at the time that our lives were going to cross paths in various places and in various ways over the next three years and beyond. At the time, she was barely 17, untamed, hurt, proud, fragile, but playful and warm. Late at night, we stoked the fire and made a bed out of two unzipped sleeping bags, crawled in fully dressed between them, and slept tangled up together like children at a sleepover. All you could hear was the sound of the water rolling, crashing, and splashing in the river while Bernarda slept between us in a warm cocoon.

The morning was cold, and we got up early, lit the fire again, and ate some leftover bread and cheese. We looked like a family of wandering gypsies. The romance of the night was gone, and we were just three hungover glue sniffers, cranky, anxious, and nervous. Hardi and Bernarda started an endless argument about whether they should get back on the road. She had to meet "Čičko," a Belgrade boy she had fallen in love with on the coast. They'd broken up, this time for good, but she still had to see him. She thought it was fixable.

Hardi was pissed off. They'd travelled for two days to get to Raška. He wanted to spend more time with me. Her habit of falling in and out of love every five minutes was getting on his nerves. The fragile girl

Sarajevo's Elusive Spring

I'd held in my hands the night before was turning into a wild cat, ready to scratch and hurt anyone who dared to touch her. Her obsession with her boyfriend was annoying me too. I was watching an immature teen materialise right in front of my eyes.

Hardi didn't have much choice. He was a long way from home, and hitchhiking on his own would have made this trip a torturous adventure. He wasn't going to send her off on her own either. That was out of the question. In these backwaters, she would have been treated as a roadside prostitute by truck drivers and the militia. We decided it was best for them to leave together and get on the long road to Belgrade as soon as possible. I had my permit until 10 am and headed back to the barracks as soon as we said our goodbyes.

Back at the barracks, my commanding officer ordered me to report to his office. At the office, he had company. I was introduced to a state security officer, who had the manners of an educated and streetwise man at the same time. Our camping had been reported, and it had caused some stir at the base.

"You'll need to give me details of your friends, and I'll pass them on to the militia (civilian authorities) to follow up," he said. "You've defamed the image of our Army by spending the night like a gypsy with these friends of yours. What did you think, soldier?" (He kept addressing me by my surname.) "You've seriously jeopardised the security of the base with your careless actions, and we seriously doubt that, what's her name, your fiancée."

Although struggling to find an appropriate response, I couldn't accept that their seriousness and security concerns were justified. "Comrade officer," whatever rank he was, "Hardi and Bernarda are my friends, and they came to visit me. None of us had money to pay for a hotel. Spending the night around the fire did no harm to the Army's reputation and caused no security risk to our camp. They gave their details at the gate yesterday, and it would be a shame to send the militia after them, since their only crime was paying a visit to their good friend."

He listened and kept silent, observing my body language intently. I knew they had no chance of catching my friends on the road. They would have been 100 km away from Raška by then. The officer went on about how we should be vigilant, how the enemy was always around, and how the times were especially challenging in this location.

"I'll certainly make sure we keep an eye on you. Don't think this business is over. If we find out that those two had some hidden agenda, we'll be talking again. I've sent soldiers to Martial Court, and they don't fool around there, don't you know?"

I sat quietly, not needing to add anything. Behind my calm façade, I was afraid of what they knew and what they might find out if they really tried. My commanding officer didn't look impressed as I left the room. I didn't really like him, and if he ever thought I was alright, that was no longer the case.

I told Iliya and Mirso about the investigation but kept the details of the night around the fire to myself. The word had already spread around the barracks, and soldiers approached me, enquiring about the details of my "awesome" experience. Sex-starved men, especially the Albanian gang, could only see it as a potential for a gang bang orgy.

"You should have invited us. We could've paid for the hotel. We're loaded. Come and see us next time, we'll pay for everything: booze, room service, cigarettes, just let us know."

In their eyes, I was a hero, connected to a world completely unknown to them. As it was, I was certainly part of a new culture, claiming a form of freedom for myself, not clearly understood by ordinary people. The government officials and the Army weren't sure if we were careless or dangerous. My Bosnian commanding officer decided to pass me on. He wasn't going to risk his rank for someone who had nothing to lose. Shortly after, I received an order for a transfer to Titovo Užice (T.U.) and a permanent new posting.

Yet Another Transfer, Army Lock Up

Titovo Užice was a great option, 200 km from Sarajevo on a direct bus line that ran twice a day between the two. I knew a few important people from the city. They were students in Sarajevo and well known around the traps. Daga was studying painting at the Academy of Art and Suzy was a student of something at the university there. They both lived at Zizi's place in a form of an urban commune.

It wasn't anything like the attics I'd seen in Nancy a year before. This was a small apartment and Zizi was charging everyone rent. The difference, and the advantage, was the fact that this place attracted a small army of musicians, poets, writers and progressive students, including young Palestinians, Libyans and Iraqis. Zizi was known as a working-class poet and a legendary freak.

I went out to town the first weekend and met everyone who was into music, dope and booze at the square. Daga and Suzy were local legends, and I met Daga's brother everyone called "Indian". That same night we all danced in a hall at the square to music played by a local rock band. They only played covers, but that didn't really matter. Everyone was friendly, girls talked to me, and people offered cigarettes and moonshine booze they had smuggled in. I felt at home and knew that I could easily manage the rest of my eight months here. The memory of Raška was fading away quickly. I missed a few friends, but this place was a great substitute.

At the end of the first week, the Army had yet another surprise for me. They were moving me along again. It turned out that they needed a phone exchange technician in a place called Užička Požega (U.P.), 14 km away. According to them, I was one of those. Fortunately, a local bus line operated frequently between the two towns, I was told. Nevertheless, I was transported across in a military van and introduced to my new crew.

We were stationed in a tiny base with a dormitory, guard house, a single commanding officer, a phone exchange and a canteen where no food was ever prepared. My soldier officer had one stripe, spoke in a soft north-western Croatian dialect, and appeared harmless and insecure. He and two Bosnian phone operators, who did all the shifts at the exchange, knew how to repair a common problem caused by a jamming relay. This small base provided a perfect post for a maintenance technician nobody required unless someone from T. U. headquarters did a roll call over the phone.

It was perfect camouflage for the elusive soldier I was. Rather than standing still and playing dead before developing escapist trickery, I used the opportunity of a quiet afternoon to slip out of the barracks and catch a bus back to T. U.

It was a warm day and a few young punks had gathered at the square. I went across and we rolled cigarettes from my tobacco box for a while. A young girl turned up with a bottle of what they called *"Klekovača"*, a sort of fortified moonshine gin. We all got into it enthusiastically. I was having a great time talking music, travel, the Sarajevo scene, freak philosophy. It isn't a typo, and I didn't mean Greek philosophy. I guess I've already exposed elements of it through my stories. It's a loose bunch of ideas, morals and experiential concepts I derived in my own head and often discussed when drunk, stoned or engulfed in tobacco smoke.

The sun was coming down, closer to the ridge of hills in the west of the city, when it became obvious that I was getting very drunk on an unauthorised outing only metres from my commanding officers on the other side of the square. I felt OK and confident about my ability to return to U. P. – until I stood up. My legs felt weak, and I could hardly walk. The punks I'd been drinking with came along for support and almost carried my half-conscious body to the bus stop.

I remember boarding the bus and recall someone getting up to let me take a seat in the overcrowded rusty bucket filled with diesel fumes and sweaty working-class commuters. I had no strength to open the window above my head, and the last thing I remember was the rattle and shake of the handle built into the framework of the seat ahead while my stomach contents pulsed up and down.

Sarajevo's Elusive Spring

I woke up in a cellar on top of a barren mattress and under an army issue blanket. My head was splitting with every beat of my heart, my mouth was dry as a desert, and I couldn't work out if the overwhelming stench came from the semi-flooded cellar, the dried vomit I had smeared all over my uniform, or my thirsty mouth. One thing I was sure of: this was a cell, and the only door in the room would most probably be locked.

By the time I gathered my wits, a soldier on guard duty came in and told me to clean myself up and report to the officer on duty. He showed me out and led me to the toilet where I did my best to make myself look less miserable. One look at the mirror over the basin confirmed that my best wouldn't be good enough. "This won't be a fashion show anyway," I thought, and walked out, placed my hat on, stumbled upstairs and into the officer's room.

"Soldier so and so, reporting, senior officer," I proclaimed as I saluted and stood at attention. He looked at me with clear disgust, as if he had never seen himself in the mirror in that same state.

"You call yourself a soldier?" he yelled. "I have no words to describe you and your behaviour." He stared at me while both of his fists sat clenched on top of a worn-out tabletop. "If I found one, it would have to come out of the book about animals," he went on. "We were called by civilian authorities to collect a soldier in a shocking state of drunkenness. Do you realise how embarrassing that was for us? We are meant to show civilians our integrity and our dignity, confirm their confidence in us as those who can protect them and their families." He stopped and shook his head, his hands still holding tight onto themselves. "Have you ever thought what Marshall Tito would have said about your sorry character and your filthy appearance?"

For a second, I looked at the serious face of our President Tito looking down from the framed picture above his head and felt as little and miserable as a mouse caught in a trap, losing hope that things could ever be the same again.

Sami Tischler

I don't know how I managed to gather strength, connect words into a meaningful sentence, but I mumbled a sort of apology and a pledge: "I'll do my best, comrade, not to disappoint you and our glorious leaders headed by Marshall Tito himself." It almost sounded like the end of a confession at a church. I half expected penance in the form of prayers I couldn't recite but didn't get any.

"Get lost, take leave, get yourself a shower and a good sleep. You are lucky, bastard. My wife delivered a perfectly healthy son while you were in a coma downstairs. I promised myself to let you off if everything went OK. And it did!" His hands were away from one another and up in the air. I knew he couldn't wait for his shift to end, and he was certainly going to get wasted in celebration at home.

"Congratulations, comrade officer, congratulations. Hope your son lives a long, happy and prosperous life," I exclaimed as I left the room.

I did take a shower, changed out of my soiled uniform, slipped on my pyjamas and went to bed as ordered.

When I woke up and paid a visit to my Bosnian friend working in the canteen, ready to get a feed and fill my devastated gut, I realised I had become a legend. He told me about my heroic drunkenness and the legendary trip from T.U. to U.P. Apparently, civilian passengers lifted me from the seat and the area covered by my vomit, carried me out of the bus, and planted me at the most prominent spot at the station buffet. The owner made sure my further actions weren't going to ruin his floor, tablecloths or furniture before he called my garrison. I was found at the table outside, in full sight of the random bus stop audience, with my face in the fresh vomit puddle delivered neatly all over the tabletop, wearing vomit-stained clothes and shoes, a perfect drunken pig.

Apparently, two soldiers who came to collect me, since there weren't Army police at the barracks in the town, carried my "dead" body into the public toilet. They weren't going to soil the floor of the jeep, so they decided to give me a "hose down". It would have been a rough wash and a tumble dry. After that they dumped the washed, dead looking body of mine into the back of an Army jeep. Believe it or not, this made me a hero amongst the troops.

All those guys who had hardly paid any attention to my existence started coming around for a chat, offering cigarettes, plotting little mischiefs against their mates, bitching about officers and Army regulations, telling me about their girlfriends and the letters they exchanged. Occasionally I was given their girlfriends' photographs for detailed analysis and approval.

The Croatian soldier officer wasn't impressed. He claimed he'd received a proper grinding from Headquarters and promised I was due to report to them and get an earful over the phone. As far as I knew, they had nothing on me, and I did report to Headquarters. I was served a similar lecture over the phone to the one I'd had at the guard house the previous day: "I have no words to describe you and your behaviour …" I mumbled a similar kind of promise: "I'll do my best, comrade, not to disappoint you nor our glorious leaders headed by the Marshall Tito himself." I understood that all of this would get recorded on my file. I didn't really care. I had no intention of impressing anyone and knew that I'd be honoured to do my patriotic duty in our self-defensive Army any time required.

As for the Marshall himself and his ever-present stare, he was an old man, and his vision was losing direction, strength and clarity. My behaviour was just a reflection of greater problems the system was facing at the time.

Sami Tischler

Army, the Slow River

Things settled down and my Army time went by like a slow river, a very slow river. Weekends at the dance hall became highlights of that period. It would generally start with hanging around the town square at T.U., having a few drinks with the punks, but only a few. I wasn't going to make a fool of myself again and go too far. After all, I had made a pledge and took my word seriously.

However, my escapes to Sarajevo were too tempting not to try again. There was a direct connection from a small bus depot to Sarajevo, about four hours' drive between the two cities. Once you bought a bus ticket, which you could do a day before, you had to slip onto the bus just before it took off to avoid the Army Police patrol. There weren't major cities along the way and Army Police weren't authorised to do ID checks inside civilian transport. Once you took your Army cap off, you weren't obvious when they visually scanned the crowd anyway. You just had to pick the right time, a weekend with a lazy, ageing guard officer who couldn't be bothered conducting a rollcall in the morning.

The rest was between you and your soldier officer. Mine was an obedient and soft-hearted gentle boy from the northern flats of Croatia. He generally didn't like drama or trouble of any kind and never reported my absence, just tended to ignore it and threaten me on my return. There was no point causing drama then.

I went home twice without a permit. Many of my close friends were doing their national service at the same time. These escapes turned out uneventful, except for my parents who freaked out every time I turned up unannounced.

Things at U.P. were going well and once I had two months of duty left, I got another transfer back to town and Headquarters. Someone who'd taken a good look at my file must have labelled me as unreliable, unpatriotic and unsuitable for any duty; hence I had no assignments of any description.

Sarajevo's Elusive Spring

Moreover, my friend Guitarist, whom I'd met in Raška, had just arrived from another location in Serbia. He had no assignments either, most likely for the same reasons. We befriended a boy from Pančevo, a city on the opposite side of the Danube directly across from the capital, Belgrade. When we talked about music, he claimed to own a bunch of rare records at home. I suggested a trip to Pančevo by bus, the three of us together. We weren't expected anywhere and had no scheduled duties.

We spent mornings by the grocery store just outside the Army barbed wire fence, asking local shoppers for small change. The Serbian population generally felt that the Army was the pride of the country, which they considered their own. The Army's Headquarters were based in Belgrade, as were the rest of the government departments including the National Assembly. Serbia had also liberated itself from the Ottoman Empire, fought against its neighbours and expanded its territory before the Great War, which they virtually started. By the end of it, the Kingdom had expanded again and absorbed all South Slavic nations, including chunks of Italian, Austrian, Hungarian and Albanian lands.

During WWII most of Tito's partisans came from Serbia, Montenegro and among the Orthodox population of Bosnia. The country expanded again as a friendly state and an ally to the West, at the expense of the aggressors, Italians, Germans and Hungarians. The Serbian and Bosnian populations were generally proud of the Army and happy to support its recruits and officers. Other states didn't necessarily share this attitude.

Local shoppers happily contributed and gave us money when asked. Luckily, no one ever squealed to Army command. This could have been another issue to discuss with the special branch dealing with disrespect of the values and virtues of our great leaders and revolutionaries. They had already forgotten that those same revolutionaries once walked around in rags infested with lice during the Great Revolution, took food from peasants and executed those who refused to support their cause, and never showed much gratitude once their revolution succeeded. No peasant in Yugoslavia received a health benefit card, an entitlement granted to all government employees and the working-class population. Yet the revolution only succeeded thanks to the peasant population and their voluntary, and forced, support alike.

Sarajevo's Elusive Spring

Three Amigos on the Road

We were certainly thankful for the symbolic support from the shoppers, and those accumulated funds were used for noble causes, quickly converted into wine and cigarettes. We took these into neglected corners of the Army compound and consumed them with *gusto* while we discussed plans for the trip to Pančevo.

I was looking forward to the adventure together, although my friends weren't very comfortable with it. I gave them a crash course in my escapist strategies and managed to boost their courage. We decided to do it, set the date, bought bus tickets, and waited it out.

On the day, we just went out through the gate with no luggage, walked to the bus stop, sat casually at the bistro there and kept our bus in clear sight. The driver was about to walk in as we boarded. As soon as we'd found our seats, the bus got on its way. By lunchtime we had made it to Belgrade bus station.

As the rest of the passengers got up, we scanned the platform for Military Police. There weren't any. All three of us, as if in a drill, slipped out and caught a cab just outside the station building on the main street. Our friend's mum had lunch ready on the stove as we walked into their apartment in a Pančevo housing block. She knew what we were up to and never asked for explanations. Her boy had explained on the phone the previous day, and we were going to have a great time with no hassle from any over-patriotic parent.

And so we did, beer after lunch in his room, cigarettes and music. Music, and more music. Using our "invisibility" strategy, we managed to return to the barracks the following day. The boys raved about it for days.

Sami Tischler

Rašo

Through my interest in music, I met Rašo. He lived in a village between T.U. and U.P., where there was a large copper manufacturing and processing plant, a prosperous kind of industry dependent on a massive supply of electrical power. Rašo worked there, and I was invited to visit on weekends.

I was so happy to be a guest of the family and enjoyed their hospitality with gratitude. We would listen to his great vinyl collection, smoke cigarettes, drink locally brewed spirits and top it off with food and cakes prepared by his widowed mother or his younger sister, Rada.

Rada was a liberated young woman, and I secretly fell in love with her, but I didn't even think of letting her know. My status as a soldier, temporarily stationed near her town, stripped me of confidence, and I wasn't brave enough to take those steps. My experience with women was limited. There was an aura of shyness around me, and I could never figure out if a woman was interested in me. The fear of failure, which I had experienced more than a few times, tended to hold me back from making the first move.

Rašo's friendship was very important to me, and I wasn't going to risk it. There was talk of a boyfriend and a broken relationship in recent times, all of which kept me away from Rada. She was sweet, friendly, intelligent, funny, open and happy in her dealings with me. I remained at a safe distance all the way through the rest of my time there.

Summer was nearing, and I was getting close to the final release from National Service. My 15 months were nearly over. I can recall the day of my release as an endless wait. My paperwork was being prepared. I guess they needed all that time to fill in the report of my service and include all those breaches of the Army code of behaviour I had committed over the previous 15 months.

I got out just in time to make it to the last daily bus to Sarajevo. Penniless, as any former recruit was when leaving the service, I could have risked an arrest by civilian militia for sleeping outside on a park bench. Instead, I was sitting on the bus climbing into the Bosnian mountains with a sense of relief, as well as a feeling of anxiety ahead of my planned trip to India.

Sami Tischler

Germany Revisited

I went to India in 1978. When I came back, five months later, there were big changes in Sarajevo. By that time, I had been virtually absent from the city for about two years. It was burning with life; cafés played groovy progressive music all over *Baščaršija*. Zizi started the new trend by offering a struggling government-owned bar "The Nightingale", a surge in business by playing progressive music and attracting young students and freaks. It worked so well that we had a new place to meet and enjoy Zizi's extensive vinyl collection. New places popped up like mushrooms around the Old Town, exploiting the same idea. The whole area vibrated with the sounds of great music previously confined to a single nightclub Cactus, well away in the New Town.

Bijelo Dugme survived the punk revolution in all major centres of Yugoslavia. They played in Skenderija for tens of thousands and invited all the major music stars of the time to join them. Anyone who was anyone in Belgrade or Zagreb came and played in Sarajevo.

Karlo came home for Christmas and invited me to go back to Germany with him for New Year. Karlo and I travelled through the Alps, covered in deep snow, in an old VW Beetle. Its heating was great, but we slept through the shortest night ever in the back of it and nearly froze our nuts off. We got up half-frozen in the early hours of the morning. Karlo kept driving, just to keep us warm.

At the time, my English, learnt from books and first practised on my trip to India, was basic, and my time at Karlo's household was a lonely affair. Suzy and Ralf, his housemates, spoke German exclusively. The only sentences I could pronounce in German were picked up from war movies, mostly set in concentration camps. It looked hopeless. I had just returned from a five-month-long adventure by land from Sarajevo to Himachal Pradesh in India and back. I wanted to tell my story but couldn't. The Germans had travelled in South America; I was keen to hear but couldn't understand.

Sarajevo's Elusive Spring

On New Year's Eve 1978/79, a group of four came to visit. Two were on their way from Berlin to Spain, the other two friends from Berlin came just for the party. One of the two women (considerably older than me, 21 at the time) was keen on talking to me. She listened to my questions about Spain, about what she did and where she had been. I was using my crude English, and she didn't seem to mind, working it out and listening patiently while I wrestled with my awkward sentence construction and pronunciation. She kept me to herself with no chance to "talk" to anyone else. I was looked after, felt like young royalty throughout the evening. She made sure I had a drink, passed me joints, laughed at my crude attempts to be funny, and took her time to comprehend my ambitious elaborations in broken English.

I felt this could have led to an invitation to join her on her trip to Spain, and a sense of anticipation was overwhelming yet comforting at the same time. Getting away from winter would have been lovely. As midnight approached, Karlo came over and invited us to watch fireworks over Kempten from a lookout point nearby. The German "lady" wasn't keen on the idea, nor was anyone else. Karlo was trying to liven up the party and failed. He needed company and, after all, I was his guest and had no choice but to join him.

I got up, dressed in warm clothes, feeling awkward about leaving "the lady" behind. We went out. The freezing cold air and invisible ice walls weren't welcoming either. I knew I shouldn't have left the perfectly cozy party for this. The cold was bitter, but the moon was out in its full glory. A magical snowscape, a natural miracle with millions of silver glittering sparkles in the snow, a gift for the brave ones.

As we were getting in the car, a young visitor, the one who came to "party", jumped into the back seat. We had hardly exchanged a few words, and I wasn't sure if she spoke much English. She was sitting behind me, speaking to Karlo most of the way. I could smell her lovely fragrance mixed with light traces of alcohol and tobacco. She had a pleasant, soft voice, and listening to the sounds of the German language in that dreamy tone so close behind me excited my senses, already overstimulated with *Manali* hash and fortified wine. I was starting to imagine her in my embrace, kissing the neck from which such harmonious syllables poured. German hadn't sounded so good since Helga spoke to me.

We parked the car at a lookout over Kempten, kept the engine running and the windows fog-free, waiting for midnight and the fireworks. I felt her warm breath close to my ear as the colours shot up and explosions cracked through the night. Her lips were on my neck, and I was melting away as we watched the changing scenery ahead of us. Magic continued with each firecracker's explosion in a range of colours over the frozen, snow-covered Alpine valley. Her hands explored my torso and face, her fingers in my mouth, her lips on my neck. With my contorted neck and head over the edge of my seat, we got into kissing.

At some stage, Karlo became aware of what was taking place, but politely ignored our foreplay. On the way back, we held onto each other and exchanged passionate glances across the backrest of my seat. During the short drive, Karlo made a few short approving comments on my advances in Bosnian. As we got out of the car, she dragged me towards the open barn entrance where she wanted to wish me a Happy New Year. We kissed for a long time and she sucked the life out of me with a creative tongue technique. She didn't get offended when I slipped my cold hands under her winter clothing, feeling the warmth of her smooth skin and firm curves.

Karlo was already inside; the sound of music and full-on party was spilling out into the freezing night. There was no point in going any further out there. I took her hand and led her quietly up the squeaky wooden stairs to the attic and the small bedroom allocated to me. It was simple and unheated, the windows already displaying frost patterns. I lit a candle and undressed quickly. She was keen to get under the blankets fast.

Cold hands, cold feet, warm breath, hot skin, swollen desire, hard urgency, juicy tongues, puffing lungs, soft necks, hard nipples, all mixed up in an accelerated tempo of movement, caress, licking, sucking, kissing, rubbing, twisting, puffing, and penetration. Deep, deep penetration into the abyss of her silky, slippery insides. She rolled with me, finishing on top, and before I knew it my hardened thief propped up her light naked body. She rode me as if welded on. By this time, she had thrown off the blanket and I was gazing at her softly lit, bouncing, pear-shaped breasts with pointy pink nipples like shooting stars in a dim-lit sky.

With her head thrown back and eyes closed, she was riding a tidal wave of passion, rocking gently on its crest. I raised my torso and grabbed her breasts, perfectly fitted to my large hands, pressing her fragile nipples between my lips. The tempo went wild, the grinding on my shaft holding my pleasure at the edge of just-bearable pain. She rose and landed back hard, again and again, rolling and grinding before rising once more and slamming down. She finally stopped once my penis was fully inside. Sitting there, she held me deep within, imploding, pulsating with pleasure as she received my semen in gulps.

We lay under the blankets in the freezing room, bathed in mixed sweat, fused secretions, overheated, the edge of the blanket left open to release the erotic fragrances and let in fresh air for our starved lungs. She snuggled beside me, satisfied and calm. I lit a cigarette, and we smoked it together, kissing between puffs.

The door opened and Ralf came in. As rude as it was, I wasn't sure what was going on. He said he wanted to talk to her. I was caught by surprise. They were in a relationship. "What a crazy idea," I thought. "We've already done it, she's still full of my passion, of my semen." I was sure she still carried the memory of my swollen dick deep inside her.

Ralf sat down beside the mattress on the floor where we lay. I lit another cigarette and watched him cry as she responded with cold, short, unfriendly phrases in a tone very different from the enchanted sounds she had produced for me earlier. She spoke to him in that cruel form of German language.

For the rest of the night Ralf took charge of my lover and did not allow me to get anywhere near her. I felt guilty for a bit and then gave up. I joined the crowd in drinking, dancing, and smoking more joints of *Manali*. The "lady" who appeared so "fascinated" by me before the "fireworks" outing didn't show further interest. I am sure she was smart and experienced enough to get away from the young "Balkan Bull" easily distracted by a young shapely tit bouncing woman. She was right and it was a shame. Spain had to wait. At the end, it wasn't really my fault. I had no idea that she "belonged" to Ralf and that I was used by her to get back at him for something he had done to her. She left with her friend after lunch next day and for the rest of my time at Karlo's there was a cold distance between me and Ralf. I never apologised, because I didn't feel I needed to, neither did he. Also, back in Sarajevo, my penis started to dribble a whitish sticky discharge. It made sense. The Ralf's girlfriend told me that she had learnt English from American soldiers residing at a US base. She lived nearby and made friends with many. It was clear that she did much more than made friends with them. A course of injection delivered antibiotics in Sarajevo STD, famous Vrazova St. Clinic, got me sorted, but I never forgot her. A few years later I will realise that my attitude towards Ralf was perfectly gauged, but I'll tell you about that later.

Still in Germany

Karlo and I did our fair share of partying and hanging around other communes in the area, the type of places my friend Hardy and I had hoped to spend the winter of 1976 in but never did. Once we drove to a small village and its guesthouse, where a band played while the Alpine winter covered its surrounds with a fresh layer of fluffy white powder snow. It was cozy inside, with a massive fireplace at one end and a great rock band at the other. Everywhere in between, young German hippies, fired up on schnapps, dark beer and the smoke of aromatic herbs, danced, spoke loudly, and enjoyed the great atmosphere. The place was swelling with beautiful young girls, often accompanied by mature freaks, ageing hippies with traces of experience and wisdom reflected in their faces, dress codes and jewellery. I was only a greenhorn but doing well, I thought.

One visit stayed in my memory for a long time. Karlo drove to a small village where we found a neat, elegant, one-storey house where Wolfgang lived. He was a successful freak who operated a jewellery workshop from a small, cozy room in the attic, where he worked gold, silver and stones, producing custom-made original pieces in high demand. He was tall, blond and handsome. His fingers seemed designed for delicate work, and he filled his small workshop with his elegant movements and well-sculpted figure so gracefully. The bench was covered with beautiful objects, unusual tools and devices I had never seen before. My *Opinel* folding pocketknife, which I used to carve and sculpt wood at the time, felt so lonely and primitive. Yet somehow, I felt that this visit was very significant, and that it opened my eyes to the world of an artist operating outside the known space and conventions. Apart from that, I had very little chance to exchange or express my views or opinions. My English, as I've said before, lacked the width, depth, range and fluency.

Following a massive snowstorm, our minimal food stocks at the farmhouse had almost run out. I was penniless, as I had been forever, and Karlo went to Kempten for groceries. I found a pair of skis in the hay barn, and the fresh powder covering the hillside below the house looked irresistible. The steep hill disappeared into the dark pine forest covered in snowdrift dunes. I had sold Christmas cards with scenes like this only a month ago back in Bosnia.

The only problem was that I didn't have proper ski boots, and the pair on my feet only allowed minimal grip and control over the slippery devices I decided to ride into this fairy tale. I had ridden handmade skis in Bosnia for years, the kind with nailed-on shoe straps, and I had a lot of skill on snow. This time, no skill would have made much difference, and the fact that my feet were hardly attached to the skis must have saved my life.

I was doing reasonably well on the way down until my speed accelerated. Panic set in once I realised I was heading straight into the forest, trees and snowdrift dunes. I knew any attempt to turn or change course would result in being ejected out of my foothold. Before I got a chance to test it, I came across a barren patch of dirt where the strong wind had blown the snow off the ground. As soon as my skis hit this spot, they virtually stopped under my weight and my whole body was ejected forward, straight onto the edge of the frozen patch, where I landed, slid across, and got buried head-first into a snow dune.

It took some time to get my wits about me, to work out where I was and how I'd ended up there. Somehow, I managed to "unearth" myself out of the snow dune, find both skis, carry them over my shoulder, and walk back through the deep snow. It took a massive effort to walk all the way up the steep hill. It was an endless hike, much longer than the short run and fall. Apart from a few scratches and bruises, I wasn't missing any parts.

Back at Home + Baba's Harem

We came back across the Alps in an old VW. Things in Sarajevo looked great. The Nightingale scene was a blast. I met Baba, who had just returned from Ceylon. He had sold his Yugoslav passport, the sort of thing usually only done by French freaks. The "Frenchies" could go to their embassy and get a trip back home paid for by their government. If you were Yugoslav, our embassy staff told you to "fuck off and find your way home the way you made it there". However, they had already taken your details, and when you did return you were banned from getting a passport again indefinitely.

Baba was an old Joša freak. He had spent years in Amsterdam, being a hippy, gigolo, hash dealer, and commune and squat dweller. He would regularly come home dressed like a cowboy and work with Gypsies at a travelling merry-go-round. He was so cool that I never even dreamt of having him as a friend. He was a godlike creature.

We sat at The Nightingale, rolled raw tobacco, drank beer, and smoked joints at my friend Chuck's place in Malešići. Besides, once I'd cleaned up my "German girlfriend's inheritance", girls just wanted to be with me. Unfortunately, most of them were barely of legal age, and my love affairs were still very platonic. By now, I had built up a decent collection of sexual encounters, including the one on the road involving a Bulgarian Gypsy prostitute who performed a great oral trick, my first one. It happened in the sleeping compartment of a moving truck, as a favour to the truck driver who had given her a lift. I wouldn't call this a success, of sorts, but it counted for something, and somehow my luck with women gradually changed.

While I was in Germany, Rašo came with his best friend to visit me. My sister led them to Malešići, where they met the mob living there. Bernarda came from Zagreb, Nada from Konjic, Hardi stayed most nights, Baba was there, and Chuck had brought Edith to live in his house. It was starting to look like a commune when the boys from

T. U. turned up. To top it off, there was plenty of free dope to be had.

Baba was the head stallion there, with an enormous penis and years of experience satisfying demanding ladies. He slept with them all, and the whole village knew when that happened. The ladies made as much noise as Ivo Andrić's characters tortured by Turks while being impaled. Somehow, Rašo managed to win Bernarda over, and shortly after my return she had moved to T. U. via Zagreb to live with him. Their passionate encounter was the talk of the town, or rather, the commune, when I made it back. Baba was a bit down, but Nada, the fresh girl from Konjic, took over Bernarda's place almost instantly. She abandoned her boyfriend, the one who had brought her there. While he slept in the communal room, she got properly impaled by Baba, to the horror of all present. Her boyfriend, also horrified and thinking of suicide, drowning in the freezing, dirty waters of the Bosnia River flowing nearby, slept on blankets on the freezing floor. Nada easily swapped lovers again, befriended Hardi in no time, and off they went.

Baba's loyalty didn't hold water either. I watched him as he was getting ready for a visit by a teenage princess and figured out other qualities of his that women must have found irresistible. He had a shower, spent an hour combing his jet-black long hair, trimmed his beard and moustache, and then cleaned up his feet and toenails, adding fragrant oil to his toes and legs, massaging it in forever. It was an unusual ritual for me, and not a typical Bosnian way of grooming for a man. However, I understood that Baba wasn't only about his big prick. Years of making a living in the business of female satisfaction had made him an exceptional lover and seducer of women's hearts. I felt that these tips might come in useful one day, and I couldn't imagine competing with him for someone's heart and coming out a winner.

Employed and Settled?

Shortly after my return from India, I started work at TAS through an intervention by my Uncle Ibrahim, an influential politician in the region. It had to happen through connections. Both of my uncles did their best to find me work. Uncle Ali worked for a large company building industrial infrastructure across Yugoslavia. I applied for a job with them as a graduate from my studies in electrical engineering. I was called for an interview and received a job offer.

While in the process, Uncle Ibrahim promised to use his powerful connections and get me a job in the local car manufacturing plant TAS at the end of my street. I applied and waited. Uncle Ali's company "Unioninvest" offered me a job on the construction of a high-voltage power grid somewhere in Macedonia. I seriously considered the offer. The idea of being somewhere in the Macedonian mountains, in remote villages where they played bagpipe, *zurna* and *tapan*, did appeal to me. When I told Uncle Ibrahim about it, he assured me that his connections were solid and said: "The job is yours if you want it."

My parents had massive faith in his powerful status in the Party and factory management, so I decided to wait. It paid off. Shortly after, I was notified that I was successful, and the job was mine, just as Uncle said. There were some complaints by another applicant. They included comments about my travel to India and touched on very personal issues, but Uncle assured me: "Do not bother with that, they cannot touch me or you. It is just idle gossip." That's how it was.

I went to the main office by the gate I knew so well. Most people who went through that gate walked past my street if they lived in town. They usually started work in their early 20s and were still there in their 60s. I was meant to feel lucky about getting a job. Most of my friends were unemployed. We were often told that someone had to die before a young person could get a job. Once you had one, you held it for life. After getting a job, you waited to get a government apartment, and you wouldn't be entitled to one of those unless you were married.

Somehow, I skipped the routine. My parents decided that I could have a one-bedroom flat in the basement of our house. I started my life as a working bachelor and had a place where I could bring friends over. That, I considered great luck. Having the privacy of my own place changed my social life dramatically. There were some restrictions about what I was allowed to do, since everyone had to pass by my parents' front door to enter my basement. Although tricky, I managed to bring over Spanish travellers who carried a load of hash, concert visitors from North Croatia (four of them, two females), other friends for small parties, as well as the occasional girl for an intimate encounter.

Friends came and I cooked rosehip tea with cocoa. We'd listen to music, talk revolution, commune, politics, literature, the future of Yugoslavia, the oppressive police state, and travel. We rarely took drugs there because there weren't any around, and when there were, we couldn't afford them. A bottle of wine always helped the lively conversation. Besides, just talking about the quantities of drugs we had consumed in India was enough to get us almost stoned.

Baba managed to get his passport back somehow. We felt that it involved Amir Latić, a drug squad detective in the Sarajevo militia, and names of small gangsters who sold stolen prescription tablets popular with punks and more adventurous youth of the late '70s in Sarajevo. His teenage princess, whom he must have groomed into a lover, lost her prince, who returned to Amsterdam at short notice.

The Princess

Ian Gillan (ex-Deep Purple singer) played in a Sarajevo sports hall. I met random friends at the entrance, and "the teenage princess, Baba's sweetheart" joined our group. Surprisingly, she stuck with me and wouldn't go away. I thought that fragile and delicate creature used my presence for safety and protection in the rowdy concert crowd. We got in and ended up squashed together on the overcrowded dance floor, music pumping and the human mass moving around us in the semidarkness. She held onto me and looked comfortable in such intimate proximity, and it was becoming more intense by the minute.

I thought about Baba and our friendship and tried hard to remain cool for a while, but I couldn't resist the affection from the sweet, gorgeous beauty generously channelled towards me. At one stage, there seemed to be a bit of space around us. I took her under her arms and swung her light body in circles, spinning full speed. I was good at spinning in those days. It was my favourite dancing move, and I used it often. This time I did it while holding onto her armpits, her head against mine. I felt her excited breathing right beside my ear as I kept her body floating and spinning above the ground, in semi-darkness and amongst a boiling crowd moving in waves. It felt like flying together until her feet knocked someone over.

It had to happen; it lasted long enough to fuse our fragile emotions. I had to deal with an angry youth whose girlfriend had been knocked over. It almost ended in a brawl. I knew I had to stay cool and preserve the sense of trust and intimacy we had created. We walked away. Gillan wasn't the man I remembered with his original band Deep Purple. Also, my taste in music had evolved much further than hard rock by that time anyway. I realised the only reason I happened to be there was to connect with the exotic little angel.

We found a dark corner at the back of the hall, behind the dense crowd, sat on my jacket spread over some piled-up plinths, and started kissing. She just wanted me there, and I decided to drop the "guilt trip" right out. It was like being in a warm nest and courting a bird of paradise just before mating with her. By the time the concert ended, we were welded together, laughing, kissing, embracing, and discovering each other.

As we walked towards the overcrowded trams, Ziyo Crazy came over and asked if I could put up some friends from Osijek, Croatia. I had never been to Osijek. My place made a perfect option for them. We managed to get into an overcrowded tram with four Croatian guests. As we got off at Skenderija, we had to run for at least a kilometre to catch the last bus to my suburb. My angel did all this with us. It was clear the only reason she came out of the house that night was to hook up with me. She only lived a five-minute walk up the road and was fine to walk home alone.

As I boarded the bus with my guests and lost sight of her delicate small figure, it felt like waking up from a dream. I wasn't sure if she, and what had happened earlier, was real. I loved what happened but hated the situation I found myself in. After all, she was Baba's girlfriend. "Baba is a womaniser, and he doesn't deserve her," I thought. "Has she taken a ride on his donkey, and if she has, what am I going to do with her?" Clearly, I didn't know what I was getting myself into, but I also felt that Baba wouldn't feel any guilt if he were in my shoes. He never hesitated to take pussy right in front of my friends' noses at every opportunity.

"Why should I? Fuck it, enjoy it while it's there. The girl is mad about you, so see what happens," I concluded as the city lights flickered and danced with the bus negotiating curves, potholes, and the ridge ahead of my suburb.

Osijek girls weren't much fun, a bit snobbish with their mix of Bosnian and Croatian dialect (a bit surprising to hear). They loved my place, and we stayed up chatting, playing music tapes and talking freak topics: police brutality, drugs, parties, bands we liked, politics, literature, alternative realities, India...

I had a great time with the "princess". One time, we hitchhiked at the edge of the city intending to take a walk through my childhood zone.

Sarajevo's Elusive Spring

We went into the hills above my village and observed it from a distance, with the mountain behind it and forested hills around us. She behaved like a fairy-tale princess, fascinated, observant, wanting to know about Bogumil gravestones arranged like a necklace at the rim of the village, and wanting to memorise the house where I was born.

On the way there, we almost got a lift with my neighbour and, who else, but my father. They were going to get some fruit trees from a nursery a few kilometres up the road. They recognised me and stopped, but I refused the lift since it was virtually useless. They didn't get a chance to meet or question the princess.

Other days, we went out to the movies, walked in the park, went to the Nightingale Bar and Club Cactus. She was so young and so sweet. We kissed and laughed a lot. She spoke an eloquent version of Bosnian, had aristocratic family members from the past, originating from Tuzla in the north of Bosnia.

Once, I walked off the bus with my cousin Ramiza from the White Mountain. She was dressed as mountain women dressed in those days. She had Turkish-style *shalvare*, a Muslim modesty scarf over her head, black rubber shoes and colourful woollen hand-knitted socks. She wore a handmade pullover she had knitted herself out of the wool she spun and dyed.

Ramiza was so dear to me, and we happened to be going in the same direction from my place in the suburbs. Her family had brought sheep to graze the last green pastures before winter, as they must have done since pre-Roman times. Ramiza spoke loudly in a heavy village accent as we came face to face with my princess and her mum, whom I had never seen before. I held Ramiza's hand gently and stopped to say hi to the princess, who introduced me to her mum.

Ramiza was extremely shy. As I introduced her, she stood well away at a safe distance, red-cheeked and a little confused. It was very brief and felt a bit strange. I certainly didn't know if her mum knew about me, if the princess had things to explain, or if the princess herself realised who I really was. I never knew that myself.

Sami Tischler

Part of me always stayed in the village of my birth, with the people and relatives there. The connection is so powerful and not only in my heart. Most of the Bosnian population came from its mountainous villages and quickly forgot their origins, or tried to disguise them by adopting urban dress, culture, language, and behaviour. I was very proud of my Bogumil and Muslim origins.

My semi-nomadic relatives were a dying breed in Socialist culture. They had the status of Gypsies, exotic but undesirable. They were expected to assimilate and accept change. In time it turned out that all those changes that made them neglect their traditional way of life and values became their demise. New industries offered economic prosperity, medical care, and educational opportunities, but destroyed forests, water and air quality, brought illness, bad diet, alcoholism. Finally, they brought destruction by those who inspired and fought the revolution, which had once brought Socialist ideology and prosperity to all.

One of my close relatives left Sarajevo during the Bosnian war and decided to fight alongside his relatives and friends from the village of his birth. Vahid died in the war, showing great courage and connection with them. Sometime before the war, when he was visiting the village of Dujmovići, the place of his mother's origin, he did what was unheard of. Villagers held a party at the spring as they would have done for centuries. This is the closest village to Ledići, where part of this story started and where Karlo and I got "arrested".

There was music and dance in the semi-darkness under the full moon on a summer's night. One of his distant cousins, who had become a policeman in the regional centre Trnovo, decided to break the party around the official "closing time". Nobody had ever heard of such nonsense in the village. Everyone was there, and noise pollution was never going to be a problem. The event was a sort of house party in the open. There was no alcohol or amplified music, and the whole thing was seen as harassment by a power-hungry policeman.

Sarajevo's Elusive Spring

Vahid would have dealt with such pricks daily in Sarajevo, where he had lived most of his young life. His brother Omer was a young policeman at the time too. Things started getting out of hand when the policeman threatened someone with arrest. Vahid grabbed somebody's jacket, threw it over the policeman's head and held it tight while a couple of boys gave the off-duty policeman the beating of his life. This technique was known as a "blanket job" in the Yugoslav National Army (JNA). It was used to send a message to individuals in power without exposing the perpetrators. It was done at a time when the majority decided that someone had gone too far in abusing their official power. It was risky business and treated as an act of aggression against authority, even against the government.

The party was over. Revellers scattered into the darkness and back to their homes and neighbouring villages, leaving the policeman to find his own way home. The whole affair didn't end there. Police turned up in force the next day and investigated the event, questioning those reported as witnesses. They were barking up the wrong tree. These people were the children of those brave villagers who had refused to be humiliated by communist guerrillas during the last Civil War (WWII), and when attacked, managed to defend themselves. They were all given death sentences by communist leaders who planned and ordered burning and pillaging. Their mistrust of the system never fully evaporated, and this was another example of their resistance. Everyone knew Vahid, and they all knew who was involved in the incident, but they decided to keep it to themselves.

As I said, I don't know what her mother thought about our street encounter. I did manage to squeeze out a small "Good day" and a nod of the head to her at the time. Coincidentally, I had not seen the princess for a while, and one day Baba turned up. He had been deported from Holland. It appeared that his work and residential permits had expired, and the record of long-term unemployment the authorities held there didn't help his case.

When he came back, things had changed. For some reason, Edith didn't want him in her house anymore. She had heard enough screams from women impaled by Baba and was trying to take control of what was going on in her home. She was tired of police raids, people coming and going, loose women hanging around, and an empty fridge and pantry. She had had enough of playing Jesus and trying to feed everyone with a loaf of bread and a jar of *ajvar*. The veggie garden we planted grew weeds and waited for someone to clean it up. Everything people damaged or broke never got repaired, and the place started to look like an abandoned drug den. She didn't want Baba back.

Chuck wasn't going to argue, as he never did anyway. He would just pick a strand of his curly hair, twist it around his forefinger and stare at nothing. Eventually, he would shake his head and walk out, often disappearing for days. Baba managed to find a share house with some art students, worked as a model at the Academy of Art, where young females came to life-draw and admire his oversized penis.

The princess went to school near a park where we often gathered. By then, I hadn't seen her for a long time and wasn't sure if she knew he had come back. Although unsure of my status in her heart, I realised that I had fallen in love with her. I feared that our affair might be at the end of its short life. She appeared out of reach for weeks. I wasn't going to show my desperation and wait in front of her school just to get a fair share of humiliation. I was getting too old for that. Baba was back, and I felt I was going to be pushed aside. I never had a chance to discuss this scenario with her and assumed that her absence meant a break-up.

One day, I sat on a garden wall in the park near her school with a bunch of people. It was my favourite place in the city. Busts of Ivo Andrić, Branko Ćopić, Isak Samokovlija, Mak Dizdar and Meša Selimović, my favourite Bosnian writers, were permanent features there. Baba was there too, with another group of friends a little further away. I was surrounded by a few girls, all good friends, and one particularly keen on me. Out of the corner of my eye, I saw the princess coming across the park. She looked like a colourful butterfly in the summer sky. Her hair flowing, black eyes shining from the distance, immaculately dressed, swinging across the space like a ballroom dancer, taking it over as she went. All eyes were on her.

I pretended not to pay attention and continued flirting with the girls. They too became aware of her presence. I was devastated when I saw her going to Baba's group and giving him a big bear hug and a brief kiss. He got up, and they went away. I froze and felt like a limp dick. All my frivolity was gone, and the girls soon decided they had somewhere else to go.

I sat there rolling my tobacco, my old beaten-up tobacco box next to me on the wall, puffing smoke into the sky, inhaling deeply and exhaling clouds. All my ships had sunk, and I was sinking with them. A small delicate hand picked up the box, and the princess materialised next to me. She flew in soundless like an angel, placed her hand around my neck, folded her little body into my lap, and offered her hot lips to my smoke flavoured mouth. We kissed like never before. It felt as if we had met again after a long absence, but afraid it could be the last kiss ever.

"I am all yours if you still want me," she whispered as she kissed my earlobe and licked my neck behind it. The warmth of her wet tongue went right through every cell of my being like a perfect electric shock.

"You have no idea how much I do want you and how wonderful it feels to have you here in my lap."

She wiggled her little bum deeper into my crotch and purred sweet words into my ears.

"If you want to know why I disappeared for weeks, I can tell you."

"Of course I do." I was keen to know now that everything suddenly felt safe and romantic.

"My grandfather fell ill, and we all went to see him a couple of weeks ago. I tried to call you, but a woman on the phone insisted that nobody by the name of UFO lives there."

Sami Tischler

I started laughing, because that was exactly what happened when other friends tried to contact me by phone. Most of them only knew my nickname and were puzzled by my mother's answer. However, my mother had no idea my friends called me UFO, and the term didn't make sense to her.

"That was my mum. She doesn't know my nickname and gets agitated by those calls and friends with no manners."

"I was nice on the phone but didn't get time to explain. She cut me off. You know me, I am a nice girl."

We kissed more and nestled our bodies together on the warm stone wall.

Her bones, limbs and muscles fitted perfectly into my lap.

Sarajevo's Elusive Spring

R.

My affair with the princess went its natural course for some time and included her visits to my love den. Nothing much happened there, we cuddled half-naked, she wasn't ready to go all the way and I loved her innocent beauty, dark skin, and her ability to melt my heart with her sweet words, fragility, and need for the safety found in cuddles with my tall muscular body.

One day we got news that Rašo and Bernarda were living together in Sevojno, Rašo's town near T.U. Hardi and I decided to visit. The old narrow-gauge railway line to Višegrad was gone by that time. We made it across somehow, must have hitched a ride across Romanija's highlands. There we were at Rašo's place. Bernarda was so excited about our visit. We had a bit of hash and spent a lot of time in his room listening to music, eating, drinking, and laughing our heads off. His mum and Rada, his sister, cooked for us. Rada was herself, friendly, more open, and freer with me than ever. Bernarda made jokes about us and the fact that I wasn't reacting to Rada's hints. I realised that she knew what I didn't, being a woman and Rada's confidante.

At some stage, Rada and I went out behind their house into a secluded spot, sat on a woodpile and smoked a small joint. She told me about her breakup with a boyfriend of many years. They were serious, the breakup was painful, and she felt like living in limbo, at home, not working, not going out. I always had feelings for her, but didn't need complications of distance, old friendship with her brother and certainly unsure of religious and ethnic issues we were always having to consider in our turbulent society. Somehow, we ended up cuddled behind the house against a limewashed wall and passionately kissing for a long time. Once we came back into the room, they all understood that we had started our romantic journey. Rada didn't hide her feelings and over the following few days of our visit expressed them openly in front of her mother and the rest of the "crowd".

We went out one night to the "Hall of Culture" dance party with the same band I danced to during my Army days. It was a blast. We all had a great time. Rada and I got very close and intimate within the semidarkness of a crowded hall, dancing, cuddling, and kissing. She discreetly pointed out her ex-boyfriend. Rada didn't hide her affections for me and blatantly ignored the boy. We parted the next day. I had my job and my princess to go back to. I invited Rada to visit me in Sarajevo, unclear if she would accept it and how I would find time and space for her.

The princess wasn't really a girl I saw a grand future with. She was young and had a whole life ahead of her. Rada was a lovely girl and could commit herself to much more but wasn't necessarily a woman I had that much in common with. At the time I was fascinated with the idea of living on the land in some remote location, I didn't know where exactly. So many open-ended possibilities in front of me. Anyhow, I was worried about how I would spend time with her without destroying my relationship with the princess. I was hoping Rada would just forget about it.

We spoke on the phone often. I called from work. My home phone sat in my parent's hallway and there was no chance for private phone time. She wanted to come. "That would be great," I said and regretted it right away. I knew someone was going to get hurt. "What the heck, we live in the age of free love and should be able to tolerate parallel relationships. Why not, it could be fun!"

Rada turned up one Friday night at the bus station. She was so happy to see me, and I loved her happy nature. She looked great, brought homemade food and cakes and a small suitcase. I never had a girlfriend who travelled with a suitcase before. We boarded a public bus and came to my apartment where she served us a beautiful meal. We ate cakes, drank a couple of glasses of wine, laughed a lot, and ignored my parents' presence upstairs. It was getting late. We had kissed before and kissed in intervals this time but didn't go much further than we did on any previous occasion. I was anxious about how this night was going to evolve.

Sarajevo's Elusive Spring

I gave her private time in the bedroom to get herself organised, half prepared to sleep on the couch. She made some commotion in there and after some time I could hear her call: "UFO, you can enter, I am ready." I walked into the room; she had her silk shawl over a bed lamp. Her small suitcase had its lid open against the wall, her colourful things displayed in it. "This is the first time that a woman moved into my space and life in a serious way," I thought. Her smiling face surrounded by curls of her brown hair lay on my pillow and the rest of her under the eiderdown. I stood there aware of the mystique that she had set up for me exclusively.

"Aren't you going to join me, I am keeping a warm spot here, next to me?"

"I cannot wait to join you, darling, this is so sweet, I am coming."

I took my clothes off, kept my T-shirt and briefs on, lifted the cover and there she was, a beautifully packaged female beauty as erotic as they come. No other woman had prepared herself like that for me before. It reminded me of Baba's preparations for his meeting with the princess, months before. Rada wore a transparent nightie, with tiny underpants showing through lace. The nightie was so minimally "symbolic" that it showed her carefully shaved body, manicured and detailed for this event.

I felt so proud and so did He, shamefully saluting in honour of her mature erotic gesture. The room wasn't warm enough to prolong the scene. Although I could have stood there forever enjoying the sight of her generous well-shaped melons, shapely strong legs, and the magic secret spot in the middle, promising an amazing night. That is exactly what it turned out to be.

Rada had no inhibitions regarding sex and modesty. She had done this before and understood her body and her needs. She held my penis without any shame, kissed passionately, and offered her swollen nipples to my lips. She let me undress her carefully and let me enjoy every part of her hot body, removed my clothing skilfully when she decided it was the right time. She mounted my penis effortlessly and rode it skilfully, ensuring not to miss her own pleasure and guiding me to hold back to a perfect climax. Her breasts bounced in my face, and she took my hands gently, placed them on her nipples, later her hips from where they happily slipped onto her buttocks moving up and down, helping her to enjoy every stroke of my swollen penis. We climaxed in a fury amongst her mind-boggling circular movements. She had her head thrown backwards, her breasts and nipples pointing to the ceiling, her hands and nails in my chest, firmly locked as she orgasmed. She was silent all the way and apart from our breathing out of control we were so well behaved.

The rest of the four days she stayed, we moved between my den and the Malešići "commune" where she met Edith and Chuck. They didn't know where to fit her. She was so nice, fashionably dressed, domesticated, immaculately made up and smelled expensive. She stood out from her surroundings, especially there, but her warmth and spontaneity won them over. Before they knew it, she was telling dirty jokes and talking knowledgeably about the music we all listened to. She discussed Kafka, Dostoyevsky, Sartre, Andrić, Crnjanski and Kapor with great insight and understanding. They were so impressed they invited her to stay.

I wasn't keen to stay and hardly ever stayed overnight before. The house had physical traces of too many people and although Edith did a lot to make it into a home, she had no physical or mental strength to do it on her own. We left and caught the last bus back to my suburb on the way to Sarajevo. All the way home we were squeezed together in the semidarkness of an old bus, vibrated by its massive rumbling engine, watching the moonlit frozen land and river Bosna gliding by. I felt her body next to mine, carrying memories of the previous night mixed with the excitement and anticipation of what was going to follow at home.

The arrival home was perfect. Lights were out and parents asleep. I started a small kerosene heater which gave my bedroom a primitive feel and set the scene for something new and mysterious. I boiled some water and made us cups of rosehip tea infused with a generous amount of rum. Its flavour and effect, combined with whispers of burning kerosene and the warmth coming off the heater, made us strip most of the winter layers we had on. Rada was left wearing a long cotton shirt and woollen leggings up to her knees. Her nipples pointed forward through the fabric, exaggerated by the dim light and strong shadow contrasts. I had to touch and play with them while we kissed.

She took my hand and walked to the bed where she helped me undress, took my penis, already starting to harden in her hand, and played with it until I was completely ready and hard. I had her shirt unbuttoned, and my hand in another pair of lacy knickers looking for her slippery lips. She appeared ready too but had a different plan in mind. She sat on the edge of my bed and held my hard tool in both hands for a bit, investigating its circumcised features, poked her tongue at it and gave it a masterful sensual treatment. It didn't take long before I was getting close to shooting my load, but Rada wouldn't want that to happen that fast. She gave up playing with my cock, fell back on the bed and offered her open legs to me.

I went on my knees, slipped her knickers off in a swift move and buried my face into her honey pot. I don't think I knew exactly what I was meant to do. I had learnt fingering techniques by then and could feel what a girl enjoyed, but having my mouth and tongue there still felt a bit disorientating. She held the back of my head gently and led me to find her sensitive areas, encouraging my strokes when they felt good. I loved every moment of it, and it diverted my mind from the excitement I had felt a minute ago. That was the best part about lovemaking, holding back, relaxing the excitement, and building it up again, extending the pleasure and the intensity of it.

Before Rada, I was lucky to have satisfied anyone in my short life as an incompetent and naïve lover. I couldn't believe what she did next. Since she was nearly ready and knew that I wasn't going to last, she pulled herself up on the bed, rolled on her side facing the wall and away from me. Just the sight of her naked back, her hair spread across the pillow and her buttocks in the semidarkness gave me shivers. My dick wasn't in its best shape but after I lay behind her and she took it in her hand, leading it into the warmth of her anus and the wetness of her vagina, it hardened within seconds.

I had only ever had Helga from behind. I had a sense of being with her for a few moments. Generous-sized buttocks and Rada's strong legs, as well as her firm breasts, nipples and the size of her compact body, felt almost the same. I had my hands on her nipples, my tongue and lips on her neck and ear, I could hear her sounds of pleasure so close and feel her pushes against my belly and onto my solid rod. When we culminated, it felt as if I had her impaled on a long hot pole and she was there absorbing my pulsing semen, shivering.

What a graceful moment! For me, a young lover, it was an overwhelming sense of pride and a powerful awareness of newly acquired skills in lovemaking. Yes, Rada taught me a lot. I was such a greenhorn. The memory of Helga and the experience of lovemaking with her couldn't match the passion of the two young lovers, fascinated by one another and connected at a deeper level.

Princess and R.

Yes, there was a feeling of guilt and betrayal about having to hide her and lie to the princess about her existence. I had to explain my disappearances during those weekends to her. My reasons didn't sound very convincing, and she was trying to hang on to me. She even volunteered to come for a visit to my basement, which I was trying to avoid with an overwhelming feeling of guilt. I was afraid of her female instinct sensing Rada's invisible presence there.

So, she came one night by herself. I waited for her at the bus stop, one before the town centre, just to avoid the unnecessary attention of all those curious small minds living in my suburb. We had a similar cuddle as any time before, not much different from those we'd had in dark passages of the city when we met there. There was a novelty I hadn't encountered before. She had her pad firmly fitted. It was meant to be a try-hard chastity belt. I found it funny because I only ever acted with consent and never forced unwanted or undesired sex.

After a wild weekend with Rada, the whole affair appeared childish and immature. I was still in love with her but knew that our sweet relationship was nearing an inevitable conclusion. I just didn't know how to deal with the one who gave so much and the other who would if she could. One was serious, a masterful lover, knew how to please her man, had her heart broken already and looked to long-term commitment. The other just enjoyed having a cool older boyfriend, already bored with her teenage admirers, unconcerned with the freedom I had in the world I had created for myself.

I also felt that life was closing in on me. I lived at my parents', worked full-time, met a woman ready to get married, had a series of relationships with very young women, fun, short-lived and leading nowhere other than heartbreak for fragile young souls. Things took their own course, and I hardly made any wise decisions on my own. Within a couple of intensive months playing my immature games between two gorgeous women, all three of us ended up with broken hearts when I decided to break up with both. I don't know why I did that. I just couldn't play this unfair cheating game anymore.

I was going out alone, spending time with friends in bars, searching for land in remote villages to the country's south on weekends, dreaming of living in a stone house beside a small vineyard and a fig tree at the back of the house. I had a plan to buy a donkey in Herzegovina and walk across and along the coast to Kosovo or even Albania. The donkey would have carried my camping gear and made me look like a local traveller to always curious peasants and militia. The range of mountains stretching along the coast appeared a real challenge, and I thought that walking on tracks between old Bogumil villages was the most marvellous thing you could waste your life on.

None of the girls I was seeing would have understood the reasons for something as profound and ridiculous as that. I started avoiding girls who were seeking my company unless they wanted to talk books, music or travel, and didn't have to go home by 9.00 pm. I discovered a whole new world out there, a world not necessarily interested in me as a man but more in what I had in my head, where my shoes had walked and what my eyes had seen. I also discovered that there were women out there who had so much more in them than looks, fragility and innocence. I felt that I was learning important aspects of life without moving my arse very far.

The city was changing, or perhaps it had never changed since the Ottomans left. I was just growing older with it. Thin layers of raw life stuck to me along the way, deepened my emotions and thoughts, and gave meaning to the simplest experiences, like a conversation, a dance in the semidarkness of a nightclub, or the touch of a woman who wasn't even interested in intercourse and penetration.

I made another trip across the range to visit Rada. Inspired by my stories of living on the land, we went to inspect a couple of charming properties on the Serbian side of the River Drina. They were typically small mudbrick houses on hillsides, surrounded by orchards and bushland bordered paddocks. Most of the villages were semi abandoned, as they were in Bosnia. An occasional old man or woman lived in a house in desperate need of repair to its roof, façade, fence, doors or windows.

There weren't any *stećci* in sight. It didn't feel like Herzegovina and its stone houses and ruins set amongst stone-fenced fields, windswept bonsai oak forests and broken shapes of limestone rock growing out of the rich red soil. Back at Rada's house I felt an expectation to take things further, beyond the casual relationship we were enjoying. I don't think Rada was unhappy with what we had, but Bernarda was desperate for the fresh urban breeze, and I was the one who was going to bring it. She was already bored with village life, Rašo's mother and her house.

She would have rather lived in T.U., but they couldn't afford the rent. She had already managed to have an affair with a guy Rašo couldn't stand, and how could he? Bernarda went out, got drunk, spent the night with a guy in the town where everyone knew everyone else, completely forgetting that this wasn't the Croatian capital, Zagreb. I liked Bernarda a lot, but I wasn't going to sacrifice my freedom and prolong her agony for a bit longer when she would eventually dump all of us and walk away to yet another sweetheart she may have dug up from somewhere, anywhere.

I felt like a real prick as I started ignoring Rada's calls or shortening our conversations when she tried to rekindle our hot affair. She decided to come and see me. I had broken up with the princess already. There was no real reason, and it wasn't triggered by a fight. I just couldn't pretend that our fairytale relationship made sense any longer. I told her that she needed to find someone younger she could enjoy more. I wasn't going to keep lying to her or substitute her with more mature and liberal women as friends or lovers. I was just being honest, and I knew I was hurting her as well as myself, but I had to get this done at the time.

Something inside was telling me that I had to come clean with myself and my lovers because I was expecting bigger things to happen. I didn't know what they were, but it seemed I was consolidating my accounts. I believed that everything led to life somewhere on the land.

I felt that by leaving space around me I was going to let things happen and that these relationships I was invested in were just getting in the way.

Rada came on a bus, and I met her at the station. She had her sweet small suitcase and looked like a doll who had just come out of the hair salon. This time I didn't need to hide her existence, and we went straight to bars in the Old Town where we both got properly drunk. She met my cousin Gev and she liked him. Gev was the most generous drunk you could ever meet. He wanted us to come and spend the night at his place and get Rada to meet his wife Sada. That wouldn't have been appropriate. Just imagine three of us drunks coming home after midnight to the basement of my Aunt Goldie's place. It was dangerous enough bringing her back to my own den.

My parents never really approved of my visitors and didn't think highly of any girl who crossed my threshold, not to mention their religion or ethnicity. The whole affair was immoral to them, and other issues just placed more weight on my conscience and guilt. By the time we made it home in a taxi, we were both completely out of it and couldn't wait to eat each other up. That is exactly what we did as soon as we got under the covers. She was giving it all to me, and I responded in the same way. I felt that she understood this was to be our last time and she wasn't going to hold back. I was determined to give her everything I had, knowing there wouldn't be more.

She let me ride her hard in a variety of tangled positions as we tried to extract maximum pleasure from the alcohol-fuelled madness. Then she got on top of me and moved herself in a fury of passion, reckless and violent at times, biting, scratching my skin, sucking on my neck like a vampire. As we collapsed, bathing in sweat and falling asleep, I had no idea where I was or what exactly had just happened. Some of it was the toxic effect of alcohol, but some of it was our two comatose souls and bodies starting to say goodbye to one another.

Sarajevo's Elusive Spring

When I woke up, I felt hungover, exhausted and used up. It wasn't a good feeling to start a day with someone who had just given you all of themselves. I decided to take Rada to Malešići commune and my friends Edith and Chuck. They were so happy to see her. They told me that she was the best thing that had happened to me in a long time. It was the wrong time and the wrong thing to say. We were about to part ways silently.

Chuck had a lump of hash a visiting dealer gave him for staying at the commune. We rolled joints, laughed, spent the day walking along the river Bosna and eating food we had brought. Rada spent some time with Edith, and we both enjoyed the day. It was great to be in the company of friends, genuine friends, the best friends I have ever had. The sad part was that we were spending our last day together.

Edith cooked a cake in Rada's honour for the evening meal. It could have been so lovely, but neither of us was in a romantic mood. An untold decision hung in the air, and the euphoric effect of THC had long worn off, making the world look greyer and darker than it really was. We arrived home late at night, and as we cuddled together, I felt her body's shivers and spasms against mine. Her face was wet, and she was crying in silence.

I told her that I loved her, and I meant it, yet it felt like an act of cold cruelty. Deep inside I understood that my life needed space to evolve further into the less familiar and riskier sphere. I just had no heart to drag Rada along this path. I still believe that I made the right decision, or perhaps the decision had already been made for me. There are those moments when our destiny takes its own path, and we must follow. This appeared to be one of those moments. Overwhelmed by sadness, our cuddled bodies cried themselves to sleep.

I escorted Rada to the bus stop the next morning. I thought we were never going to see each other again.

Sami Tischler

Free in Sarajevo, Heading East Again

Finally free of a stable relationship in Sarajevo, I felt light and dangerous. I had already casually applied for Permanent Residence in Australia. It was just another in a series of coincidental events when Hardi and I heard from his brother that the Australian Embassy was advertising and recruiting young migrants who held electrical and building qualifications. We fitted the profile perfectly. Hardi was trained in Civil Engineering, and I was qualified in Electrical Engineering and working in my profession.

We sent a written request for the documentation and received packs of forms and information booklets in return. We both filled them in and sent them back, accompanied by the documents they requested: work references, police record summaries, qualification transcripts, etc. Time went by and I received a request for more documentation. Hardi didn't. We figured out that I had been selected to continue since I was employed and working in my profession. I sent more documents back, and by this time I had almost forgotten about the Embassy.

We had originally hoped to seek fortune in Australia together, earn some money, and travel through Asia, possibly fly to South America. Now that Hardi wasn't in the picture, I was losing interest. For some strange reason, I decided to continue with the process and see where it would lead, just for the fun of it. It had potential as another option, small door opening. Besides, I had been searching for land with limited funds. I thought that earning big money somewhere in "the West" (rather, the far southeast) could put me in a better buying position.

In the summer of 1979, free of any serious commitment and looking at how to spend my first ever paid annual leave, my young fan "Ziyo Crazy" asked to travel with me somewhere, anywhere. I wasn't too keen. Ziyo's nickname should tell you a bit about him. He started off as an underaged hippy, hanging around the "Cactus" with girls even younger than him. They looked like portable harem around him. Then punk came through and broke all music and cultural conventions. All eyes were on the English scene, but great punk bands were surfacing all around the country taking everyone by surprise.

Ziyo found himself somewhere between a freak and a punk, which I liked about him. Many of my freak friends had already attached themselves to a progressive band or two and wouldn't venture any further. My idea of music was that it had an inexhaustible potential for exploration. I am so glad I never abandoned that idea. There is always more music around the corner, and more of it being made as we speak, and I want to hear it all, or as much as I can possibly digest.

I met Ziyo at the "Nightingale" bar frequently, and he kept pushing the idea of joining me on a trip. I could tell it meant so much to him. I suggested that we could hitchhike to Istanbul during our summer holiday. He was so happy about the idea that he kept bringing beer to my table until I had a hard time getting up. Both of us were working at the time. Somehow, I couldn't visualise Ziyo sweating in the workplace as much as he couldn't imagine me slaving in an office. I had my doubts about how long I'd last there, but it suited me for the time being.

I was really hoping to find a house with some land in a deserted village and try to live off the land. I had a decent lump of money saved, but purchasing land wasn't easy. Due to frequent changes of government and land ownership in the last 100 years, purchasing land in former Yugoslavia had its complications. Private land was often divided amongst the family, and everyone knew what they owned, but deeds were left unchanged, which meant you could not transfer land ownership if you had bought it. It was notorious in remote areas of Bosnia, and I wasn't getting anywhere with my intensive search.

We took off in June during the collective holiday season and made it to Sofia by catching free rides. In Sofia we caught the "smugglers' coach" on its way from Novi Pazar to Istanbul. The main item everyone carried was boxes of nails, in high demand in Turkey and plentiful in industrialised Yugoslavia at the time.

We had a great week in Istanbul, hanging around mosques, Aya Sofia, the Blue Mosque, and the Pudding Shop. At the Pudding Shop, we struck up a conversation with a shady-looking Turk. He said he could give us a good deal on some Turkish hash. We told him we were interested and followed him to a small back lane. I didn't think it was a good idea, but the prospect of smoking a few joints while in Istanbul was too tempting.

The last time I was in Istanbul, I had been in the company of a friendly couple from Belgrade. I'd met the young man from Kosovo and his girlfriend at Sultan Ahmet Hotel in Tehran. The ceiling in my room was decorated with fresh bullet holes. I was coming back from India by land. Iranian Islamic revolution had started as a massive civil unrest. The army came out and shot at protesters while I chilled in Himalayas and smoked *chillums* with Indian *sadhus*. We were waiting for dawn at a checkpoint on the outskirts of Tehran. The city was in a curfew. None was permitted to enter during the night. I was the only Westerner on the bus and driver offered his opium pipe while we waited. "I've been smoking every time we stopped." he proudly declared. He took us through the rugged mountain ranges between Mashhad and Tehran in an overnight trip completely stoned. I was asleep on the bus most of that time. Iran had imposed draconian laws against narcotics trade and use. I couldn't believe that drug use was so commonplace amongst population.

The friendly couple had gone as far as Tehran and planned to smuggle a quantity of hash back into Yugoslavia. They had it worked out: buy it in Istanbul from a safe source, board the Orient Express, remove a panel in the toilet, hide the hash in the cavity, refit the panel and observe what happened at border crossings from a safe distance. If safe, once back on home territory, they would recover the dope from the cavity and leave the train.

Sarajevo's Elusive Spring

We found a shop owner in the Old Bazaar, originally from Kosovo. He looked clean, businesslike, and respectable. We walked to his home nearby. When we got there his young wife was sitting on the sofa bed, breastfeeding an infant. We sat in the kitchen, drank some tea, and waited for her to finish. She took the baby to the bedroom, and the shopkeeper pulled the seat up as a lid. Below, he had a couple of kilograms of uncompressed hash in a heavy-duty clear plastic bag. A set of scales sat beside it. They worked out a deal, weighed about 200 grams, packaged it, and we walked back together to the Old Bazaar. We parted as best friends. Later I found out their plan had worked. Our mutual friends in Belgrade confirmed seeing the man in the street.

This time, though, we were in a deserted lane with the shady guy, looking nervously around while he held a chunk the size of a matchbox of what looked like hash, wrapped in clear plastic. I was holding 100 DM, as nervous as him, and we were about to do the swap. Somehow, I felt the whole thing was a scam. You typically ended up buying hair dye known as *khanna*, which looked very similar in colour. I pulled my hand back and walked away with my 100 DM. The shady guy hung onto Ziyo and tried to convince him the deal was genuine, but I had already made it back to a busy street and the deal was off.

This time, buying only a small quantity of dope turned out to be an ugly and dangerous undertaking. I did try to find the shop, but they all looked the same, and buying such a small amount of hash would have been embarrassing. Luckily, there were other freaks who managed to get some, and we smoked a few joints with them at the hotel where we stayed. I know it meant a lot to Ziyo, who bragged about it back in Sarajevo.

We hitched rides along the Sea of Marmara, stopped at a small Turkish seaside village, and mixed with a bunch of teenagers from Istanbul on holiday. Ziyo, a born entertainer, amused everyone with a few words of English, German, and plenty of Russian he knew. Girls were falling over in all directions, and kids brought food and sweets to the beach where we stayed.

I cannot say I had the greatest time, my jealousy got in the way, but I had to give it to him, he had a gift, and I had to learn a thing or two about impressing girls. Not that I wasn't able to play a fool's game, but I thought it the most boring method to get to a girl's heart and ultimately into her pants. That's exactly why I wasn't getting much attention, and he was getting plenty.

The small Turkish seaside town started to look like Sarajevo, where we both dated young girls who had to be at home just when things got exciting. We'd both seen too much of that back home. On weekends, parents of the teenagers came from Istanbul, and they weren't allowed to hang around us anymore. Ziyo was suffering a kind of cold-turkey withdrawal, with no girls in sight. It was time to leave.

The next day we crossed the border and entered Greece. Beaches were full of Western tourists, Greeks so happy to take their money and we were nobodies there. Everything had to be paid for. We hung around a festival site dedicated to the god Bacchus and managed to get in at half price, only an hour before it closed. Inside the half-empty site we drank as much as we could from the free-for-all barrels and managed to catch the end of a great performance by a Greek folk band, while the revellers danced the night away.

By the time we got into it, the show was nearly over, and we left the site heavily drunk on cheap wine we'd paid dearly for and shortchanged for the lack of entertainment. The following day we suffered the worst hangover on the beach, no friendly girls around, unbearable sun overhead, and a cheap version of Greek burek for lunch that just sat in your stomach like a rock.

I had fantasies of visiting the monasteries on Mount Athos. Their monks looked so much like Indian sadhus, and it was a romantic, hash infused idea that could have been amazing, but for one thing. Both of us, my friend Ziyo and I, were Bosnian Muslim freaks, circumcised virtually at birth. Just imagine us on a red carpet on Mount Athos, greeting monks with *Selam Aleykum*. Perfect opportunity to lose what was left of our pricks.

By the end of the following day, we made it to Thessaloniki, an ancient port city on the Aegean Sea. The major Macedonian River Vardar drains into a grand delta nearby. We met a Pakistani sailor at the park near the docks and talked about hash prices in Sarajevo and the lack of it. We plotted about smuggling a large quantity into the country through our newly discovered sea connection.

He said he'd do it and confirmed that his ship sailed into Dalmatian ports frequently. "We sail to Rijeka at least once a year. I'll bring a kilo in," he assured us, adding, "That shouldn't be any problem, it's easy." It sounded great, too good to be true, however unbelievable. I wrote Ahmet my postal address on a used cigarette packet.

We spent the night at the park listening to the bustle of the port, the sounds of horns from large sea vessels, and the comings and goings all around us. The next day went slowly. Cars leaving the city, overloaded with families returning from their summer holidays in Greece, had no space for two hitchhikers. International cargo semitrailers, so close to the border, hardly ever considered taking an additional traveller. The whole day on the road took us only as far as Gevgelija.

Macedonian youth at a disco in the evening softened our sense of hopelessness from the long road ahead and the slow progress of that day. Although hardly anyone there had seen Sarajevo or Bosnia, we seemed to be the centre of attention amongst boys and girls. Not many young travellers hung around places like Gevgelija. The most exotic visitors would have been unlucky soldiers from other Yugoslav states serving their national military service there.

We slept outside, and with all the attention we had received before closing time, it was disappointing that no one made any accommodation offers. That's why we considered our sleeping bags our most treasured possessions. In those days, I hardly went anywhere outside Sarajevo without one.

Sami Tischler

Next morning, we decided to hitch rides separately. We knew that from there on, road luck was going to take over and send us in unpredictable directions. I took off first and made it successfully to the Macedonian capital, Skopje.

I was walking along a tree-lined avenue at the entrance to the city with my shoulder bag and a rolled sleeping bag strapped to it. The previous lift wasn't ideal. I had to walk all the way through the city to its opposite end before I could hitch rides further towards Sarajevo. The morning was still fresh. I was pacing at a good tempo, keen to get through the city before the late-morning heat.

Out of the corner of my eye, I noticed a car had pulled up. A voice called in my direction, and I turned sideways. I looked at a small Citroën under a large load on its roof rack. A girl's head poked out of the window, calling and waving. A few seconds later a tall, handsome blond stranger stepped out of the car, and I recognised Wolfgang, the silversmith and jewellery maker I had met in Germany the previous winter.

I couldn't believe it. We were both fascinated by the coincidence as we exchanged bear hugs and short greetings. I found out they were returning to Germany and planning to follow the Dalmatian Coast all the way to Slovenia. They were about to drive across Kosovo, through Sandžak and Montenegro on the way there. This must have been one of the most exotic and hazardous drives one could have chosen through Yugoslavia.

Having a local friend as a guide and meeting me on the road the way they did, was nothing short of a miracle. They must have felt like they'd just met a guardian angel in broad daylight in the middle of a godless Yugoslav socialist state. Wolfgang was travelling with a blonde woman. They easily made space on the back seat for me. My "baggage" didn't need much space anyway. Before long we were on our way through Skopje, the Kosovo plains, and the city of Peć.

By midday we were ascending through the mountain range to Rožaje in Sandžak. I spotted a great camping spot by a crystal-clear mountain

Sarajevo's Elusive Spring

creek, just outside the town. They were surprised we could camp just like that outside an allocated campsite. Rožaje didn't have one anyway, and I didn't care what the local militia might think about our decision. I would have been more cautious if I'd travelled on my own, but I knew militia would save us their antics for the sake of Germans.

We spent a great night cooking by the fire and finishing off a bottle of Greek wine before settling in for the night.

It got quite cold before sunrise, and I woke up early. Sleeping on the ground in my light sleeping bag didn't help. The chunky piece of dry driftwood we'd left burning the night before had almost died out. I got up and went to the creek, where I stripped off my clothes and washed in the freezing water. It was bitterly cold but rejuvenating. It felt great as I emptied my bladder into the clear stream, watching the steam rise as it touched the chilly surface.

The last grains of Aegean salt washed off, and I made some growling sounds as I struggled to warm up. I stood on a rock lit by the morning sun to dry. I never carried a towel on my trips; any surplus luggage added to the load, and I often used my T-shirts instead. This time I was going to wear the same one I'd stripped off a few minutes before. Droplets of freezing water drained away, my skin was drying, and warmth was returning to my muscles as the sun rose higher over the trees.

I lit a cigarette and stood there enjoying it with my eyes closed. I felt an erection coming on, that wonderful sensation which starts in the groin and spreads into previously dead muscles that suddenly come alive, bringing strength, power, and desire for flesh. I gave my erection a gentle stroke and arched my body. It felt so good that I did a few more, completely forgetting for a moment where I was. My penis felt hard, warm, and powerful in my hand. I gave it a slap and watched it swing when I suddenly realised I wasn't alone.

As I turned, there she was, perched on the riverbank above me, squatting and ready to take a leak, with the most innocent grin on her face. Her open legs displayed blonde-haired, pink lips in their full glory.

"I've seen yours, now you can watch mine," she whispered. "I'm very impressed, hope you will be too."

Resting her face on the palm of her right hand, she placed a focused, shameless gaze at my erection. At that moment, I didn't care, it was so unexpected, and I had no idea what to do with my hard on. I watched her beautiful lips as she dribbled a few drops and then let out a hissing torrent. Her stream shot out towards the creek and splashed into the water, only possible with a dick, I thought.

She looked relaxed, happy, innocent, and sexy as she performed her call of nature for me. As the last drops trickled out, she said, "How am I going to wash her now? Ooh, I know, you could give me a hand!"

And so I did. I cupped water in my hands and gave her pussy a gentle, almost analytical wash. She was enjoying it so much, cold water over her hot flesh, sizzling in the palm of my hand. She purred like a cat, eyes closed, head tilted back, neck arched, her breasts straining against the fabric of her T-shirt, sharp silhouettes of erect nipples showing through. A tiny streak of steam rose from her delicate blonde hairs, lit magnificently by the morning sun.

Greta's golden pubic hair glistened as if cast from metal, forged by the cold water in my hand. I wanted to stay there forever, playing with her silky flesh as she purred and moaned, squatting on the bank.

"Greta! Gretaa! Where are you?" we suddenly heard Wolfgang calling out.

"I'm coming, just having a leak, won't be a minute," she responded. She rubbed her drying snatch into the palm of my hand with reluctant movements, looking down at me, disappointment in her eyes. Using my hand to prop herself up, she stood and lifted her dress, showing off her wet blonde pussy and swollen, sun-tanned lips crowned with golden hair.

Sarajevo's Elusive Spring

My penis stood there, red-headed, excited, powerful, proud, and disappointed. She blew me a kiss and walked back to the campsite, wiggling her arse across the clearing just for my pleasure.

I dressed quickly, struggling to find room in my jeans for my hard-on, scrambled some dry firewood from the bank, and walked back to the dying fire.

"Good morning, Wolfie," I said.

"You've got exactly what we need!" he replied enthusiastically.

"I'm your man, aren't you lucky to have me," I grinned, looking down at my erection still too obvious in my pants. I was sure he noticed it too before he rolled onto the blanket, laughing.

Greta came out from behind the car wearing a gorgeous linen dress, delicately embroidered between her large breasts, her nipples standing proud beneath the fabric. The part where her strong legs started was barely covered by its minimal length, and it was obvious she wore nothing underneath.

It took most of the second day to descend towards the sea and the city of Dubrovnik. Wolfgang booked all three of us into a small apartment and we spent the early evening there, as all tourists do, cleaned up and changed into our best clothing. Stradun looked so chic, and I felt so proud as if I owned it, which I did in a way. I felt that all of Yugoslavia belonged to me, and as much as it was a bit of a mess, places like Dubrovnik gave me a sense of confidence that my world could get better and that we weren't too far from that objective.

When we came out into the Old Town, Wolfgang looked like a German Prinz and his lady the sexiest creature on the road. She wore a floral dress, and her blonde hair and suntanned skin made her a perfect living statue. Everyone scanned this blonde goddess as we negotiated the crowded promenade.

It was the first time in Dubrovnik I'd eaten at a restaurant where we emptied a bottle of Dalmatian red. My previous visits often ended with me being evicted from the city. Eventually, I'd found a sleeping spot high above in the hills, a place where I left my "baggage" and made myself less visible to the local militia and plainclothes police who combed the city for penniless hippies, drifters, and small-time criminals.

This time I was legal and certainly not penniless. We stayed in a large apartment, and I had a room of my own. They left the city for an early night, while I stayed with a few Sarajevo freaks until the early hours on the rocks beside the fortress. Bottles of wine kept turning up, and I struggled up the long, steep climb, carefully negotiating endless cobblestone steps to the apartment.

As I approached the entrance, I saw the amber glow of a cigarette. The smell of hash was overwhelming, and I recognised Greta sitting under a grapevine trellis in the faint moonlight.

"I've been waiting for you. I wanted to give you another chance to meet my pussy in a more romantic setting. What do you think?" she whispered.

"That sounds like music to my ears. I had it in my hand, washed it clean and fantasised all day about licking it dry."

She laughed. "That's my boy. I cannot wait to feel your and her lips kissing."

Her hand extended with the joint and I sat beside her. Before I even raised it to my mouth, an invitingly fresh scent reached me, something animalistically erotic. There was a faint odour of sea creatures, forest moss and lavender surrounding her lightly clad, voluptuous figure.

I took a long puff with my eyes closed, then another. When I looked again, her mouth and face were so close, ready for a "smoke barter". We brought our lips just short of kissing, and I blew the smoke slowly into her slightly open mouth. Her eyes were closed as she inhaled, her nipples pressed hot against my chest, as if a low voltage surge shot through.

She took the joint and repeated the routine, while her hand searched for what was already growing in my pants. Within seconds my fly was undone. As I was finishing the joint, she took care of what had grown in my pants, her mouth wrapping my swollen tool in its warm, slippery embrace. She worked its head and shaft while massaging my balls. I was about to shoot my load when she suddenly stood, pulling her nightie over her head, exposing her belly and the smooth lips of her vagina right before my wide-open eyes.

I buried my tongue into its silky warmth, those scents of sea, moss and lavender pouring into my mouth. I gripped her breasts, swollen nipples between my fingers, pleased to hear her moan. She didn't seem too concerned, letting long groans escape. My penis stood eager, ready, when she ended the game by collapsing onto it, smashing down with such force the bench squealed and cracked as if it might collapse beneath us.

We locked tight as our juices burst, holding back our breath, sweating profusely. We stayed there what felt like forever, hidden in silver-blue patterns of moonlight filtered through vine leaves. The bell of St. Vlaho rang four times as we returned to reality.

"I've left my Wolfie alone, you know, just to get the taste of your circumcised beast. This was my first one ever," she whispered, snuggling against me, holding my fading hero in her hand.

"At your service, madame. Any time. The pleasure was mine. Hope Wolfie doesn't feel left out," I teased.

"He'll get his share in a minute. He isn't very possessive. In fact, he gets excited when I score a great cock. He'll want to hear about yours for sure," she giggled, before sliding her mouth back onto it. My cock stirred again, and she took it deep, sliding hard along its shaft. I couldn't hold back, she took it all, licked it clean, and kissed me warmly before slipping back upstairs to Wolfgang.

I found a blanket on the railing and stretched on the bench, my fingers brushed across a wet patch. I was curious and brought them up to my nose, I could still smell sea creatures, moss, lavender, and my own semen enriching the mix.

"Where have you been all night?" Wolfgang asked, surprised, when I walked in.

"I slept outside. I'm used to it. Hotel rooms make me claustrophobic. Besides, it was so warm, and the moonlight reflections through the grapevines were magic."

As I spoke, Greta made a cheeky gesture behind his back, licking her lips, pointing her tongue rudely at me, and squeezing her nipple through the nightie she'd worn in the moonlight. Her full figure and arse, crimson-red love bites on her neck that weren't mine went on display as she slipped into the bathroom

"Horny bitch fucked Wolfie right after she came off my dick," I thought. Soon "Rockin' the Night Away" blasted from the shower while Wolfgang poured coffee, completely relaxed, graceful and handsome.

"I love it when she's happy," he said. "Must be something in this country she enjoys so much." He looked puzzled. "What do you think?"

"I don't know, Wolfie. Women are a big mystery to me. I've got a lot to learn yet," I dodged, trying to avoid embarrassment.

"You do, my friend. You certainly do," he concluded.

On the way to Opuzen a bit later, Greta slipped her hand quietly onto my leg. I squeezed it gently, and we said our goodbyes there with a short embrace. By afternoon I was in Sarajevo, meeting Ziyo "Crazy". He eventually made it to Skopje, where he caught a bus to Sarajevo, but he lacked the nerve, or the luck of a phantom traveller like me.

Naturally, I wasn't about to share my trellis experience. I felt like laughing. A bit of English and a little luck had gone a long way with a hot, mature lady who had no qualms about sharing her pussy and passion with two well-hung, gorgeous men.

Untimely Troubles with Baba's Harem on the Road

Buying land and property had stayed on my agenda for a long time, and travel to distant destinations was only possible with decent funds. Since I was employed and had good work and study references at the time, I was ushered through the immigration process with the Australian Embassy in Belgrade. Over a period of two years, they requested my qualification documents, work references, medical and police records. I managed to provide various documents swiftly.

When invited for an interview at the Embassy, I managed to hold a conversation in English with an Australian official without a translator. Once they requested my passport, I had no idea whether that was a good sign or not. The officials and their methods reminded me of the Yugoslav Militia (police). I chose not to ask too many questions and left them to do their job. They certainly did that and took their time doing it.

I'd always been a good citizen and an excellent student. My police record had no stains on it. The same couldn't be said for my military file. Considering all those escapades during 15 months in the Army while on National Service, my file wouldn't have looked so clean. However, the Embassy had no access to those records, neither did I.

While the immigration process dragged on, my official reputation went progressively downhill. I managed to get myself in trouble more than a few times. I got jailed for vagrancy in Belgrade and spent two weeks in Padinska Skela with my friends Boldy and Hardi. That didn't appear on the record which went to the Embassy.

On my return from India, I visited Hardi, who was serving his National Service in a Serbian town called Ćuprija. I'd said that we were going to make it to Ćuprija (bridge in Turkish) someday. Two truck drivers who'd taken me and Hardi across Bulgaria in the summer of 1976 lived there.

Sami Tischler

I got caught in the cellar of an apartment building with two female friends, commune dwellers at the time. Both Nada and Bernarda were Baba's consecutive lovers and my fellow travellers. We were trying to stay out of the freezing cold night and found an empty cellar where we cuddled close together in our sleeping bags.

The local Militia couldn't believe that two good-looking, perfectly respectable girls travelled in the company of a wandering, jobless, penniless freak who couldn't offer them anything better than free accommodation in a cellar. The three of us spent 10 days inside for vagrancy, in separate wards, of course. Including my time in Rotterdam, this was my third time in jail for vagrancy.

All the male inmates, generally small-time crooks and Gypsies, treated me like a king, offering cigarettes, keeping a spare seat for me around the communal tables and handing over surplus food at mealtimes. They were all convinced I was a pimp "on tour" through small Serbian provincial towns, and that my two girlfriends were available for "hire".

"Why else would you be dragging them around with you bro?" a Gypsy crook openly questioned my moralistic story. My denials were ignored and only added to my so-called glory.

Somehow, after all this, I still managed to get proof of a clean criminal record from the Ministry of Internal Affairs. Police records across the country mustn't have been linked. Computers were as big as wardrobes in those days, and most of us couldn't understand what they were made for or where that technology was heading.

Central data storage irritated progressive youth in Germany. When I was there, young freaks discussed databases and central intelligence digital records of each citizen with anger. Some had already demonstrated at these locations against government control and the files kept on everybody. The Baader–Meinhof Group had just been terminated. Members of the Red Brigades in Italy were either shot or jailed. The German government and Mossad weren't going to let that mess evolve further.

Sarajevo's Elusive Spring

The Jewish State was happily expanding in the East, the Germans had already done their ethnic cleansing, and the Palestinians were being pushed into the sea. Everyone was happy and couldn't see the trouble brewing, where a new form of fascism and ancient forms of state terrorism established roots and dug deeper into the historical and religious garbage of the Holy Land.

Later that year, my six cannabis plants, casually planted in my cousin's neglected garden, were discovered by a sleepy neighbour employed as a security guard at my TAS factory. He recognised them as "hemp plants". Bosnians had grown hemp for centuries. God knows if they'd ever had a smoking variety.

However, a clever peasant's nose worked it out and he invited the police to the party. They raided the garden and found another four plants behind the apartment at my parents' house. A greenhorn journalist tricked me into giving him an interview. I spoke about society's lack of tolerance for drugs and suppression of personal freedom. I promoted the advantages of using *ganja* over violence and issues in a society fuelled by rakija, cognac and beer.

An article came out in a popular Bosnian weekly magazine, The World. The whole story got blown out of proportion. The young journalist wrote it just as I'd said it. The only wrong thing was that the timing and the place for saying it were wrong. Everyone in Bosnia was told that I was a "criminal", and they mostly believed it, because it was announced in the papers.

Australian officials couldn't have cared less about a Bosnian magazine with a pompous title like The World. In Canberra at the time, this offence wouldn't have been considered a crime or produced a criminal record. But Bosnian police, forever paranoid of anything different and new, made sure this sort of behaviour wasn't going to go unnoticed or unpunished.

I served another three weeks in Central Jail (Sarajevo) while they further investigated my "crime". I shared a small cell with an Orthodox priest accused of Serbian nationalism, a serious crime against the state. Pop Neđo had celebrated his son's christening and invited the local Borike intelligentsia: teacher, forest keeper, council official and some neighbours. After a big drunken party, they sang banned Serbian patriotic songs. One of his guests must have dobbed him in.

The other two cellmates were Muslims. One was accused of attempted rape and had an infected wound on his hand from a young waitress's teeth. Poor girl, his employee, clearly didn't see sex with the boss as part of her job description. She must have been traumatised, since the incident marked the end of her employment. He never admitted his guilt, but the teeth marks had no valid excuse.

The fourth cellmate had fleeced his boss, the butcher, for a large amount of cash. He admitted it and wasn't sorry for his crime.

As for my crime, I couldn't see anything wrong with planting some herb, which turned out to be a male and impotent drug. Police ripped it out before it could have acquired any potency anyway. That was the real crime in my books. They weighed the green plants and used that measurement as the "amount of narcotic found", justifying their sentence delivery.

I was further investigated while in jail and allowed to defend myself as a free citizen. Pop Neđo got seven years, and the other two never came up in the media. I engaged a private lawyer, who asked for my references from work. He suggested that being employed was very important and insisted I keep my job.

I had to put up with a lot of social discomfort at work. All my workmates became hostile towards me. Many people who "didn't know me from a bar of soap" yelled abuse at me in broad daylight as if I was the biggest criminal ever. These same people had watched young criminal bullies terrorise me and other kids in town for years and never said a "booo". I guess I was a peaceful, outspoken, harmless hippy who deserved what he got.

I did deserve it, for looking ahead and seeing the changing world devouring our overinflated, righteous socialism. Highly polished

Sarajevo's Elusive Spring

heroics with the trailing paranoia, rigidity and aggression comfortably coexisted and flourished in the proletarian swamps. It felt like a sort of "Biblical stoning" to me, while the proletariat all felt grand doing it.

"You shouldn't have to fear the Militia if you have nothing to hide or if you haven't done anything against the law!" Exactly, why should you?

Why should you ever confront the system, traditions, hierarchy, conservatism, violence, racism, state terror, when all you can get is trouble? And worst of all, the judgement of people who have no courage, wisdom or foresight to recognise the real enemies of the society they were guarding?

Their leader, Marshall Tito, wasn't one who conformed. He never feared anyone or anything and certainly never closed his eyes or mouth when searching for causes and solutions. Even their admiration for him must have been something they accepted blindly, like their religions. You get it, you keep it, you die for it. No questions asked. Who cares about your fellow man?

It was a ripe time to think about disappearing from that damned place in the Bosnian mountains. The Bogomils had gone. They left only their bones and tombstones; the sole remains of anything decent in its turbulent past. Weathered and monolithic, they sat there in their remoteness, neglected, abandoned and misunderstood. Victims of the expanding corporations of Catholicism, Orthodoxy and Islam.

Sami Tischler

Mia

My jail experience had elements of prophecy. What a mix: a Serbian nationalistic chauvinist priest, and Bosnian Muslims: a rapist, a thief and a convicted marijuana user and grower. What a great blueprint, prophecy, and future mix for the upcoming Bosnian nightmare. None of us knew exactly what was going to come out of the fermenting society of Yugoslavia. Tito had only been dead a short while. The immediate post Tito period was marked by shortages and an increased police presence. The economy was struggling. Foreign currency was precious, and Yugoslav companies were pushed to export, earn dollars and repay the strangling foreign debt accumulated during the "prosperous" period of easy living on IMF loans.

I had already met Mia, my lifetime partner, in the most natural and spontaneous circumstances, in the most significant of places on the map of Bosnia and Herzegovina. I didn't know that my new girlfriend was to be my last. We hooked up during a trip to Čitluk, a small town within a crow's flight of Međugorje. This small village in Herzegovina had become world-famous since the Virgin Mary appeared and delivered messages to a group of local shepherds. Just another event that paralysed, confused, and completely surprised Tito's antique socialist government. When everyone heard the message, "You have to keep the peace", they made it into a farce, believing there was no danger to peace in the United Federation of Yugoslavia.

As I had already found out, nobody with a "healthy mind" had any reason not to trust the government, militia, Yugoslav Army, and its leadership. We were led to believe the whole system was clean, transparent, trustworthy, and based on immaculate morals and values born in the revolutionary struggle of the glorious nations of the South Slavs. As it turns out, and as I had feared for a long time, the system was already falling apart. We all clung to Tito's name and legacy as something solid, but Tito was an ailing old man. His cronies and poltroons weren't to be trusted.

Sarajevo's Elusive Spring

We went to a village near Čitluk on an invitation from a student friend who came from there. This location, just over a rocky ridge beside the Adriatic Coast, fitted the profile of our extensive search for land and abandoned properties perfectly. We left Sarajevo in three groups and travelled by hitchhiking. All three (Hardi, Chuck and UFO) had a girl or two with us as travelling partners. "Stop", as we called it, never really worked unless you had a female partner. In the best of circumstances, it was very slow. Once you were with a girl, drivers felt comfortable, turning hospitable and generous during the trip. They would offer cigarettes, stop and pay for meals, hoping to impress the girl you were travelling with.

We were paired randomly. I travelled with a girl I knew, and we were good friends. The plan was to meet in Mostar, the famous city on the river Neretva, 50 km inland from the coast. The trip was uneventful. We met in the evening at a well-known local hangout. The rain was drizzling outside, and our local hippy friends led us to a cellar of a public building. It was a perfectly safe place to spend the night and stay dry. We had our sleeping bags with us, found some dry cardboard boxes and settled for the night. None of the girls brought anything with them. Our local friend, a student in Sarajevo at the time, promised to arrange a place for them to crash. Three friends, Mia being one of them, went away with De, and we stayed in the cellar. A few cigarettes later we were all sound asleep, the rain intensifying throughout the night. Its drumming in the downpipe sounded like a lullaby.

Hours passed. I was woken by commotion and muffled conversation in the semi-darkness. It sounded like a police raid. "Cops, what the fuck, another jail term for vagrancy is all I need now." I was relieved to see our girls coming through the door. They were back, soaking wet, cold and miserable. I woke up, we smoked cigarettes and heard how they had travelled on a bus to Military Cadets' College accommodation quarters. Once there, De led the girls to three empty beds in a small room while she disappeared with her cadet boyfriend somewhere in the building.

They never properly settled to sleep. Hours later, cadets, the owners of the beds they were occupying, returned from their weekend outing and found our girls in their beds. "We wouldn't mind sharing our beds with you," they said. "It could be fun, now that we've gathered so nicely, let's not waste such a great opportunity."

Our girls weren't impressed. They packed up and got out, into the drizzling rain, on the road in the early hours of the morning. The girls looked like abandoned army whores. They had no idea which way to walk and asked a shift worker, the only person they met: "Which way is Mostar?" The guy showed them the way, and they walked for kilometres. Luckily, they found our cellar and sneaked in unnoticed, soaking wet, cold and miserable.

When we offered to share our sleeping bags, they had no complaints. Mia crawled in beside me. I helped her get warm as discreetly as I could, but after a while I was starting to feel cramped and uncomfortable. We weren't friends nor lovers, and I felt this forced intimacy a bit embarrassing. I knew that Mia couldn't settle into sleep for the same reason. Neither could I. "I'll get out and give you a chance to warm up and get some sleep!" I said as I unzipped the bag to get out. "You don't need to do that for me," she whispered. "Happy to do it for you, enjoy it, and don't feel offended, please."

Chuck did the same, and we sat, smoked and chatted while the girls took their beauty sleep. Beauty sleep didn't help much. We looked pretty worn out, messy and dangerous as we emerged onto the street and walked into a pastry shop for breakfast. Rain had stopped, warm pastries and a cleanup at a street fountain changed everyone's mood.

We reached the town of Čitluk in three groups easily, found Vanya by phoning him at home, and took a bus from the town centre to the nearby village. The whole town had its eyes on us while we waited with Vanya. If he hadn't been there as a local, we would have been arrested for sure. We stood out so much, like a band of Gypsies. "No reason to be afraid if you weren't doing anything wrong" kept ringing in my mind throughout my ventures in small towns, villages and provincial centres of Yugoslavia.

Sami Tischler

My Mia

We spent two days and two nights in a dilapidated stone house, listening to music, conversing, and taking short walks through the semi abandoned village. A woman over 90 years old was the only permanent resident there. Her radio produced sounds from an unstable reception, emitting sound effects we often heard at rock concerts. We later joked about baba listening to experimental electronic music on her radio, broadcasted from "The Dark Side of the Moon".

Back at the house, I was copying quotes from a Buddhist text into my notebook when Mia came close, wanting to know what I was doing. I told her a bit about what I thought to be the essence of my understanding of Eastern philosophy, Hinduism, and Buddhism. But what did I really know? My trip to India felt so unreal by that time. The greyness of my existence in Sarajevo had settled in, and memories of India were becoming as distant as India's geographic position.

The search for land and a radical change of lifestyle wasn't getting much further than fantasies about its possibilities, its advantages, and endless arguments with everyone about its viability. Most of our friends were studying to become doctors, lawyers, engineers, politicians, and there I was, talking about a stone house, goats, bees, vineyards, olives, cheese, while still virtually living with my parents.

She asked a few challenging questions about my plans but didn't show much enthusiasm for these "return to nature" ideas. She was calm, bright, and loving. She had a soft voice, lovely skin, and beautiful green eyes magnified by the thick lenses she wore. She dressed simply and hardly projected any of her femininity outward. Yet she appeared very fragile and gentle. I thought she was very attractive. Still, there was a sense of distance I wasn't prepared to travel, and she appeared cautious.

I did pay attention at close range. After all, we spent the weekend in a single room dwelling, listening to music in semi-darkness. Candles provided the only light and charged the space with suspended intimacy. It was unlike Chuck's "commune", where people often made love in the dark with everyone present in the same room, or listened to screams and moans caused by Baba's enormous tool in the room next door. None of us were lovers, and there were hosts present in the same room. There was an overwhelming sense of decency, and my own presence often commanded respect among people who didn't know us well. I tended to be the keeper of high morals among the troops, something like a commissar in a partisan guerrilla unit.

On Sunday morning, we regrouped for our return trip. Mia and I were paired together. We were the last in line at the start. By the time the other two pairs left, I felt strangely comfortable with Mia. She was pale and weak, and I guessed she had her period. The stop went well, we made it quickly to Mostar and caught another lift straight to Sarajevo, 90 km away, over the range of Bosnian mountains. It was a father and son returning home from Mostar who drove us. The old man was pleasant and intelligent. I led a smooth conversation with him and soon realised that Mia was struggling with pain.

I placed my Indian Hare Krishna shawl over my lap and offered it to her as a pillow. She appeared relieved and happy to curl up and rest her head there. As I spoke to the driver, I started caressing her hair, keeping it away from her face to ease her pain. I looked at her closed eyes and realised she felt completely comfortable with me. At one point, she opened her eyes and gave me a faint smile. She wasn't wearing her glasses.

"My God, she is so beautiful" I thought.

Enchanted by my discovery I graced her with more tender touches to her face, closed eyes, ears, and hair. She responded by making herself more comfortable in my lap. Her features drew my eyes like a flower attracts a bee. She slept in complete safety, calm and angelic. I couldn't help myself when I sneaked in a small kiss as she opened her eyes somewhere halfway up the steep winding road towards the Bosnian highlands.

As we walked towards the tram in Sarajevo, we held hands and kissed at the back of the rattling tram. Next time we met our friends, they knew we were together.

I spent several nights in the house she shared with two girls who had come with us to Čitluk, high above the city, in Soukbunar, almost in the clouds. In those days, when the city choked under winter fog and pollution, it felt like you could jump into the soft cloud below and descend into the city.

A month or so later, I suggested we move in together at my place. On another return from a weekend trip to the Baćinska Lakes on the coast, we boarded a tram to the city and realised something was wrong. People looked different, quiet, and depressed, as if a dark cloud had descended on them. You could tell something tragic had happened. Someone whispered that Tito had died a short time ago.

A few weeks earlier, we had gone to Ljubljana in Slovenia, where he was hospitalised. By that time, playing music at Sarajevo cafés had been banned. Only revolutionary and classical music played on the radio. Fully armed militiamen guarded government buildings. Yet Ljubljana radio stations played punk bands, and life there appeared normal.

I couldn't see the logic in this paranoia and fear of its own people. When should we be strong if not now, when our great leader was dying? It worried me greatly, this lack of trust in our own Unity and Brotherhood.

He was dead. "He is dead. He is really dead now" I kept thinking over and over, "and I am in trouble with the law."

Mia stood by my side through all that drama, 21 days in jail and the aftermath of it, including the trial. We were lucky she came from a city in the north, and much of the publicity didn't reach her family. They didn't know about my existence at the time anyway.

Sarajevo's Elusive Spring

I was handed a 15-month suspended sentence for two years. Funnily enough, the same length as national service, as if my service had been deemed invalid. I was terrified at the thought I could end up in jail for that long. My previous jail terms were brief in comparison, but they all left scars and traumas I wasn't fully aware of. One of them was a growing resentment and mistrust of the regime, its suppression and restrictions. It certainly had a great capacity for terror and humiliation, and I wasn't keen on challenging it further.

During those three weeks in jail, my father came to visit. He told me my passport had come back from Belgrade with a visa in it. I just couldn't believe my luck. Australian immigration authorities had cleared my documents just before my situation deteriorated.

Sami Tischler

From Bad to Worst

Police, family, and the local township community were making my life real hell, and the idea of going to Australia for a change looked better and better by the day. I met Mia in the spring, and she stuck with me through this time. Her family wasn't aware of our relationship, and we were looking for ways to disappear before they did.

I lived in the basement of my parents' house, and just across the road, overlooking my windows, lived local policeman Rade "Drot". He spent much of his free time keeping an eye on who was coming and going from my apartment. If he noticed a gathering, he'd phone the station and a cop car would bring a militia squad to the door for an unofficial raid. One night, two cops came uninvited, wanting me to present my passport. I lied, saying it had been sent to the Australian Embassy. I knew they couldn't check, and I had no time to think of anything wiser. They bought the story and left. My passport was safely upstairs with my parents.

Police had the power to confiscate passports and often used it unofficially to punish nonconformists as well as real criminals. This time, I got off the hook. The cops must have thought that confiscating my passport would have been a great additional punishment. They had no official warrant, but I was nervous and worried, nevertheless. As they left, I felt like a "marked" man, unsure what might happen in the coming days. I was at the mercy of a low-ranking police officer, my next-door neighbour, and his bored mates, looking for some excitement in life and glory at work.

Around this time, a letter arrived in the mail from the port city of Rijeka. It looked suspiciously tampered with, I could swear it had been opened. The letter came from Ahmed (a Pakistani sailor Ziyo and I had met in Thessaloniki more than a year before). I freaked out when I read that he was in Pula and had what "we talked about", asking me to come down and collect it. I was already in deep shit over a nonsignificant quantity of low-grade weed. There was no way I could find enough courage to take the trip, and I'm glad I didn't.

I never found out if the local drug squad cop, Amir Latić, had his fingers in it, or if Ahmed's letter was tampered with. I was terrified that Ahmed might decide to take the trip to Sarajevo personally, since he had my address. I wasn't going to write back to him. Weeks passed, and nothing came through the mail.

I tried to live like a good citizen. I went to work, came home, went to work again, and spent evenings in the usual dives of the Old City filled with students, freaks, and hordes of punks, the latest trend hitting Sarajevo. I had to be very careful. I had a visa to Australia in my pocket, but the two-year suspended sentence was hanging over my head. Getting caught with possession could have triggered a 15-month jail term. Police ID checks were always a reality. They easily led to body searches, but luckily hash availability was so random.

At the end of the year, with the help of Karlo's brother Davor, well connected in the Old Town mafia circles, we set up a small business venture. I call them mafia, but they were nothing like the real mob. They controlled small stall sales of smuggled goods like jeans, handmade jewellery, fashionable leather items, and seasonal goods like flowers for Mother's Day or Christmas cards. Hardi and I had already made a small fortune selling Christmas cards door-to-door. Now that I was working full-time, I had no time for that.

Through Davor and his connections, we scored a location right in front of the main shopping mall in Sarajevo. It was undercover, and Mia was going to run it with the help of Karlo's youngest brother, Miro. Business went well until the policeman patrolling that area smelled money. We didn't have a formal permit, only a reference to some guy I had never met. His name was supposed to scare off baksheesh hungry cops.

It was a nightmare. Mia would call me at work to say the cop had ordered them to dismantle the stall by 10 am. I'd have to sneak out from work, catch a bus, walk a mile, and wait until the pompous nobody turned up, then argue our entitlements or beg for mercy. We never paid any bribes, didn't even know how to, but managed to stand our ground while making a small bundle for ourselves and Davor. As soon as we had the cash, we converted it into German marks, plentiful during the Christmas season with all our expats home for the winter break from German factories.

We started looking at exotic locations for winter travel. Morocco appeared attractive. We knew you could get hash there, and its ancient Islamic culture at the edge of the Sahara sounded worth the trip. The idea of African warmth, the Atlantic coast, and the Atlas Mountains grew more realistic by the day. Hardi had already taken off, planning to travel through Africa. Davor talked about going there with his wife once we mentioned it. Mia had her share of the money, and I was cashed up anyway. My passport had an Australian visa in it.

The decision to travel to Morocco was crucial to my final move to Australia. I knew I was going to resign from my job any time now. I didn't need it anymore. I had my suspended sentence behind me and no reason to play the role of obedient citizen. It was a liberating moment. I had a clear road to travel on.

At the end of that year, I joined Karlo for Catholic Christmas Mass in Visoko. Kraljeva Sutjeska, nearby, was the last pre-Ottoman Bosnian capital, while Catholicism came to Bosnia with Franciscan missionaries in the 1700s. Kraljeva Sutjeska and the fortress of Bobovac are full of medieval Bosnian history, only 15 km from Visoko. The first mosque in Bosnia was built there, and it is believed that most former Bogomils converted to Catholicism and Islam.

The small church was swamped by the faithful, something I had never seen before, and Mia couldn't go in, her fear of crowds was feeding into her emerging claustrophobia. Karlo invited both of us back to Germany. At the time he lived with Gerda in a village apartment. The village was covered in deep, clean snow, the crystal whiteness shining with pure magic, perfectly set for romance.

Sarajevo's Elusive Spring

Mia and I lived ours, taking walks through the old village, along snow-covered roads through pine forests weighed down by heavy snowfall. Mia accidentally walked in on Ralf fondling pregnant Gerda in the kitchen. It turned our visit into a conspiracy plot. Unsure what to do with the incriminating evidence, we chose to keep it to ourselves.

Privately, I felt I had already avenged my friend Karlo by sleeping with Ralf's girlfriend during my last visit. I busied myself, making a small sculpture of Gerda with her pregnant belly out of a piece of firewood, which still sits on the windowsill of their house.

On the way back home through snow-covered Austria, we spent the night in a small hotel room, clean, heated, and cosy. While levitating snowflakes whirled outside, rarely falling, whispering their unique silence, my commitment to Mia deepened and opened gates of trust and dedication between us. We talked about the triangle of Gerda, Karlo, and Ralf, and felt lucky that we loved each other. We had so much, and yet we had nothing. Orphans of the world, caught in a storm on a highway.

On returning to Bosnia, I resigned from my job (something unheard of in Yugoslavia, where you kept your job for life). I had decided to leave the country before my visa expired in August 1981. The honeymoon with revolutionary romanticism was over. It had been killed in the cradle for me by Prof. Phillip, the judges of local small courts across Yugoslav territories, Rade "Drot" and his agricultural bully comrades in the local militia station, Amir Latić, try-hard drug squad detective, and just about any other person in power who systematically destroyed the illusion of a safe, prosperous future in the country of my birth.

Their interpretation of socialist governance and justice labelled my free-range lifestyle as something unacceptable and dangerous. As naïve as I was, I could tell that my life in the country wasn't facing a great future. I had seen "labelled" citizens without a passport or a job pushed against the wall into crime and illegal activities out of desperation and necessity. I was ready to leave and try my luck elsewhere.

Mia and I knew that we were destined to spend our lives together. We heard of a wedding by proxy and arranged for my father to act as my representative once I had gone to Australia. I had my permanent residency visa as a single immigrant and wasn't allowed to marry before my arrival in Australia. My mother wouldn't give her blessing to our union. I had to sit down and have a conversation with both of my parents a few days before my departure.

"I'll be gone in a few days, and I don't know when or if I'll be coming back. I love Mia and we have decided to spend our lives together. I have no intention of changing my mind. I have given her my word. She is a good girl. You can accept her as my wife, and that is the only way you will continue to have me as your son."

Tears poured down my face as I spoke. I hated the ultimatum, but I wasn't going to give them any choice. My mother was crying too, and my heart was falling apart. I had already been through a similar situation when I respected their decision and broke up with Bella at the age of 16. I wasn't going to repeat that mistake now. I was a grown man and about to leave my parents, the house, my country, friends, and my maiden behind.

"Mum will be OK, I know that you've made the right choice. She will get to know her, and Mia is a nice and respectful girl, I can tell," my father said as he held my mother's hand. "She will look after you, Mum, as well as our daughters would if you give her a chance." It was in August 1981 when I immigrated to Australia.

On the day of my departure, I arrived in Belgrade one day too early by mistake and bumped into Rada on the street. This turned out to be one of those meetings with destiny. An unbelievable coincidence: meeting her at that exact moment, a consequence of misreading my departure date. The following day, at the airport, I was told that my trip would be delayed for another day due to a strike by air traffic controllers in New York, where the plane had been held up. The JAT

Sarajevo's Elusive Spring

airline provided overnight accommodation at the airport hotel for all of us caught in the delay.

When I bumped into her on the street, I had been considering spending the night at the atomic shelter, which I had used previously during my wanderings in the capital. Our meeting was brief, polite, and warm. She looked great, and I was so happy to see her like that, gorgeous, sexy, fashionably dressed in cosmopolitan Belgrade. She didn't show any grudges, just surprise that I was leaving for Australia, mixed with a bit of sadness. We never questioned or revisited our affair other than through the certain sadness I saw in her eyes as she looked at me speechless.

In just a few minutes on a busy street, with her female friend standing by, she managed to say that she was studying at university and was happy living in Belgrade. She wished me well and had to go.

Without realising that I was going to spend another night at Belgrade airport, I ended up staying as a guest of a heroin addict who lived in an inherited grand apartment. My host, obsessed with blues, exclusively played Taj Mahal records, his only possession, while sleeping in the smallest room of the grand apartment, possibly a pantry. The apartment was normally rented to African students during the academic year. Over the summer holidays, empty rooms with worn-out, stained, abandoned mattresses didn't look very inviting. But what choice did I have? Luckily, I had my sleeping bag, my only piece of luggage and the place was in the very centre of Belgrade. Taj Mahal wailing blues guitar sung the most appropriate farewell to a freak in the dusty dilapidated drug den. It was the end of an era. I was going on a journey and had no immediate plans to return any time soon.

I had been brought in by Zuba, an old friend I'd known for years, whom I ran into as I wandered around killing time. Most of the people I knew in Belgrade were street kids, and that's where we had met and built our friendships over the years. I had no idea where they lived and had never seen their homes or met their parents.

Sami Tischler

I knew then that Rada wasn't meant to live with a person like me. She was fascinated by my freedom and unconventional lifestyle, but she fitted so well into a life of cool glamour and elegance. She was a dame and deserved to remain one. In a way, I was proud of her, but also jealous that she had already found herself while I still had a long way to go. That was the last contact I ever had with her.

Out of the Trouble Zone

In two days, I landed in Sydney completely disorientated, fell asleep in Central Station Park. I was lying on my unrolled sleeping bag while the city rumbled on. Only a few people walked through the chilly August morning and across the park. My train was scheduled for the afternoon. I was heading for the capital.

When I woke up, the park was filled with people. Most of them sat on the grass and the benches by themselves, next to little lunch boxes, eating their sandwiches in silence. It almost felt as if I had landed amongst an alien race in a parallel universe where everything looked like the known world except the people, who were humanoids programmed to work and run the place.

"What the fuck am I doing here? Why am I here, and was this a bad move? Is this what I've been searching for? Why did I think it may be here?" All these questions flooded my confused and exhausted mind. I had been on the train, on the road and in the air for the previous five days. I understood that this trip had a greater purpose, other than pure fun and curiosity.

The absence of any familiarity with Australia, the strangeness of its landscape seen from the air, and the humanoids around me eating in silence gave me shivers and unsettled thoughts. The rumble of city traffic swallowed the superficial illusion of nature and the orderly greenery around me. I was struggling to put my mind at ease. I had to get these questions out of my head. Otherwise, I'd be heading to a travel agency and purchasing a ticket back to Belgrade. Fortunately, I wasn't a coward. Besides, I didn't have enough cash for it. I felt embarrassed even considering it.

"My time in that swamp has expired. This is going to be a new life, a chance to reinvent myself, live wiser, quieter, and try to be invisible for once." I was trying to settle the panicky, fast-paced line of thoughts. "You've been too honest and open, you've let your guard down, so naïve and enthusiastic against hardcore agricultural, oppression happy, try hard revolutionaries." I almost laughed at my own sarcasm.

Finally, I made it to the correct platform and sat on the train. Wooden benches in two rows, like the local trains or those dating back to Austro-Hungarian times in Bosnia, surprised me with a strange sense of familiarity. Once the train left Sydney and rattled through the open land, I was hit by jet lag again. The half-empty train slipped into the night through the land inhabited mainly by sheep.

At some stage, I woke up, completely groggy, and looked across the aisle where a young, bearded man held a joint in his hand, stretched across towards me.

"Of course, I'd love a puff, thanks."

That was exactly what I needed at that moment: a welcoming gesture by another freak in this strange place. It was perfect. I joined the group for a chat and a cone. They didn't care that everyone knew what we were doing, neither did I. I couldn't believe how relaxed everyone was.

They were curious about my existence and my destination: Canberra (Keembra, they called it). They told me they were travelling to do their turn at the "Nuclear Free Embassy". It sounded like what was happening in Germany, but I had no idea what exactly that involved or where. I told them about my own journey in my crude English while struggling to understand their Aussie drawl and fast Sydney dialect. I didn't really care. I was so impressed by laid-back attitude and the fact that they were so inclusive.

We made it to Canberra railway station late at night, where they waited for someone. I expected to find some form of transport to the suburbs where I had a Bosnian contact. I spoke to a bus driver before the only bus departed, and he told me it would be impossible to get to my destination on public transport at that time of night.

My friends' lift had just arrived. It was another long-haired, bearded character with a VW Combi wagon.

Sarajevo's Elusive Spring

"Why don't you come with us?" someone said. "We'll spend the night in a tent ourselves. We'll get you sorted in the morning."

I didn't have to think long. "Sure, that would be great, thanks!"

I couldn't believe my luck. These guys were unbelievable. After a short drive, we came to a well-lit white official building with black writing on it: "Australian Parliament House". Just across the plateau, on the grassy paddock, stood two tents. One had a banner with "Aboriginal Tent Embassy" and the other "Nuclear Free Embassy" handwritten on it. There were other crudely written messages around both.

There were fires and people sitting around them. My friends exchanged greetings with a bunch of people manning their tent. They talked about the progress of their protest. That would have been the handover, and the previous group left. We settled around the fire and smoked more joints. A few policemen patrolling the grounds didn't seem to be bothered by our presence, the log fire, or the pungent smell spreading through the air.

The combination of multiple joints and exhaustion from the fourth day on the road was knocking me around. The VW driver looked at me as he was leaving.

"You look like you could do with a good sleep. I have a spot for you in my van if you want. I can take you to your contact in the morning too."

That was so generous and hard to believe. I said my goodbyes to the crew, and we drove somewhere out of the city. He parked the van, and we set up for the night. I was exhausted and slept like a dead man.

I woke up in a nature reserve, near the river. I got out, washed my face, stretched my legs, and listened to strange sounds coming out of the bush: crows crying like a small child, the screeching of cockatoos, the singing of magpies. The morning was chilly in August, refreshing after the scorching summer heat of Belgrade.

Sami Tischler

I was sitting on a bench with a cigarette for breakfast. My host came out of the van, stark naked, and walked into the river for his morning shower. I wasn't even thinking about joining him in the freezing stream, but he seemed to be enjoying it, splashing and screaming out of sheer joy. I loved his heroic act but wasn't into it myself. I watched the steam rising from his body in the sunlight amidst the untouched forest and wooded hills all around.

Shortly after, he boiled water for tea on a small gas burner and pulled out a tin with biscuits for our breakfast. He told me that he lived out of his van, travelled up and down the coast of NSW, camped where he liked, worked when he had to, and enjoyed the simplicity of his existence and the frequent change of scenery.

I had questions about the legality of his lifestyle and his interaction with the police.

"I've registered a permanent address with friends, I collect "the dole" (unemployment benefit), and I work when I find work. My car is registered, and I try to find locations where I can camp for a night or two, nature reserves, remote beach car parks, suburban wastelands and the like."

I was impressed by the similarity with the gypsy existence in my homeland. "You live like a real gypsy. I'm so impressed and glad that I've arrived in a country where you wouldn't get in trouble with police for it. Where I come from, all that is illegal and rarely tolerated. Combined with smoking pot, you can get in trouble with the law in no time."

Soon I figured out that I was going to enjoy the benefits and radical changes brought on by the Whitlam government in the late '70s. Things were changing and rapidly deteriorating following the Liberals' *coup d'état*. The Yugoslav expat community appeared divided, anti-Communist, uneducated, badly informed and chauvinistically religious. Croat extremists were numerous, nationalistic and militant. Their terrorist activities on Yugoslav territory were well known and caused great concern for the government.

I found myself defending Yugoslavia's socialism as a fair deal for its people, the only way to maintain unity, and the only way forward for its diverse ethnic and cultural mix. Considering my reasons for leaving my homeland, this was a strange position to be in. Besides, as a Bosnian Muslim and a Yugoslav, I didn't quite fit into any of its divided groups. Neither did Mia, with her combined Serbo-Croatian heritage. For many years we looked for friends and allies amongst the Australians, new and old.

Within two years we had accepted Australian citizenship. During that time, we married by proxy, Mia came to Australia holding a permanent residency visa, and we had our lovely daughter. Over that period, I worked in concrete precast manufacturing, at an abattoir, studied English for migrants, learnt to drive taxis, cleaned for a Greek contractor, and finally became a house painter. Small house renos and painting jobs paid well. We lived simply, saved money, and felt notoriously homesick.

We had serious intentions to return to Yugoslavia. My parents complained about the poor state of the family home my father had built on the cheap in the 1960s. We decided to rebuild and extend the original structure out of our own savings. That was meant to secure a place for our return.

Our social life in Australia flourished. We discovered the hidden alternative culture evolving around art, music, dance and theatre, and started expanding our social circle. We were invited to wild parties, went to great concerts, performances, exhibitions, bars and dance clubs. My work in wood as a sculptor led me to the Art School and studies of Furniture Making and Design with the legendary English designer George Ingham. By 1990 I had graduated from the Art School, worked on the New Parliament House project for two years, and bought a small house, better described as a shack, in a rundown suburb of Canberra. We were over the moon. We owned our house, well, the bank really owned it, but the feeling was great, nevertheless.

The New Parliament House project came to an end, and we moved to Sydney where I worked as a freelance joiner, fit-out carpenter, and all-round renovator. Life in Sydney didn't quite work out for us as a young couple without family support. The property market was completely out of our reach. The city at our doorstep offered little benefit with a small child at home. School in Erskineville looked gloomy, overcrowded and unfriendly. One year of driving on unkempt, congested and inadequate Sydney roads took its toll.

We decided to move back to our little shack and build a workshop with the money we had saved. I was going to drive taxis, build the studio, renovate our ugly duckling, and try to develop my own freelance mixed bag furniture and building career. Between a collective workshop, founded by friends, Art School graduates, and my own improvised workshop, now under a solid roof at home, I started getting small, fine detailed residential projects.

I refined and fused together a wide range of skills I had acquired by that time. Painting, building wooden structures great and small, carving and furniture making, wood machining and finishing, making and installing cabinets, doors and windows, laying floors and pavers, all were highly regarded skills with my expanding client base.

I scored a lengthy well paid employment period with a respectable high-end joinery. At the end of it we decided the time was right for my first visit back home. Things were changing there. Import regulations eased off. There was a sense of radical change and talk of great political and economic reform. Ante Marković was the name on everyone's lips. New wave rock bands we were listening to from cassettes brought across by friends, sounded great and openly shouted criticism and demanded the change. At the same time dangerous nationalistic and separatist rhetorics were popping up in the new "liberated" media. Serbia's response to Kosovo crisis came in statements and speeches of its radical leaders with Slobodan

Milošević at the helm. Croatia was preparing for its first multiparty elections and Serbian minorities on its eastern borders talked about atrocities they had endured during the last Independent Croatian State and *Ustaša's* terror. Old monsters in new clothes started crawling out of dark holes. We were really excited by fundamental changes, but extreme nationalism wasn't one of them.

Sami Tischler

Sort of an Epilogue

I went back to Yugoslavia in 1990. Hardi and I took a few trips to meet old friends around the central Bosnian towns. We found Dino in Visoko. Dino was Hardi's companion on the trip over the Algerian Atlas Mountain range all the way to Nigeria. They had some wild times in Lagos in 1980. Hardi went on and spent two years travelling through Africa penniless.

We met Slav "Šego", my college-days Catholic friend, in a bar in Vareš. He was divorced, teaching Serbo-Croatian, and courting a young waitress. We spent a second day with him walking up Joša Creek and smoking hash at the bank of the River Bosna.

One night we went to Iliyaš and met up with Soma, Igor, Ziyo and Davor. Davor, Karlo's elder brother, told me he kept a canister of petrol in his cellar. He was going to use it and leave the place when the time was right. In the meantime, he lived off gambling big money with the local criminals. It reminded me of the character in "Deer Hunter" who played Russian roulette for the thrill of it. Davor wasn't too keen to leave the excitement of the war zone.

Ziyo, Chuck's friend, had spent a year in a juvenile detention centre for vandalising a classroom as a teenager. He came to visit family and check out the Bosnian situation. Chuck, who joined him in the fun, spent 15 months in jail as he was over 18 at the time of the "crime". Chuck managed to get a passport in the mid-80s, went to India with a plan to meet Karlo. But Karlo became sick on arrival to India by plane from Germany and couldn't make the appointment. Chuck wrote a couple of letters, sent a few pictures dressed like a Sadhu, and disappeared without a trace.

Ziyo had sold heroin on the streets of Frankfurt for an Albanian "brother", lived with a German addict girlfriend, missed his old mate Chuck and could smell trouble in the air. Soma, a new-age manager saving firms before collapse, couldn't see where things were going, unaware he would spend the rest of his life in Australia. I would be the one to link him with his uncle, the Australian sponsor.

Sarajevo's Elusive Spring

Igor, already recruited into the army of Serbian Neo-Nazi thugs, travelled between Yugoslav capitals with hordes of them, fully sponsored by the "Red Star" football club, which covered their accommodation and booze. Igor spoke perfect Belgrade lingo and openly raved against Croats. Pompous, arrogant and chauvinistic, he thought himself dangerous but only found strength in the herd.

A potent, volatile scene evolved at the local night club "Diana." I had a hard time digesting it. The small prefab structure was full of local drunks, freaks, gamblers, uniformed police on duty, whores, and small-time new age criminals. Typical small-town mentality, soon to turn into a society of armed thugs and killers.

I travelled all the way from Ljubljana to Berlin with Hardi. They had just demolished the Wall. Germany was reuniting. We drove into the eastern section of the city. It was so depressing. We almost recognised elements of our own country there: neglected parks, great buildings in disrepair, poor street lighting, absence of glamour, potholes and cobblestones, empty shops... West Berlin certainly looked modern, lively, prosperous, elegant, well planned and immaculately clean.

The nightlife we experienced only briefly, over two consecutive nights, appeared dynamic, cultured and world-class. German autobahns were instantly flooded with colourful plastic Trabants and East Germans checking out the West, camping along the highways and truck stops.

On our way back we visited Karlo and Gerda in their own house in Siefield. It appeared that Karlo didn't trust Gerda and that she was possibly living parallel lives with other men. Their house was a hive of activity. Parties with music and hash added to the magic. They had bought an old original Bavarian farmhouse on a small plot. Karlo managed to preserve and upgrade the house and farm buildings. The house had an additional studio/workshop and a massive barn attached. It sat on the slope of a small hill overlooking the valley.

They had two boys by then. I had conversations with Gerda in English, and she introduced me to a sculptor living nearby. He made contemporary sculptures using wood and found objects. It was very impressive work. They appeared very close. Everyone in Germany tended to ignore conventional ways between sexes and I could never tell who was shagging whom.

Hardi had fallen in love with a young single mother in the 1980s. He was in Sarajevo at the time, and I had already gone to Australia. He wanted to impress her. They drove to Germany to visit Karlo. As soon as they got there, she befriended a German man, a friend of Karlo's, and disappeared with him. Hardi had a broken heart and never forgave her. He never saw the woman again. That was the way they lived. We were more attached, expected loyalty and commitment, just old-fashioned Balkan peasants.

I was back in Australia in 1992 when the war broke out in Bosnia. I had a short conversation with Karlo on the phone at the beginning of it. It appeared we had different views on the situation. At the time, I found many people dumped their frustration onto the first available recipient. For us two friends at opposite ends of the world, there weren't others to blame nearby. We both copped it from each other since we were there with the phone in our hands.

My parents, exiled to Sarajevo from Joša Township where they had left their house, all their belongings, property titles, personal documents and family photographs, drove through a roadblock into the hell zone reserved for those destined to suffer the Siege of Sarajevo for the next four years. The township and surrounding hills, access roads, airport and railway lines became the lines of separation and encirclement.

The positions, armament, artillery and ammunition originally controlled by the National Yugoslav Army were handed over to Serbian nationalists. They completely controlled the city, food, international aid, power, water and the lives of its inhabitants. They fired bullets from automatic weapons, telescopic rifles, tanks, machine guns and antiaircraft guns. They shot grenades and projectiles of all calibres indiscriminately at buildings, houses, mosques, libraries, marketplaces, public fountains, TV and communication towers, graveyards, funeral crowds, schools, children playing. Snipers even shot at street dogs.

At the very beginning of the war, they bombed the National Library and burnt everything in it – over two million items of unique Bosnian heritage in text and image. They behaved as if the city and the people in it weren't their own. Citizens of Sarajevo called them "hoof-ians" (aliens on hoofs).

When Russians invaded Afghanistan in 1980, I seriously considered joining the Mujahedeen. When the Bosnian war broke out, I was a different man. I lived in a country with no history of conflict other than the extermination of the native Aboriginal population. I was following the progress of the conflict and the world's reaction to it. Bloodbath followed by negotiations led by Western diplomats, followed by more bloodbath.

A well-organised army, which I knew well and had served in for 15 months, starved, terrorised and slaughtered its own population in the tens of thousands, destroying infrastructure and cultural heritage our own people had created with their bare hands. None had the guts to stop it. I had no guts to join the fight either. I felt guilty about it, of course. Not that it made any difference.

By the time the Dayton Peace Agreement was signed, we had managed to arrange refugee visas to Australia for Mia's and my parents. Mine left the city through a primitive tunnel dug under the runway controlled by the UN and the Serbs all through the war.

Karlo and I both housed refugees and family who managed to escape the violence, and both had clean hands and pure intentions. Karlo's house became a "refugee centre" during the war: family and friends came and went, including Fako and Di, Sarajevo freaks I knew in the 1970s. They lived at Karlo's for a year before coming to Australia.

At some stage, through my communication with Fako, I managed to contact and reconnect with Karlo. By then, Karlo had serious cancer, and he was dying. He chose to follow a non-intrusive and naturopathic course. I commended him on his courage and his loyalty to his convictions. In one of our last conversations, he wanted to know the exact name of the village we got "arrested" in back in 1977. It appeared the experience had haunted his memory since then, and he was going to "look it up" on Google Maps.

He told me how he had become a stonemason, and we discussed the possibility of a visit to Australia and a project together. Six months later he died with his Dutch wife, his two sons, Gerda and Ralf, by his side. I couldn't comprehend Ralf's presence there. I guess I would love to have as many of my great old mates by my side too. Unfortunately, most of them are gone. Must be the reason I've been writing this book.

Back in Ledići

On 6 July 2022, Mia and I visited Ledići spontaneously on the way to my inherited plot of land called Brda (The Hills). It was intentional, but I wasn't going to make it obvious. I had no idea if my rented VW Polo could handle the roughly cut track lined with oversized crushed limestone road base. The rough, unsealed road led to the village, nestled against the forested side of Bjelašnica.

Mia was paranoid about my reckless decision. I had to see the place again. There was so much unresolved in this experience – memories of it and the evolving story. A road sign directed visitors to "Tito's wartime house". Burnt-down houses came into full view as we descended into the village on a narrow, dangerous gravelled road. Roofless white limestone walls overgrown with ivy looked almost idyllic.

As before – *déjà vu* – a man came out of nowhere onto the village road, washed by the crystal-clear morning sun. Everything followed as before: "Good day, good day" Where are you from? What's your business here? Tito's house is up the road, not much to see there, just a plaque on it. You can go and see it if you like. Are you interested in honey?

Of course I was. They knew the village of my birth. The man was about my age and knew my relatives. His wife brought out a large jar of honey. They were friendly. The small potato field behind them, the one they were working that day, looked just like the one my parents had in our village 5 km away. I paid a fair price for the honey – not too little, not too much.

There was something human in the exchange, a sense of forgiveness – *"Hallalosum"*, as a Bosnian Muslim would say. There was nothing threatening in our encounter. I felt a weight lift off my shoulders. Glad to have revisited my emotions of sadness and anger from the past. I felt light and childlike happy as I descended back to the parked car near the village spring where Mia had decided to wait.

Sami Tischler

I found Mia seated at a small memorial to 24 civilian victims killed in 1992 when my people "cleaned up" the village. The list of victims ranged from 2 to 76 years of age. Two women were born in 1957 – they would have been my age. Some of the victims could have been those who "arrested" Karlo and me 45 years ago.

My feelings of anger and disappointment about the event in 1977 were no longer there. It was tragic that the village had become the scene of a war crime, and it wasn't what it once was. None of the villages were. My village Trebečaj had just a single house and one smokehouse left intact. All the others – Muslim and Orthodox Christian alike – had been burnt down.

The Muslims rebuilt, but the Orthodox Christians didn't. Most of them now live in Trnovo, the original regional centre 5 km away on the main road between Sarajevo, Foča, Kalinovik, Gacko, Trebinje and Dubrovnik, on the old caravan road. They have their own territory of Republika Srpska, carefully carved out of Bosnia and Herzegovina and strategically connected to Serbian borders and territories.

Once neighbours, they now sell land bit by bit, ensuring that the politics of ethnic cleansing and permanent separation remain forever.

The glass jar filled with amber-coloured honey, collected by a solitary Orthodox Christian in Ledići on the territory of the Bosnian Federation, was shared over the length of our visit with many special people. Every time I opened the jar, the rich aroma of field flowers, herbs and mountain air came out with its healing power – healing my memories, emotions, and the sense of helpless frustration about the history of my people and their inability to find a way with each other.

"There aren't any Bosnians in Bosnia anymore," is what I say when depressed. What keeps me optimistic is that the Bogomil necropolises remain – mysterious, unexplained, defiant and proud as they have always been.

Back of the Book's Jacket:

At the age of 15, a young "freak" (post-hippy) takes an eventful journey from adolescence to adulthood. The story follows his fearless, penniless road trips through the Balkans and Western Europe. While searching for an alternative lifestyle in the 1970s, he makes likeminded friends, meets passionate lovers, confronts conventions, fights restrictions, and exposes the rigidities of Yugoslav socialism and the hypocrisies of Western capitalism.

His lived experiences on the road, as a small-time smuggler, jailed vagrant in Belgrade, Ćuprija or Rotterdam, clochard in Paris, penniless freak in Istanbul, Dubrovnik, or Venice, are as convincing as they come. His beloved city, Sarajevo, is experiencing its own ascendance to a well-deserved historic cultural Spring. A whole generation of freaks, avant-garde musicians, artists, and freethinkers believe it possible. Their destinies appear to steam ahead together while the dark cloud of historic inevitability looms over the city.

The resolution to the fundamental dilemma of the storyteller, what to do with his own life, where and how, could not stop Sarajevo's bloodbath and destruction. Here it is: a book based on real-life events, characters, and lived experiences under an oppressive political system, told through the story of travel, family history, adventure, friendship, steamy erotic play, army and prison life, all infused with fumes of black resin and the sounds of rock 'n' roll.

www.ingramcontent.com/pod-product-compliance
Lightning Source LLC
Chambersburg PA
CBHW041302240426
43661CB00010B/989